THE VICTORIAN SOCIAL-PR

Also by Josephine M. Guy

THE BRITISH AVANT-GARDE: THE THEORY AND POLITICS
OF TRADITION

POLITICS AND VALUE IN ENGLISH STUDIES (*with Ian Small*)

The Victorian Social-Problem Novel

The Market, the Individual and Communal Life

Josephine M. Guy

First published 1996 by
MACMILLAN PRESS LTD
Houndmills, Basingstoke, Hampshire RG21 6XS
and London
Companies and representatives
throughout the world

ISBN 0–333–62843–8 hardcover
ISBN 0–333–62844–6 paperback

A catalogue record for this book is available
from the British Library.

10   9   8   7   6   5   4   3   2   1
05   04   03   02   01   00   99   98   97   96

Printed in Hong Kong

Contents

Preface

As I explain in Chapter 1, yet another book devoted to a sub-genre generally acknowledged to comprise 'second-rate' works may seem extravagant. However, this group of novels continues to be popular on undergraduate courses on Victorian literature, not least because the topical reference which defines them as a sub-genre provides a particularly useful illustration of a fairly common practice in English Studies of reading (and teaching) literature 'in context' – that is, attempting to establish the relationships between particular works and the historical conditions which produced them. Such ambitions, however, are complicated by the fact that 'doing' history (in English Studies at least) is now no simple matter. Today there are not only profound disagreements about the relationship between literature and history (or, more accurately, between literary value and historical knowledge), but there is also little agreement over more general historiographical issues, such as the status of historical knowledge, the role of historical causation, and so forth. In practice these kinds of differences can result in very different explanations (and evaluations) of the same works – a situation which can be confusing for the modern student who is often unsure which account of a particular work is 'right', or even how to decide on a criterion of 'rightness'. The critical history of the social-problem novels provides a case in point, for the various accounts of them map in miniature many of the changes in the practices of literary history which have taken place in English Studies over the past four decades. In Part One, I examine these accounts in some detail, drawing out the historiographical assumptions which underwrite them in order to show how a particular view of history produces a particular evaluation of the novels in question. My account, though, is critical as well as descriptive, for I also highlight what I see as the limitations of these ways of doing history, and I offer to the reader an alternative historical method which attempts to overcome these limitations. In this respect one aim of this book is to use the example of the social-problem novel to provide the student with a practical illustration of some of the general problems involved in 'doing' literary history. More particularly, I attempt to provide some suggestions about how the familiar (but deeply contested) concepts which literary historians now use – such as 'discourse', 'ideology' and 'authority' – might be more accurately and fruitfully deployed.

The second and more specialist ambition of my book is contained in Part Two where I use the historical method sketched in Part One to offer some new insights into the literary history of the mid-Victorian period. More specifically, I attempt to provide the grounds for a re-evaluation of the social-problem novel. I do not claim that these works are 'better' or more 'worthwhile' (in whatever ways we might wish to define these terms) than, say, more familiar Victorian novels, such as *Bleak House* or *Middlemarch*, but simply that they have been misread. I suggest that the 'weak-nesses' typically attributed to the social-problem novels (for example, alleged incoherences of plotting and characterisation) have been the result of misunderstanding the kinds of social questions which these writers set out to answer. My argument is that when viewed in the context of mid-nineteenth-century debates about the nature of what I term 'the social' the novels turn out to be much more coherent (and in some cases more challenging) than has often been realised. In documenting these debates about 'the social' in Chapter 3 I have drawn upon information which, though familiar to intellectual historians and sociologists, will be largely foreign to students of literature. Rendering this complex body of work both manageable and accessible has inevitably resulted in simplifications. However, I have tried to balance the dangers of reductiveness against my ambition to suggest that an attention to a variety of other, 'non-literary', discourses reveals some surprising but revealing continuities in mid-Victorian conceptualisations of 'the social' and social life. In such a scheme the kinds of details which will be of interest principally to the economic historian or the sociologist have necessarily been omitted.

My attempt in this book to address two kinds of issues – specialist concerns of mid-nineteenth-century literary historio-graphy as well as more general debates about the relationship between literature and history – inevitably holds some pitfalls. Most obviously, the student of the social-problem novel, interested primarily in the minutiae of Eliot's or Dickens's fiction, may find the length and detail of the argument of Part One taxing. If so, they are recommended to skip the lengthy exposition in Chapter 2, and proceed from Chapter 1 (which summarises the main points of the second chapter) to Part Two. My hope, though, is that most readers, alert to the vexed relationship between 'theory' and 'practice', will see the value in taking the time to understand the theoretical foundations which underpin even the most simple and apparently neutral critical activity.

Nottingham   JOSEPHINE M. GUY

Acknowledgements

Thanks are due to the Department of English Studies at Nottingham University for the provision of an equipment grant which speeded up the preparation of this book, and for my employers for a sabbatical semester which permitted it to be finished on time. In particular I would like to thank Ron Carter for recognising the difficulties of balancing the demands of teaching and research.

J. M. G.

Part One
Literature, History, Value

1

Evaluating the Social-Problem Novel

The mid-nineteenth-century novels which we now call 'social-problem' or 'industrial' novels – principally *Hard Times, Mary Barton, North and South, Alton Locke, Sybil* and *Felix Holt* – were not described and identified as a group by their nineteenth-century readers or critics. In fact the label has a relatively recent origin for it dates only from the 1950s.[1] The forty years since that time, though, have seen a sustained interest in the novels as a group, and various readings of them have been produced. However, common to nearly all of these readings is the conclusion that the works are in some way flawed – that they are marked by incoherence and contradiction and that they possess fundamental weaknesses of plot and characterisation. The modern student of Victorian literature is thus confronted by a paradox: on the one hand there is a considerable body of critical work devoted to the social-problem novels; but on the other, most of the judgements about them appear to be negative. Such a situation in turn provokes two further questions: why should works with such widely acknowledged shortcomings have continued to attract so much attention? And why do we need yet another book devoted to them?

The terms 'social-problem' or 'industrial' novel are generally used to refer to a body of English fiction written in the late 1840s and 1850s which allegedly takes as its subject-matter large-scale problems in contemporary British society, problems which in turn were the product of changing demographic patterns and changes in work practices associated with the accelerating industrialisation of the British economy.[2] This literary engagement with contemporary affairs in turn depended upon what was claimed to be a new kind of relationship between the novel and the social and political worlds which produced it. Social-problem novels are typically distinguished from earlier novels, and from other works contem-

3

porary with them, by their attempt to comment on, and stimulate debate about, matters of general public and political concern. Thomas Carlyle's portmanteau phrase, the 'Condition-of-England question', is often used to describe these social matters; they centre on the perception that social order was under threat from conflicts between various interest groups in society, and particularly from the discontent of the increasingly impoverished and degraded working classes. The intentions of the writers who address these issues are assumed to be both serious and, more importantly, political. So social-problem novelists are commonly credited with the intention of trying to educate, and therefore by implication to change, the opinions and prejudices of their readers. In so doing, they are seen to be implying that the novel can, and should, have an important role to play in social and political life. As a consequence the moral authority often associated with Victorian fiction and the didactic function which proceeds from that authority are given a new dimension in the social-problem novel. The principal distinction of the sub-genre, then, exists not so much in any formal features or properties (the works in question are not formally innovative or experimental), but rather in the non-literary ambitions which certain authors were assumed to have held. Where critics have differed is in the various ways they have described and explained those ambitions. These descriptions and explanations have in turn depended upon the principles which have informed their historical research, and the kind of historical evidence which they have adduced as relevant to understanding literary works.

One way of accounting for both the number and variety of critical works which have been written about the social-problem novel is in terms of the changes which have taken place since the 1950s in the practice of literary history. As new ways of understanding the relationship between literature and history have been developed, and as new 'stories' of the past have been written, so historical sub-genres, such as that of the social-problem novel, have been redefined and reinterpreted. In this respect it is significant that in the 1950s, at virtually the same moment as social-problem novels were being brought to the attention of the reading public, the main point of contention among literary critics was the role which historical knowledge (then loosely called a historical 'context') should play in literary judgements. For some, such as the Oxford critic, F. W. Bateson, historical knowledge was seen to be a necessary condition for a proper or informed literary judgement. For other critics, most famously F. R. Leavis, literary or aesthetic judgements were held to be necessarily anterior to, and therefore independent of, any historical enquiry or any amount of contextualisation. In this view a context was only necessary once the literary worth of a work had been agreed upon. What many saw as the pervasive topicality of Victorian novels in general, and of social-problem novels in particular, posed what amounted to a test case in this dispute. A novel such as *Hard Times*, for example, which self-consciously addressed itself to a contemporary economic and political state of affairs (its full title is *Hard Times for These Times*) seemed to demand that modern readers pay attention to its historical circumstances. Today we will probably dismiss these early debates as theoretically naïve and, as a consequence, intellectually uninteresting. Nevertheless, the fundamental issue which the disagreement between Leavis and Bateson identified – that is, the *nature* of the relationship between the literary and the historical – has remained a contested one, and it has been largely responsible for generating the continuing interest in the social-problem novel.[3]

Broadly speaking the various accounts of the social-problem or industrial novel can be arranged into three categories. All three categories have in common an attempt to explain social-problem novels in terms of the historical circumstances which produce them. Where they differ is in the particular kinds of circumstances (the particular historical 'events') which they see as relevant to that explanation. In simple terms, each account constructs a different story about the past, because each presupposes a different way of thinking about the relationship between literary value and historical knowledge. Unfortunately, these categories do not follow each other in a tidy chronological order, for the simple reason that developments (or, to use a more neutral word, changes) in academic literary criticism have not themselves been sequential: that is, the arrival and acceptance of a new 'approach' or theory does not necessarily lead to the supersession of earlier approaches and theories. This has led to a situation where different theories are held simultaneously by different critics; or, in the case of social-problem novels, where different kinds of explanations simply coexist, and where the student understandably finds it difficult to choose (or to know how to choose) between them.

The first of these categories can be called 'political'. It is derived from Marxist literary criticism and is informed by a Marxist view of history in which all historical events are seen to be shaped by a particular story of economic alienation and class struggle. Like the others, this political category encompasses diversity: it includes the work of early Marxist critics such as Raymond Williams and Arnold Kettle in the 1950s and early 1960s, the more detailed and more politically urgent criticism of John Lucas in the mid-1960s, and the sophisticated materialist criticism (often referred to as 'cultural materialism') of the American cultural historian Regenia Gagnier in the 1990s. The central aim of all these critics is to uncover the political processes which underlie fictional representations, and as a consequence individual works are valued in terms of their use or anticipation of the political categories of Marxism. Of all the ways of reading the social-problem novels, political criticism has been the most significant; its influence can be seen in, for example, David Craig's and Stephen Gill's Penguin editions of *Hard Times* and *Mary Barton* or in Michael Wheeler's characterisation of the 'social-problem novel' in his survey of Victorian fiction.[4]

The second category I have called 'contextualist'; it is distinguished from the first category by virtue of the fact that it does not trace (or even recognise) the specific political narrative which informs Marxist history. So rather than examine works in terms of their understanding of, say, the determining power of the economic base or the inevitability of class struggle, this category tends to pay attention to explaining the minutiae of a novel's topical reference. Typically the concern is with the accuracy of representation of specific events – such as, for example, the nature of Chartist agitation, or the extent of urban poverty. It is in terms of that accuracy that the novels are valued. In this category we once again find critics of otherwise varied dispositions: it includes the detailed historical scholarship of John Holloway in the 1960s and Sheila Smith in the 1980s, as well as the broader sweep of Louis Cazamian at the beginning of the twentieth century and Kathleen Tillotson in the 1950s. It is perhaps worth noting in passing that the work of this group both precedes and extends beyond that of the first group, despite the fact that one of the ambitions of Marxist historiography was to expose as 'naïve' the assumptions underlying a 'contextualist' view of literary history. One simple way of understanding the distinction between the two approaches is in terms of the different ways they explain the relationship between text and context. In 'contextualist' history, the historical context is seen to illuminate, but to be in some sense inferior to, the text; in Marxism, by contrast, this hierarchy is virtually reversed in the sense that texts are merely evidence for the particular historical process (a narrative of class struggle) which underwrites Marxist politics.

The third category is smaller and newer than the first two, and is represented by the work of another American critic, Catherine Gallagher. It can be broadly labelled 'new historicist', and it draws upon one of the most recent ways of theorising the relationship between literature and history. The starting-point of new historicism is an acknowledgement that modern values inevitably colour the way texts from the past are identified and interpreted. In order to minimise this potential distortion, new historicists treat all documents from the past as if they possessed an equal status or value. That is, they refuse to grant a special privilege to any kind of text, or to place texts within any kind of hierarchical structure. For new historicists literary works, like all other texts, become merely one 'signifying practice' among many. Moreover because such signifying practices are multiple and – in principle at least – endless (significantly 'circulating energies' is the metaphor used by one critic to describe new historicism's object of study),[5] knowledge of them is assumed to be fragmentary and limited. It follows, then, that for new historicists the traditional distinction between a text and a context breaks down, and the relationships between texts which the new-historicist critic identifies can only ever amount to correlations. Causal relationships (that is, the processes by which one text can be said to influence or determine elements of another) demand that individual texts possess a different authority, status or value, but the whole process of assigning status and authority to texts is of course exactly what new historicists try to avoid. These kinds of principles inform Gallagher's study of the social-problem or (to use her preferred term) the industrial novel. So on the one hand, there is an attention to historical detail which is similar to the researches of some 'contextualist' critics, but on the other hand, she does not possess their accompanying trust in the factual status of historical evidence. Gallagher thus limits herself to documenting a number of what she terms mid-Victorian 'discourses' about industrialisation; there is no attempt to describe any determining or causal relationships between various fictional and non-fictional discourses, nor is there any attempt to evaluate them in terms of their relationship to 'real' events. At the same time, though, Gallagher,

like the other critics, still sees in the social-problem novels fundamental contradictions; she simply describes and explains them in
different ways.

Given the variety of these historical narratives, and the diversity
of assumptions which inform them, it is perhaps surprising that
they should produce such similar judgements of the novels which
they examine. As I have suggested, despite their different stories of
the past, most see the works as 'minor'; marked by confusion and
inconsistency, they are seen in some sense as failures. Such a situation strongly suggests that despite their obvious differences, there
is nevertheless some principle or assumption which each of these
accounts has in common. Moreover, it seems likely that this
similarity will concern some aspect of the sub-genre which is not
seen to be subject to historical determination, and which is therefore immune from the different kinds of evidence produced by
various historical explanations. A clue to explaining why this is the
case is provided by a number of accounts of the social-problem
novels which so far I have not mentioned, mainly because they
only examine works on an individual or *ad hoc* basis. They are not
concerned, that is, with the generic relationships between them, nor
with the notion that the social-problem or industrial novels comprise a distinct sub-genre of Victorian fiction. The reason is that
(in distinction to the other accounts I have described) the critical
practices of this last group deliberately set out to minimise the role
of historical knowledge in literary judgements. Ignoring the political and social topicality of social-problem novels, these accounts
have instead identified in them archetypal patterns, with the result
that individual social-problem novels are seen to have more in
common with, say, eighteenth- or twentieth-century fiction than
with that of their Victorian contemporaries. It is all the more
surprising, then, that these 'ahistorical' readings should turn out to
have much in common with the historical accounts described
earlier. As I shall explain in detail in Chapter 2, this common
ground concerns an anachronistic reading of certain aspects of mid-
nineteenth-century culture whereby the modern critic assumes that
late twentieth-century ways of thinking were available to Victorian
writers. Of course such anachronism is to be expected in accounts
which deny or marginalise historical specificity; the surprise is that
we also find it in accounts which make a virtue of their sensitivity
to historical circumstance. I shall further argue that the most
striking form of this anachronism is to be found in a body of

twentieth-century assumptions about what constitutes a problem in society – about, that is, the subject-matter which the social-problem novels allegedly address, and which, in historical accounts, defines them as a group. Ironically it turns out that the very feature which has been taken to identify the historical specificity of the sub-genre – an attempt to address large-scale *social* problems – has itself been understood ahistorically; that is to say, the definition of the social, and therefore of what is to count as a *social* problem (as opposed to a problem in society), is not seen to be an issue which is historically contingent.

None of the accounts I have mentioned seem aware of the fact that to identify a problem in society (that is, to point to conflicts between interest groups, threats to social order, and so on) is not necessarily to see it as an underlying *social* problem requiring a *social* solution – a solution, that is, which requires changes in social structures or institutions. A simple but striking example of such a distinction is provided by drunkenness. Drunkenness is commonly seen to cause problems in society in that it can lead to conflicts between individuals or groups of individuals which in turn may result in violence and damage (to both people and property), activities which are often held to pose a threat to the social order. Today we tend to see alcohol abuse (and its consequences) as in part a *social* problem in the sense that it tends to be seen as connected with other problems such as poverty and unemployment which are themselves also seen as having social causes and therefore requiring social solutions (such as, for example, the implementation of economic policies which will encourage job creation). By contrast, a mid-Victorian public tended to see drunkenness as a form of personal immorality, the remedy for which lay in a personal commitment to teetotalism – a solution perfectly captured by the Victorian phrase 'taking the pledge'. In both cases drunkenness is seen as a problem in society; but only in the first instance is it understood as a *social* problem, one which requires a social solution. The argument of this book is that the Victorians' understanding of drunkenness as a personal rather than a social problem is not an isolated case; rather it is the product of a frame of reference – of what I term a 'conceptual set' – which ensured that mid-Victorian writers (of whatever political persuasion) tended to understand problems in society in individual, rather than social terms. In Chapter 3, I argue that the intellectual climate of mid-nineteenth-century Britain afforded the social-problem novelists a limited but complex set of intellectual tools with which to understand their society. Fundamental to it was an emphasis on the individual as the basic unit of enquiry. That is to say, an understanding of the social, and therefore of social causation and social change, was always made by reference to individual agency. Poverty and disease, conflicts between masters and men, inequality of wealth, and so on – all these large-scale issues were addressed by recommending changes in *individual behaviours* rather than changes to social structures. Such a frame of reference, however, was not politically or ideologically motivated; rather it set the boundaries within which politics and ideology operated. It is in terms of that frame of reference that the radicalism of the social-problem novelists needs to be measured.

The distinction which I am drawing may seem nit-picking, but, as I show in Chapter 4, an appreciation of it has important ramifications for the ways in which we interpret the social-problem novels. Most dramatically it reveals that the adverse critical judgements of them have largely been the result of anachronistic readings. Critics have tended to castigate novelists for the incoherence of the solutions which they offer to contemporary problems in society – an incoherence which is allegedly exhibited in weaknesses in characterisation and plot. My argument, however, is that the 'solutions' which Victorian writers prescribe are solutions to problems in society which they perceived and defined quite differently from the ways in which a modern social commentator would. Moreover, when seen in relation to the specific ways in which they formulated a problem, the solutions we find in Victorian social-problem novels are perfectly coherent, and the fictional devices employed to formulate and articulate them are wholly appropriate. To put matters bluntly: my contention is that the social-problem novels have been judged as failures simply because they have been assumed to have been answering questions which their authors would never (and could never) have recognised. The modest aim of this book, then, is to try to uncover the kinds of questions about society (and problems in society) which *would* have been comprehensible to the 'Victorian frame of mind' (to borrow Walter Houghton's famous phrase). For it is only when we are in possession of this information that we will be in a position to judge the success of the answers which these novelists offer.

At the same time, though, it is necessary to exercise some caution in using the term 'success'. In claiming that the social-problem novels are less confused or contradictory than critics have hitherto judged them to be, I do not in any way imply that their solutions to problems in society are therefore 'right', and should be recommended as examples we might follow today. On the contrary, judged by today's standards, the Victorians' understanding of society is certainly naïve, and their proposed solutions to, say, unemployment, inequality of wealth, and so on, are woefully inadequate. Indeed social-problem novels can tell us almost nothing about how we might resolve our own social problems (and we should be surprised and perhaps alarmed if they could, or if any critic seriously proposed that they could). What I do insist, though, is that within *their own terms*, within the context of mid-nineteenth-century intellectual culture, these solutions, far from being confused and contradictory, were thoughtful. They were also logical; and in some cases, they were quite challenging. The modern student is therefore recommended to read these novels because they tell us something interesting both about the Victorians and about literature. The social-problem novel, in distinction to other contemporary works, shows us a group of writers using the resources of literary representation in order to try to resolve some large-scale problems in their society, problems which their politicians, economists and statisticians seemed to them to be wholly unable or unwilling to address. These novels thus provide us with evidence of certain kinds of attitudes towards social life which might otherwise be invisible, and they thus provide a special sort of evidence in a social or cultural history of the nineteenth century. At the same time they also show us that some mid-Victorian writers were thinking about literature, and its social and political functions, in new ways. In this sense the social-problem novel also marks an important moment in the history of nineteenth-century taste.

When discussing the 'Condition-of-England question', Thomas Carlyle, impatient with what seemed to him to be the inertia and irresponsibility of Parliament, had ominously claimed that 'something ought to be said, something ought to be done', otherwise 'something will *do* itself one day, and in a fashion that will please nobody'.[6] The question of course was *what* to say, and *what* to do. The answers given by Dickens, Gaskell, Kingsley, Disraeli and Eliot to the problems they identified in their society are certainly not the answers we might give; but then again, as the argument of this book proposes, they did not ask exactly the questions which we would.

2

The Social-Problem Novel and Literary History

Two kinds of critical practice which consciously set out to minimise the role of historical knowledge in literary evaluation are the so-called 'humanist' criticism of F. R. Leavis and structuralist criticism, particularly that practised by David Lodge in the late 1960s and early 1970s. Both Lodge and Leavis wrote essays on *Hard Times*; indeed *Hard Times* has probably received more attention and been the subject of more disputes than any of the other social-problem novels. A close examination of Lodge's and Leavis's arguments reveals some fundamental limitations in their 'ahistorical' approach. In particular, their tendency to ignore or marginalise the novel's topical reference leads them both to partial and in some ways tautologous readings. This shortcoming is most apparent in their attempts to explain weaknesses in the novel's plot and characterisation. For my purposes, though, the significance of their readings of *Hard Times* lies in some features which they share with the historical accounts, despite the fact that these accounts seem to be diametrically opposed.

Unlike historically-orientated critics, Lodge and Leavis discuss only one social-problem novel. Indeed they make no attempt to locate *Hard Times* within any sub-genre. By contrast their discussions of the novel centre on its archetypal qualities – that is, on features which they suggest it shares with all literary works. So, for example, Leavis draws comparisons between Dickens and other writers in his 'great tradition' – D. H. Lawrence and Henry James – rather than contemporaries such as Gaskell, Kingsley or Disraeli. Lodge identifies affinities with Shelley and E. M. Forster. In both essays scant attention is paid to the topicality of *Hard Times*, or to its local reference; moreover no account is taken of its political functions. For Lodge and Leavis, the failures and successes of *Hard Times* have nothing to do with what might be called its 'Victorian' qualities. Indeed by dwelling on its archetypicality they abstract the novel from the moment of its production and reception. In general terms the validity of this ahistorical approach depends upon two factors: upon the assumption that the category of literature is essentialist – that is, the features which define works as literary are transhistorical and transcultural; and (this being the case) upon the accuracy with which particular archetypal features are identified. However, Leavis and Lodge identify a different set of archetypal features: for Leavis, successful literary works are defined in terms of their ability to embody a form of moral knowledge – what he famously called 'life'; for Lodge, it is a particular kind of 'verbal activity' or 'rhetoric' which distinguishes the literary from the non-literary. In both cases, the quality or qualities which define 'life' and 'rhetoric' are assumed to be independent of historical and cultural circumstances; they are absolute in the sense that they can be applied to any work produced at any moment in time.

What is immediately striking about Leavis's account of *Hard Times* is his overall valuation of it as a 'masterpiece', whose success is 'complete'.[1] While such wholehearted admiration is unusual in modern accounts of the novel, it is nevertheless also true that Leavis admits that there are some elements which present the critic with problems, particularly the caricatured portrayal of Slackbridge and the unions and the sentimentalised treatment of both Stephen Blackpool and Sleary's circus. As I shall argue later, it is precisely these weaknesses which are seized upon in historical accounts of the novel. In what I have called 'political' accounts, for example, these moments are taken to be the strongest evidence of what are alleged to be Dickens's bourgeois politics; and it is these politics which are in turn cited as the chief reason for the novel's failure. On the surface, Leavis's interpretation of the same episodes could not be more different. In his view, *Hard Times* is 'intended' as a 'moral fable', and the 'significance' of every character and episode (including those which later so offended critics such as Raymond Williams, Arnold Kettle and John Lucas) becomes 'immediately apparent' once we read the novel in these terms.[2] Leavis argues that the defining feature of a moral fable is an 'intention [which] is peculiarly insistent'; in other words, all the features of fiction, such as plot structure and characterisation, will always be subservient to the fable's moral imperative. In this particular instance the moral of the fable (the articulation of an insistent intention) is 'the confutation of Utilitarianism by life', a message which is conveyed, according to Leavis, with 'great subtlety'.[3] This argument allows Leavis to

explain those elements of the novel which other critics would later
see as flaws (such as its use of caricature and its sentimentalising)
as exaggerations which are completely necessary to the fable's
overall purpose and design. Hence Leavis argues that the charac-
terisations of Sleary's circus and Stephen Blackpool have value as
'symbols', and should not therefore be judged in terms of their
verisimilitude; rather, they should be valued in terms of their
ability to suggest or embody certain moral ideals. Leavis readily
admits that a real Victorian travelling circus would in all likelihood
be distinguished by 'squalor, grossness, and vulgarity', qualities
which he sees consorting oddly with Dickens's description of
Sleary's people's 'remarkable gentleness and childishness ... a
special inaptitude for any kind of sharp practice'.[4] However,
according to Leavis this evident disparity does not mean that
Dickens's symbolism is 'sentimentally false'. What is important for
Leavis is the function of the symbolism in the novel as a whole,
and the validity of the *qualities* which the circus is intended to
symbolise:

> The virtues and qualities that Dickens prizes do indeed exist, and
> it is necessary for his critique of Utilitarianism and industrialism,
> and for (what is the same thing) his creative purpose, to evoke
> them vividly. The book can't, in my judgement, be fairly charged
> with giving a misleading representation of human nature. And it
> would plainly not be intelligent criticism to suggest that anyone
> could be misled about the nature of circuses by *Hard Times*. The
> critical question is merely one of tact: was it well-judged of
> Dickens to try to do *that* – which had to be done somehow – with
> a travelling circus?[5]

Unsurprisingly Leavis concludes that overall Dickens's efforts were
well-judged, and that the success of the circus as a symbol of
'humanity' – or of what he later calls 'life' – is 'complete'.
Moreover, Leavis stresses once again that this success depends
upon the reader judging the novel from the outset by the right
criterion, that is, as a moral fable. 'Success', he argues, 'is condi-
tioned partly by the fact that, from the opening chapters, we have
been tuned for the reception of a highly conventional art.'[6]

Leavis's entire argument rests upon what is fundamentally a
Platonic view of morality – that, for example, moral values about
'life' or about 'humanity' exist independently of historical or

cultural circumstances. Criticism of this view (and indeed of Leavis's 'humanism') is so well-known and so thoroughgoing that it does not need to be rehearsed in detail here. It is sufficient to observe that critics since Leavis have emphasised what has become a commonplace of twentieth-century social thinking, that the definition of terms such as 'humanity' or 'life' is historically and culturally contingent. In this sense Leavis judges *Hard Times* by using anachronistic criteria; he does not take account of the fact that the Victorians might have had their own way of understanding terms such as 'humanity' and 'life', and that these were derived from their own (and local) moral values. The limitations of this kind of anachronistic thinking become clearer when we see the relationship between Leavis's moral Platonism and his assertion that *Hard Times* is 'intended' as a moral fable. I use the word 'assertion' because Leavis never actually argues his case: he provides no evidence from outside the text to prove that Dickens wrote his novel as a fable. Rather, we are asked to believe that Dickens wrote the novel as a fable simply because it makes sense as one. But when he demonstrates how it makes such sense, Leavis only draws attention to those aspects of the novel which fit his hypothesis. In so doing he ignores or dismisses the novel's many ambiguities, particularly its ambivalent attitude towards sexual transgression in, for example, the contrasting characters of Louisa and Sissy. The reason is not hard to find, for fables, by definition, cannot embody moral ambiguity. Hence any moral complexities in the novel have to be described by Leavis as 'subtleties' in the fable's design, evidence merely of the 'flexible' and 'inclusive' nature of Dickens's 'art'.[7]

It is worth recalling at this point Leavis's argument that the accuracy of the novel's social reference has no bearing upon its moral meaning. Of course, it is obviously true that fables are not realistic; but the obverse does not necessarily follow. It is not the case that an absence of realism – in this case Dickens's sentimentalising tendencies and his use of caricature – are sufficient reasons to categorise a novel as a fable. What makes *Hard Times* a fable is, in Leavis's eyes, an absence of realism combined with simple moral oppositions between the self-evidently 'bad' Coketown and the self-evidently 'good' values of the circus. The obvious difficulty with such a view lies in its circularity: the moral meaning which Leavis finds is used as a reason to label the novel as a fable in the first place, while at the same time, the novel's identity as a fable is used as evidence for the particular nature (and the particular form) of the moral message. Identifying the novel as a fable permits Leavis to ignore the moral complexities which confuse or undermine a simple opposition between 'good' and 'bad'; but at the same time, Leavis's assumption that such a moral framework is an appropriate way of criticising Utilitarianism leads him to marginalise the moral complexities in the novel and thus identify it as a fable. Leavis's argument, in other words, is tautologous, and the main reason for the tautology is a refusal to take account of the novel's historical and cultural specificity. Leavis assumes that 'Utilitarianism' and 'industrialism' (the targets of Dickens's moralising) meant the same thing to Dickens as they do to the twentieth-century reader (and in particular to Leavis himself). This assumption in turn leads him to separate the activity of criticising – writing a moral fable – from the specific social phenomena which are being criticised – what Dickens means by Utilitarianism and industrialism. The result is that Leavis's account tells us a good deal more about his own values than it does about Dickens's.

David Lodge's account of *Hard Times* appeared in 1966 in *Language of Fiction*, in the same year as the 'political' account by John Lucas, but nearly two decades after Leavis's essay.[8] In some ways it marked a significant change in the practice of literary criticism, for it was distinguished by a linguistic approach to texts which in turn derived from Lodge's own interest in structuralism. Jonathan Culler has pointed out that structuralism is a difficult term to define exactly, for it encompasses a wide variety of critical practices which range from Claude Lévi-Strauss's analysis of myths to the semiotic analysis developed by Roland Barthes, Roman Jakobson's 'poetics' and A. J. Greimas's emphasis on semantics.[9] These differences certainly do exist, but there are nevertheless several important analytical threads which are common to all structuralist analyses, and they are helpful for understanding the general orientation and significance of Lodge's essay on *Hard Times*. The most important of these threads (and one which links Lodge to the anti-historical biases of Leavis) is an emphasis on what is termed synchrony rather than diachrony. Applied to the study of language, synchrony refers to an attempt to reconstruct a language system as a functional whole. A diachronic analysis, by contrast, refers to the investigation of the historical development of a language's various elements. More important, perhaps, is the assertion that both activities must be thought of as separate. Indeed Culler argues that to conflate the diachronic with the synchronic is to 'falsify one's synchronic description'. He goes so far as to assert that 'language is a system of interrelated items and the value and identity of these items is defined by their place in the system rather than by their history'.[10] A synchronic analysis of a literary text therefore requires the critic to ignore its specific historical location; rather, he or she is confined to investigating the structures (which can include, for example, grammatical features, linguistic signs or forms of address) which purportedly allow a text to function *as text* at any time.

A second important basic tenet of structuralist criticism is the assumption that the descriptions of texts which structuralism produces are value-free. One of the claims of early structuralist accounts was that they were objective or scientific: they described a system which was simply 'there'. Indeed much of the initial popularity of structuralism in the 1960s, when Lodge began writing, derived from its claim to have provided a critical method which corrected the subjective biases allegedly inherent in the work of critics such as Leavis (as well as Marxists such as Raymond Williams and Arnold Kettle). A third fundamental tenet of structuralist criticism is the assumption that literary texts can be described in the same terms as non-literary texts; that literary texts contain no linguistic features which cannot also be found in non-literary texts. In his popular and influential anthology, *Modern Criticism and Theory*, Lodge included two pieces of work by Roman Jakobson, published in 1956 and 1958. They set out what Lodge claimed to be Jakobson's most significant contribution to modern literary theory: in the first place his 'identification of the rhetorical figures, metaphor and metonymy, as models for two fundamental ways of organizing discourse that can be traced *in every kind of cultural production*' (my emphasis); and in the second his 'attempt to understand "literariness"' by defining 'in linguistic terms what makes a verbal message a work of art'.[11] Jakobson (as anthologised by Lodge) starkly argues that 'many poetic features belong not only to the science of language, but to the whole theory of signs, that is to general semiotics. This statement, however, is valid not only for verbal art but also for all varieties of language since language shares many properties with some other systems of signs or even with all of them'.[12]

Lodge took this last tenet as his main point of departure. In his Introduction to *Language of Fiction* he argued that most literary criticism assumed 'that the lyric poem is the literary norm, or the proper basis for generalizing about literature; and that there are two quite different kinds of language, the literary and the non-literary'.[13] Lodge further suggested that this false opposition has led to an impoverished understanding of prose fiction, the language of which tends to be much more discursive. The main aim of Lodge's Introduction is to describe a critical practice which is capable of analysing all literary forms – poetry and prose fiction – in the same terms. The underlying principle of this new practice is the proposition (which Lodge adapts from J. M. Cameron) that 'all poetic fictions exist only as certain words in a certain order'. If the fictional world of the novel 'is a verbal world, determined at every point by the words in which it is represented' then, Lodge suggests, 'there can be no essential difference between the criticism of poetry and the criticism of prose fiction'.[14] In each and every case, the critic is simply analysing how language is used to produce certain effects. Over the course of *Language of Fiction* Lodge described the methods which such an analysis might use, taking care to distinguish between his new critical practice, and that adopted in linguistics or stylistics. The most important difference concerns the role played by value-judgements; Lodge suggests that an analysis of the language of a literary text must be preceded by a judgement about its literary value. And it is the ability to make such judgements which separates the literary critic from the specialist in linguistics:

> The language of the novel, therefore, will be most satisfactorily and completely studied by the methods, not of linguistics or stylistics (though these disciplines can make valuable contributions), but of literary criticism, which seeks to define the meaning and value of literary artefacts by relating subjective responses to objective text, always pursuing exhaustiveness of explication and unanimity of judgement, but conscious that these goals are unattainable.[15]

The role of a verbal analysis, then, is to explain language use in those works which a critical community labels as literary: in this sense, the critical practice Lodge was outlining was an attempt to give an objective explanation of a series of subjective responses. Lodge was obviously aware that such prescriptions could seem to be very similar to the 'close reading' practised by F. R. Leavis, and he added a rider about evaluation which was deliberately intended to distance his views from those of Leavis. He suggested that judgements about morality – Leavis's definition of 'life', for example – have little to do with literary value; the critic should be concerned with the effectiveness with which a work communicates, rather than prescribing the kind of (moral) message it ought to communicate. And it is a judgement about the effectiveness of language use which determines whether or not a work has a literary identity:

> In the last analysis, literary critics can claim special authority not as witnesses to the moral value of works of literature, but as explicators and judges of effective communication, of 'realization' ... In reading *Tom Jones* or *Clarissa* or any other novel, we enter a unique linguistic universe; we learn a new language designed to carry out a particular view of experience ... If this language has its own internal logic and beauty, if it can consistently bring off the feat of realization, we adopt it, and give our assent to the beliefs of the implied author, for the duration of the reading experience. But if this language is characterized by confusion, contradiction, internal inconsistencies and expectations unfulfilled, we will not adopt it, even temporarily.[16]

This paragraph represents an important caveat, for it suggests that judgements about literary value are solely judgements about language use, a conclusion which in turn provides the justification for Lodge's linguistically-based criticism. Lodge's propositions, however, beg some very important questions. For example: What is the measure of effectiveness? What counts as good 'communication'? What are the criteria of 'logic and beauty'? Importantly, Lodge has tried to divorce all these questions from any (subjective) judgements about the moral validity or truth functions of the ideas which a work might express. Instead he uses only linguistic criteria: effectiveness and communication can be measured by what he terms a 'structural approach' – that is, by tracing 'significant threads through the language of an entire novel'.[17] He glosses this definition in the following way:

> The structural approach has the obvious attraction that it tries to discuss the work as a whole, with a beginning, a middle, and an end. By tracing a linguistic thread or threads – a cluster of images, or value-words, or grammatical constructions – through a whole novel, we produce a kind of spatial diagram of the accumulative and temporarily-extended reading experience.[18]

It is important to notice here the replacement of the term 'significant threads' with 'linguistic threads'. This substitution disguises a fundamental question – what defines, or is to count as, 'significant'? Is it what we can for brevity call the ideas expressed in a novel? Or is it what we can call the novel's use of language? Clearly Lodge wants to argue that judgements about the appropriateness of certain kinds of linguistic devices (the use of repetition for emphasis, for example) predetermine our views about significance. The difficulty with this proposition is that it leaves unanswered the question of *which* linguistic devices the critic chooses to analyse. As Lodge himself admits, the critic must 'select' linguistic devices; he or she must 'take a certain path' through the novel. The principles on which that selection is made – the manner in which one linguistic path is chosen rather than another – these crucial questions are left unresolved. In fact there is more than a suspicion that it is ideology which determines these choices; so in the critic's mind there exists a prior judgement about the validity of certain ideas which then directs the critic towards a positive identification of those linguistic forms which have been used to represent them. As Lodge had suggested earlier, 'language is designed to carry out a particular view of experience' – a proposition which suggests that it is the critic's initial identification and valuation of 'a particular view of experience' which directs him or her to analyse the effectiveness of the language 'designed' to convey that experience. This dilemma (and its implications for how a novel is to be judged) can be seen more clearly in Lodge's account of *Hard Times*.

As I have suggested, Lodge's essay on *Hard Times* was written in explicit opposition to the moral interpretation of Leavis. In contrast to Leavis, Lodge focuses exclusively on what he terms Dickens's 'rhetoric', and his aim is to define the success and failure of *Hard Times* solely in these terms. The words 'success' and 'failure' of course imply a value-judgment, and Lodge's concern, no less than that of Leavis, is to decide whether *Hard Times* is indeed a good novel. The difference is that Lodge's account of the work, by being limited to a description of its textual features, gives the appearance of being more objective; that is, it does not obviously depend upon contested or anachronistic judgements about what constitutes 'life' or 'humanity'. On closer examination, however, and despite these differences, Lodge's essay turns out to share many of the limitations of Leavis's account of the novel.

The easiest way to glimpse these limitations is by comparing Lodge's account of what he calls the novel's successful and failed rhetorical strategies. Like Leavis, Lodge begins by noting the strength of Dickens's opening chapter; and again like Leavis, he judges the portrait of Gradgrind's school to be entirely successful. For Lodge, that success is the result of Dickens's 'rhetorical patterning': his 'manipulation of repeated words' and his use of 'metaphors of growth and cultivation'.[19] And again like Leavis, Lodge goes on to argue that this rhetoric 'works to establish a symbolic atmosphere' and that the efficacy of the rhetoric has nothing to do with the accuracy of the novel's representation:

> Whether [the chapter] represents fairly any actual educational theory or practice in mid-nineteenth-century England is really beside the point. It aims to convince us of the *possibility* of children being taught in such a way, and to make us recoil from the imagined possibility. The chapter succeeds or fails as rhetoric; and I think it succeeds.[20]

Lodge then turns to what he perceives to be the novel's weaknesses, and he concentrates on exactly those episodes mentioned by Leavis: the portrayal of Slackbridge, the unions and Stephen Blackpool. Unlike Leavis, though, Lodge does not try to revalue these episodes; but nor does he attribute their failure to the conservatism of Dickens's politics or to the alleged limitation of bourgeois ideology. Lodge rather argues that the problem is simply one of rhetoric. He suggests that the reader is dissatisfied because Dickens's rhetorical devices are inappropriate: indeed at one point he claims that the metaphors are not sufficiently 'inventive'. In a revealing paragraph, Lodge uses this example of failed rhetoric to demonstrate the overall importance of his linguistic approach:

> the failure of understanding here reveals itself in the first place as a failure of expression; the portrait of Gradgrind, on the other hand, though it probably derives from an equivalent misunderstanding of Utilitarianism, succeeds.[21]

A basic definition of rhetoric is that it is language use which is consciously designed to persuade; successful rhetoric is therefore language which succeeds in persuading us. If a consideration of 'rhetorical patterning' is to form the basis of a judgement about

Hard Times, we might ask: about what exactly is Dickens trying to persuade us? At this point the limitations of Lodge's emphasis on language become apparent. In his account of the novel, Dickens's persuasiveness – his rhetoric – is completely unrelated to an understanding of the novel's reference, of actual events; so Lodge paradoxically argues that Dickens can be 'wrong' about Utilitarianism but still persuade us of the rightness of his criticism of it. The shortcoming of this argument is that it obscures the fact that the values which allow us to make such a distinction must themselves be nonrhetorical. More simply we might ask: what criteria is Lodge using to define rhetoric as successful? At this point there is once again more than a suspicion that the term 'successful rhetoric' is a way of defining those views which map on to Lodge's own values; and that unsuccessful rhetoric refers to views which Lodge disagrees with. To put matters bluntly, it is ideology which is silently providing the criteria for judgement about rhetoric. This suspicion is reinforced towards the end of the essay, when Lodge elaborates another rhetorical strategy which the novel employs: that of the fairy-tale. Lodge notices that the devices of the fairy-tale are used by Dickens with varying degrees of success:

> where Dickens invokes the world of the fairy-tale ironically, to dramatize the drabness, greed, spite and injustice which characterize a society dominated by materialism, it is a highly effective rhetorical device; but where he relies on the simplifications of the fairy-tale to suggest means of redemption, we remain unconvinced.[22]

The paradox here is one not dissimilar to the tautology underlying Leavis's account of the fable elements of the novel. It is not clear whether it is the devices of the fairy-tale – the 'rhetorical patterning' – which determine the validity of the views expressed; or, conversely, whether it is the validity of the views expressed which determines the appropriateness of the devices of the fairy-tale.

At this point it is helpful to return to Lodge's general account of criticism. As I suggested, it is unclear whether he assumes that certain linguistic devices are inherently pleasing, or whether he assumes that certain ideas are 'right' and in turn direct the critic towards an approval of those linguistic forms which represent them. His analysis of *Hard Times* seems to suggest the second possibility: the appropriateness of the fairy-tale – its 'effectiveness' as a means of communication – seems to be defined in contextual rather than absolute terms; that is, the properties of the fairy-tale (its simplifications) 'work' when expressing some ideas – of which Lodge approves – but not others. The implication here is that 'effectiveness' requires some sort of 'fit' between a rhetorical device and an idea expressed. (To repeat again Lodge's formula, 'language is *designed* to carry out a particular view of experience'.) But what criteria will allow us to define this fitness? How do we judge the appropriateness of the 'design'? In the case of *Hard Times*, it would seem that the fairy-tale is a fit device to critique Coketown's materialism because materialism itself is assumed to be amenable to the simplistic moral dichotomies which characterise fairy-tales. Similarly the fairy-tale is not a fit device to persuade us of 'redemption' because redemption is assumed to be too complex a phenomenon to be encompassed by the simplistic morality of the fairy-tale form. The important point to notice here is that 'fitness' is not being determined by any properties that inhere in rhetorical devices, but rather by a value-judgement about what constitutes materialism and redemption – about, that is, the 'view of experience' which the language expresses. More importantly, we should note that these judgements are *Lodge's*, not Dickens's. So it is possible to imagine a writer holding to a different definition of redemption (which the critic may or may not agree with), one for which the rhetoric of the fairy-tale would be an entirely appropriate and convincing medium. Lodge's argument, then, contains exactly the same kind of limitation as that of Leavis, for Lodge too judges the effectiveness of the novel in terms of what would constitute an appropriate response to Utilitarianism or materialism when those phenomena are defined and valued from the point of view of the twentieth-century critic. As a consequence, his account turns out to reveal much more about himself, and his own values, than it does about those of Dickens; more significantly, it collapses that important distinction (which Lodge had earlier insisted upon) between an objective description of a text and a subjective (literary) response to it.

In one sense the anachronisms which (I have argued) limit the work of Lodge and Leavis are to be expected, for their ahistorical approach to literary works simply would not see as significant conceptual discontinuities between, say, the 1840s or 1850s and the 1950s or 1960s. More precisely, their critical precepts prevent Leavis and Lodge from seeing that such discontinuities might be relevant to how we interpret *Hard Times*, and to how we judge the effectiveness of its polemic. We might expect that accounts which make a virtue of paying attention to historical contingency would avoid this kind to anachronism, and would therefore provide a less restrictive reading of the social-problem novels. However, somewhat surprisingly, this turns out not to be the case: as I will show below, 'political', 'contextualist' and 'new historicist' accounts of the social-problem novels all betray a similar sort of insensitivity to the specificities of historical circumstance; it is simply that these insensitivities take different and very much more subtle forms.

I

The individual works which are now commonly categorised as social-problem novels attracted the attention of a variety of critics in both the late nineteenth and early twentieth centuries; but a stress on the writer's political or social (as opposed to a literary or aesthetic) conscience made it inevitable that the generic relationship between the individual works (which was needed in order to categorise the social-problem novels as a distinct sub-genre) was first established systematically by a group of Marxist critics – Raymond Williams, Arnold Kettle and, principally, John Lucas. The linking of the novels in this way can best be understood as part of a larger project in literary historiography, an attempt to use some Marxist critical paradigms in order to challenge the assumptions underlying the critical hegemony which had been established by previous critics, and particularly by F. R. Leavis and his prescriptive view of the 'great tradition'. The restriction of Leavis's 'tradition', it was argued, had literally prevented him from 'seeing' social-problem novels. As a consequence the identification of the social-problem novels as a distinct group by Williams, Kettle and Lucas became a vindication of their new historiographical method, for without it what they claimed to be important 'events' in literary history simply went unnoticed and so unmarked.

What was new about their literary history was the locating of literary understanding within a revised notion of historical context, one which encompassed social, cultural and principally economic circumstances. Underlying such a view was an adaptation of a popular Marxist literary historiography in which works of fiction were to be analysed in terms of the attitudes which they took towards the economic base of a society. This view in turn assumed

that knowledge of those attitudes was the most important information to be derived from works of fiction.[23] The social-problem
novels seemed to present the paradigm case for such a historical
method, because it was suggested that in them literary or aesthetic
ambitions are most clearly subordinate to political or social
concerns. In this history, then, the most significant attitudes to the
economic base were those which Marxism assumed to be most critical of the demoralising tendencies of bourgeois capitalism. As a
result social-problem novels were to be valued chiefly in terms of
the radicalism of their political critique.

The nature of that radical critique (a particular way of viewing
class relationships) was laid out in advance by Marxist thought.
This qualification is important, for it means that what is to count as
a problem in society (and an appropriate solution to it) is determined not by nineteenth-century novelists, but by the twentieth-
century Marxist critics who engage with their works. One caveat
never entertained in this Marxist literary history was the possibility
that definitions of 'society' – more generally definitions of the
'social', and therefore of what is to count as a 'social' problem –
might themselves be historically unstable. In other words, Marxist
critics were not alert to the possibility that there are pre-Marxist
ways of defining both society and the social, and that these may
have more relevance to understanding the problems in society (and
the solutions offered to them) identified in pre-Marxist novels. Like
Leavis and Lodge, political accounts of the social-problem novels
have failed to distinguish adequately between the conceptual
schema employed by the twentieth-century literary critic, and those
concepts available to the nineteenth-century author. A more
detailed examination of the work of Williams, Kettle, Lucas and
Gagnier (who draws upon the line of argument established by the
earlier three critics) will indicate just how pervasive and distorting
this shortcoming can be.

Raymond Williams's *Culture and Society: 1780–1950* (1958) is often
rightly cited as a seminal work of cultural history. In it Williams
devotes a chapter to what he calls 'the industrial novels', a chapter
which describes one moment in a larger historical sweep which is
characterised by a series of fundamental changes in what Williams
calls the 'structure of meanings' – that is, changes in 'our characteristic ways of thinking about our common life: about our social,
political, and economic institutions; about the purposes which
these institutions are designed to embody; and about the relations

to these institutions and purposes of our activities in learning, education, and the arts'.[24] Williams goes on to identify five key terms, the definitions of which map these changes in the 'structure of meanings'. The terms are: 'industry, democracy, class, art, and culture'. He then discusses a number of works (both fictional and non-fictional) which he argues provide evidence of the changed meanings of these key terms. It is through an examination of these works, and the changed modes of thinking which they embody, that we are able to glimpse the 'tradition' which, Williams argues, produced modern British society.

According to Williams, the significance of the group of works which he calls 'industrial novels' (*Mary Barton, North and South, Hard Times, Sybil, Alton Locke* and *Felix Holt*) lies in their articulation of a 'common criticism of industrialism', one which has 'persisted ... into both the literature and the social thinking of our own time'. The main limitation of the criticism, and one which characterises all of the novels in the group, is that a 'recognition of evil was balanced by fear of becoming involved. Sympathy was transformed, not into action, but into withdrawal'.[25] In other words, the industrial novelists all fail to confront fully what Williams terms the 'evils' of industrialisation, and they also fail to provide any satisfactory way of countering them. Williams goes on to argue that such failures were a consequence of what he terms a 'general structure of feeling' which exists independently of what he calls the 'facts' of industrial society, and which determined the intellectual, moral and political imagination of the novelists in question.[26] In all of this, the main aim of examining a nineteenth-century sub-genre was to shed critical light on modern modes of thought, for the limitations which Williams identifies in the industrial novels are also the limitations of 'our own time' (of, that is, the 1950s).

The labels 'structure of feeling' and 'structure of meanings' have been criticised for their inexactitude and they might perhaps strike the modern reader as quaint. Nonetheless Williams's work provided the generation of critics who followed him with a powerful way of analysing the relationship between literature and the society which produced it. We now tend to subsume what Williams was describing under the umbrella term 'ideology', and what Williams tried to identify as 'meaning' and 'feeling' are now defined as part of a much larger group of social phenomena. Indeed, if we recognise a theoretical continuity between Williams's concepts and those developed in more abstract Marxist thinking, his writing seems

much less dated. Nevertheless there are anomalies in his work, and
these apply equally to his successors: in other words, they apply to
the principles underlying the Marxist paradigm which Williams
was instrumental in helping to establish and popularise.

The first anomaly concerns Williams's assumption that 'facts'
(about industrialisation or whatever) are simply self-evident, and
that they exist independently of the values, prejudices or politics of
the individuals who identify them. The second is the contradiction
between his assertion that a 'structure of feeling' is 'determining'
and his subsequent criticism of novelists who fail to resist it. Both
anomalies are a direct result of Williams's (and Marxism's) failure
to perceive the anachronisms which a Marxist historiography produces – the failure, that is, to separate the conceptual schema of the
Victorians from that of the present. Williams's dilemma is a local
example of a larger problem in philosophy (and particularly in the
philosophy of history) concerning the relationship between facts
and values. In principle, the number of facts about any given
subject is always infinite. When we talk about 'facts' we always
assume that certain criteria of relevance are in operation: the term
'facts', in other words, refers only to those facts which are considered relevant to any particular topic, and relevance is in turn determined by criteria specific to both history and culture as well as to
the particular values, prejudices and politics of the historians or
critics concerned.[27] So, what are to count as the facts – the relevant
facts, we should say – about industrialisation will always be
identified in different ways (depending on the historical and cultural location of the values, principles or prejudices of the individuals who are making the identification). Facts about industrialisation
will therefore invariably differ and will probably be contested.
Williams's 'facts' (which he assumes are the *only* facts) are in
practice derived from the values of Marxist politics which identifies
as important certain kinds of economic facts, such as the allegedly
class-based nature of the means of production. It is clear that any
individual who does not share (or in the case of the Victorian
novelist, could not possibly have access to) Marxist schemata, and
thus to Marxist value-systems, will identify a set of facts about
industrialisation which could be very different indeed: for these
individuals industrialisation could quite literally be a different
phenomenon. Consequently, the way in which Victorian novelists
analyse and explain the problems of industrialisation – and hence
the solutions they find to those problems – are also likely to be dif-

ferent. What Williams fails to acknowledge is that a 'structure of feeling' and the 'facts' which indicate a problem in society are causally related to each other. So the 'structure of feeling' which determined the Victorians' frame of reference may have prevented them from recognising the facts about industrialisation which Williams was later to identify. In this sense it is simply unhelpful to criticise the Victorians for their 'fear of becoming involved' (with the facts) and their subsequent 'withdrawal' (from the facts), when the whole domain of what are to count as facts (and how those facts are to be interpreted) will be contested because of the non-identical value-systems by which Williams and Victorian novelists identify different facts.

In the same year as Williams published *Culture and Society*, another Marxist critic, Arnold Kettle, drew attention to the importance of the self-same group of novels, but he emphasised rather different elements in them.[28] Rather than label them 'industrial novels', Kettle employed the term 'social-problem' novel on the grounds that most of the works in question are concerned with the poor in general rather than factory workers in particular. Kettle acknowledged that subjects such as social disturbance and economic inequality – in brief, 'social' issues – were not in themselves at all new in English fiction; he suggested that they can be found in a 'tradition' stretching from Hogarth through to Swift, Defoe and Fielding. However, in Kettle's eyes, what distinguishes the attention given to the poor by some mid-Victorian novelists is the *quality* of their insight, and he coined the term 'social-problem' to try to capture this quality.

In fact the first word in Kettle's label – 'social' – was not his invention. It was derived from an older description and categorisation of the novels made by critics such as Louis Cazamian and Kathleen Tillotson, who used the simple phrase 'social novels'.[29] Kettle argued that such terminology was inadequate because all novels are in some sense 'social novels' – they are all, that is, in some sense about society. By contrast, what matters for Kettle is precisely the attitude towards, or engagement with, society. In this sense, the second item in Kettle's label, 'problem', identifies the special nature of the Victorian novelists' social interests. Kettle went on to argue that to think in terms of 'problems' presupposes a certain kind of reification, one characterised by a remote 'abstraction': that is, by 'the limit of involvement – emotional and artistic rather than social and political – concerned'. The social-problem novelists, in other words, are distinguished by the fact that they 'preach' where that preaching or 'didacticism' is 'incompletely fused', the term 'fused' standing for some kind of emotional identification by the novelist with the subjects of his or her work.[30] Kettle refines his definition further by arguing that the degree of abstraction and the degree of identification or involvement is significant. So social-problem novels are also marked by their intensity, a quality which is explained by comparing them with works such as William Godwin's *Caleb Williams* and Edward Bulwer-Lytton's *Pelham*. The latter two novels, according to Kettle, are 'socially-conscious works', but they fail to be 'true' social-problem novels because they are 'disastrously and often ludicrously abstract ... one has the sense that what is being written about is not life but ideas about life. Even when they become involved with a specific social situation ... they manage to dehydrate the reality into an abstract generalization'.[31] Social-problem novels, in other words, are abstract and 'preaching', but they also possess elements which are strongly 'concrete'. What determines this concreteness – this attention to the details of 'life', or to 'reality' – are 'changing social conditions and forces and also partly ... ideological developments':

> In the first place the actual size and urgency of the problem of poverty was so great and so obvious by the forties that it was almost impossible to treat it from a largely theoretical standpoint. In the second place, with the Reform Bill of 1832 and especially with the Chartist movement, political action had become more than a future possibility.[32]

In all of this we have a body of value-judgements and assumptions which are very close to those of Raymond Williams. So Kettle, like Williams, judges the social-problem novels principally in terms of their understanding of 'life', and he comments (again like Williams) on the limits of their involvement – their tendency, that is, to also remain detached or withdrawn from life (that is, to be abstract). Significantly, what defines 'life' or 'concreteness' (which, in Williams's terms, is an attention to the 'facts') is again simply assumed by Kettle – it is 'reality'; and abstraction, the analysis of those concrete details, is again seen as an entirely separate activity, one strikingly similar to Williams's 'structure of feeling'. Not surprisingly, some difficulties arise when Kettle attempts to evaluate a novel's understanding of life in terms of the relationship between the concrete and the abstract. In the case of Disraeli, for example, Kettle admires the 'conscientious use of documentary details' but at the same time he admits that such concreteness does not 'guarantee the novel's status as serious writing'. In Disraeli's novel, seriousness is to be found in the analysis of details, but when indeed he turns to this analysis, Kettle complains that there is an 'artificiality, which is sometimes more than a little ridiculous, a glibness we are right to hold suspect'. The paradox is that the feature which defines Disraeli as a social-problem novelist – his abstraction, 'a quality of limited engagement' – on inspection also turns out to be his work's most serious shortcoming. A similar dilemma occurs in Kettle's account of *Mary Barton*. Here, too, he admires concreteness – that is, Mrs Gaskell's involvement 'with the actual life of the people' – but he is critical of that specificity on two grounds: that in this case there is simply not enough abstraction (or analysis), and that when abstraction does occur, it equivocates – it becomes 'fence-sitting'.[33]

It is possible to suggest some reasons for Kettle's unease with accommodating Victorian novelists' emphasis on specificity with his notion of their abstraction. It is worth recalling his initial premise that abstraction implies a kind of withdrawal or limit to the novelist's involvement. It should now be clear that the identification of this shortcoming derives from the discrepancy between what the documentary detail in the novels (their 'concreteness') suggests to Kettle, and what it suggests to the individual novelists. Simply put, that detail is not interpreted or analysed by the Victorians as it is by a modern Marxist critic; and the limitation of Kettle's account is his failure to provide any adequate explanation as to why this should be so. He suggests, rather unhelpfully, that it is related to an absence of 'emotional and artistic' involvement – that it is, in some sense, a personal failing. Significantly, he does not see that the discrepancy might be historically determined, perhaps because his concept of historical determination is limited to explaining how the 'reality' of poverty – the 'actual size and urgency of the problem' – forced writers to take note of it. Another way of putting this point is to say that Kettle takes the documentary detail in the social-problem novels to be evidence of 'reality', without realising that 'reality' for the Victorians (that is, their understanding of the kind of social problem poverty gave rise to) might be different from Kettle's 'reality' – that is, from *his* reading of mid-nineteenth-

century social history. In these respects, Kettle has repeated exactly
the strategic errors which Williams makes: by assuming that certain
facts about mid-nineteenth-century society are simply self-evident,
his literary history makes inappropriate historical judgements
about the works it identifies. That is, the judgements which Kettle
makes once again tell us more about his view of nineteenth-century
problems in society than they do about the views of the Victorian
novelists.

The next significant Marxist account of the social-problem novels
was a long and detailed essay by John Lucas. Entitled 'Mrs Gaskell
and Brotherhood', it was contained in another influential work of
literary history, *Tradition and Tolerance in Nineteenth-Century Fiction*,
a book of essays by John Goode, David Howard and Lucas published in 1966. Lucas begins his account of the social-problem novel
with a definition familiar from Kettle's work: a social-problem
novel is a novel which 'includes among its definitive concerns a
conscious attempt to solve what are seen as problems'. Lucas adds
the important rider that 'the reduction of the living complex to a
problem comes to the fore only when whatever political attitude is
implied in the recommendation takes over as a shaping force in the
novel'.[34] The terms are vague, but the drift of his essay seems to
follow Kettle's argument; like Kettle, Lucas seems to be suggesting
that the distinctiveness of the social-problem novel resides in the
prevalence of an author's political, rather than imaginative, judgements. Indeed he sees the two existing in a virtual contradiction to
each other, believing that an attention to the political 'is bound to
get in the way of the novelist's exploration of his characters' lives
and interrelationships; demands will be made on plot and theme
which must damage the novel's essential freedom, its integrity'.[35] It
is clear that Lucas is defining integrity in terms of an artistic or literary imagination – a caveat which, as I shall argue, is important to
bear in mind when viewing his work in relation to Marxist theory
in general. The basic premise of Lucas's argument, then, is that
there are two ways to approach problems in society – one via the
imagination or literary conscience, and the other via the political.
At first sight it may appear that Lucas is doing little more than
reworking the oppositions to be found in Kettle's argument, for
Kettle had also suggested that a preoccupation with what he called
'the social and political' inevitably led to the marginalisation of 'the
emotional and artistic'. Moreover Lucas repeats Kettle's critical
verdict that an attention to the political at the expense of the imag-

inative has unfortunate consequences – it is the principal cause of the 'failings' of the novels. All these points are familiar from Kettle's work; where Lucas is new, however, is in his attempt to explain *why* this alleged 'failing' occurs so consistently in social-problem novels.

It might be helpful to note in passing that Lucas uses the terms 'political' and 'imaginative' in a very restricted manner: he uses 'political' to refer to a particular party-political position – to what he calls 'stock political attitudes'.[36] Such attitudes are later defined more exactly as the recommendation of a brotherhood of united interests which could provide a solution to social problems. The term 'imaginative' (or literary) on the other hand is defined purely negatively: it refers to ways of thinking which reject or transcend the limitations of party-political ideology. Lucas argues (like Kettle and Williams before him) that in social-problem novels, a predictable political analysis – those 'stock political attitudes' – 'takes over' from a literary or imaginative integrity, and he characterises the moment of this 'political takeover' rather melodramatically as a 'retreat from the abyss', or a bridge over 'imaginative lacunae'. Lucas's reliance upon rhetoric is significant, for it takes the place of a sustained argument. Both the 'withdrawal' described by Williams and the 'lack of involvement' noted by Kettle imply a notion of authorial choice or agency; it is suggested by both Williams and Kettle that the opposites of withdrawal – engagement and involvement – were possibilities consciously and deliberately rejected by the social-problem novelists from the outset. Lucas's more dramatic vocabulary, with its echoes of apocalypse ('retreat from the abyss'), points to a very different situation, one where an intellectual critique was initially begun, but then abruptly halted. Lucas appears to be proposing that a rejection of a dominant ideology (for this is what 'stock political attitudes' amount to) is initially contemplated; at some point in the novel, however, the author finds that such a stance is intolerably difficult or dangerous, and then retreats into the safety of conventional views.

The phrase Lucas uses to describe this situation is a 'split between intention and achievement',[37] where 'intention' appears to mean the decision to contest a dominant ideology and 'achievement' appears to mean the final endorsing of it. Moreover, what is important for Lucas is the precise moment in the novel when this split occurs. Crudely put, the later the retreat from the 'abyss', the better Lucas finds the novel: indeed the best works in the sub-genre are those where intention most fully 'contradicts' achievement. So Lucas admires Mrs Gaskell's *Mary Barton* where a disjunction between intention and achievement seems to occur about mid-way through the novel; but he criticises Dickens's *Hard Times*, a work whose attitudes – its 'achievements', that is – are allegedly 'predetermined' from the outset. Lucas identifies these disjunctions by reference to changes in the formal conventions which a writer employs. For example, he argues that *Mary Barton* is composed of two different styles or kinds of formal devices: documentary realism in the first half of the novel (which he admires), and melodramatic devices in the second half (which he criticises). The split between intention and achievement – the 'retreat from the abyss' – occurs at exactly the moment when realism gives way to melodrama. In the case of *Hard Times*, Dickens's 'predetermined attitudes' are identified with his highly metaphoric style, particularly his descriptions of Coketown. Given that Lucas connects (what he judges to be) valuable or appropriate responses to problems in society (the initial 'intentions' of the writers) with the imaginative faculty, it may seem odd that he appears to be critical of those elements in a novel which are most insistently fictional – those elements, that is, which draw attention to the novel's status as an artefact. However, the paradox disappears once we realise that he is using the term 'imaginative' in a wholly evaluative way. As I explain in more detail later, it simply refers to those ideological positions with which he himself agrees; importantly, it has no reference to the literary or imaginative criteria of the Victorians themselves. There are of course some difficulties with this line of argument. First, it is by no means self-evident that the devices of realism are inherently more or less 'literary' (or imaginative) than those of melodrama; and second, it is not clear that the Victorians valued realism and melodrama in these terms anyway. These difficulties notwithstanding, Lucas's final task in his essay is to explain the causes of the split between intention and achievement. Once again we are given a rather general explanation: it turns out that middle-class novelists draw back from the 'abyss' when they realise that to question the dominant bourgeois liberal ideology, particularly the belief in 'progress', is to undermine the middle-class's *'raison d'être'*.[38]

In contrast to Kettle and Williams, Lucas's essay certainly provides a more detailed and sympathetic account of the constraints under which mid-Victorian novelists worked. Williams's loose and problematic terms 'structure of feeling' and 'structure of meaning', and Kettle's general allusion to 'ideological developments' are, in Lucas's essay, refined to the more manageable notion of 'stock political attitudes'. Indeed there is also some attempt to engage with the Marxist concept of ideology. Unfortunately, however, what is absent from Lucas's argument is anything which resembles an explanation of those 'imaginative resources' which possess the potential to oppose the dominant ideology. As I suggested above, Lucas tends to define 'imagination' only negatively: it is the opposite of 'stock political attitudes'. In practice, Lucas's essay specifies as 'imaginative' and 'honest' anything which coincides with his own (Marxist) analysis of nineteenth-century social problems; anything which fails to do so is characterised as a 'stock political attitude', and its alleged presence in the novel is attributed to the latent bourgeois liberalism of the novelists he discusses. In such a scheme, the most valuable social-problem novels turn out to be those whose authors are most ambivalent about their own class interests: those, that is, who indicate the greatest disquiet with the appeal to nationhood made by nineteenth-century bourgeois politics – the 'brotherhood of united interests'. Here we can see the limitations of Lucas's opposition between the imaginative and the political, for it turns out that the kind of understanding which is described as imaginative is in itself no less political than 'stock political attitudes'; and to identify it as 'imaginative' (a term ironically derived from a pre-Marxist Romantic tradition) is to suggest, rather misleadingly, that the imagination exists in, or has access to, a realm outside politics and history – that in some unproblematic way it embodies a 'truth' which is simply 'there' and which Victorian novelists (for political reasons) chose to ignore. This turn in Lucas's argument is thus ironically reminiscent of the attitudes of F. R. Leavis. Leavis, whose own definition of the relationship of life to literature was instrumental in provoking the hostile Marxist reaction of the 1950s and 1960s, had also asserted that literature (or, more loosely, the imagination) has the potential to provide an understanding which goes beyond politics, and that it thereby achieves some kind of privileged access to 'life'. The chasm between Leavis and Lucas of course lies in their different definitions of what is to count as 'life'. We ought to note, however, that neither definition is one which would necessarily coincide with the mid-Victorians' own views on these matters.

The fundamental difficulty in Lucas's account exists in the different and contradictory ways he conceives of the opposition between his two different modes of thought – the political and the imaginative. So political thinking ('stock political attitudes') is accounted for in historical terms: that is, it is produced by a dominant ideology in the nineteenth century. By contrast 'imaginative' thinking appears not to be historically located; it seems to belong to a category of intellectual activity which is individual and is thus free from social constraints and historical determination. The relationship of such a category to literary works is vexed, for the whole idea of a non-social novel is not an easy one to grasp, and it rather tends to contradict a central premise of Marxism, that works of art, like every other human activity, are socially produced. In fact the dilemma here is not one confined to Lucas's work: a central theme in Marxist theorising in the 1960s was the problematic relationship between the concepts of ideology and of social determinism. Briefly, the central question in this debate was how an ideology can be resisted. If ideology is determining, then resistance to it must come from a non-ideological realm. The problem for Marxism (and particularly for Marxist critics interested in art and literature) was that the identification of such a realm with works of art tended to imply that art itself is non-social; but the whole idea of non-social explanations of human products or human phenomena is precisely what Marxism rejected. One disappointment of Lucas's argument is his failure to make any reference to these larger debates.[39]

In practice, of course, Lucas's account avoids confronting these and similar problems by implying that imaginative thinking is either simply the 'truth' or that it offers an unmediated access to it. Such a view amounts to saying no more than that the imagination represents a particular way of thinking about society which Lucas approves of, and to which he holds. In this 'sleight of hand' there is a strong suspicion of what the American philosopher Richard Rorty has called 'doxography' – the reconstruction of nineteenth-century history in terms of the analogies which can be can made with modern, twentieth-century views. A typical strategy of doxography is to evaluate the work of past writers in terms of their ability to answer questions defined from a modern (that is, late twentieth-century) point of view. Moreover, underlying such a practice is an assumption that there are fundamental conceptual continuities across large historical periods. It is precisely these views which Lucas appears to hold, for he assumes that the imaginative thinking which he values as the 'truth' – a radical way of contesting nineteenth-century bourgeois ideology – was available to the social-problem novelists and their readers in *more or less the same way* as it is available to him, and that therefore those Victorian readers and writers who eschewed it were either intellectually limited or morally dishonest. Indeed Victorian novelists are criticised in exactly these terms throughout Lucas's essay: some social-problem novels, he argues, are characterised by their 'failure to deal honestly with social experience'; more precisely, the 'retreat from the abyss' represents 'a failure of imaginative honesty [and] ... the writer's unwillingness to follow the implications of his given situation through to the end'.[40] (The use here of the terms 'honest' and 'honesty' is, of course, highly significant in that it assumes a criterion of truth – analogous to the 'facts' or 'concreteness' mentioned by Williams and Kettle – which Lucas presents as a given, but which he never feels constrained to justify or defend.)

A modern reader might feel that Lucas's assumption that his own understanding of social problems was available to the Victorians, and that there were conceptual continuities between the mid-nineteenth century and the 1960s, should at least be demonstrated. Of course some Victorian social concepts may have survived into the twentieth century (it would be odd if they had failed to do so); but we need to know exactly *which* concepts these are. More importantly, we also need to know how the status of those concepts changed. It might be the case that the Victorians, like Lucas, possessed a concept of 'class-consciousness', but it is quite possible (and indeed likely) that to employ such a concept in the intellectual climate of the 1860s meant something very different from employing it in the 1960s. The term 'socialism', for example, has been in use in British culture since the early nineteenth century, but its meanings and significance have changed profoundly over that period of time. In this respect, it is not really helpful to think in terms of large-scale conceptual continuities, because the meaning, significance and status of concepts undergo constant modification in relation to other social, political, cultural and intellectual developments. These points aside, there is a further and much more obvious drawback in Lucas's account. His essay consistently demonstrates that *his* analysis of social problems is simply absent from mid-Victorian fiction – at least it is not present in any sustained or committed way. Lucas never considers the (perhaps too obvious) possibility that the Victorians do not reproduce his

views because those views were simply not available to them or
that they did not formulate social problems in the same way as he
does. Lucas's 'truth', like Williams's and Kettle's 'life', is exactly the
opposite; it is not *the* 'truth', nor can it be assumed to be the
Victorians' 'truth'. Simple though this observation may sound, it
opens up a new way of investigating the social-problem novels,
and a new way of valuing them. Rather than trying to be proto-
Marxists and failing, the social-problem novelists might have had
very different ambitions which they pursued in ways which were
successful in their terms. The split which Lucas identifies between
'achievement' and 'intention' may simply be the result of a
mischaracterisation of nineteenth-century novelists' intentions (of
the way they formulate problems in society), in turn the result of an
anachronistic reading of certain aspects of mid-nineteenth-century
intellectual culture.

It might be thought that the kind of history which Lucas
practised is now rather dated, and that more sophisticated forms
of Marxism developed in the 1980s and 1990s would perhaps have
avoided some of its inconsistencies. It is all the more disappointing, then, to find that one of the most prominent and sophisticated
of recent materialist critics, Regenia Gagnier, in her account of
nineteenth-century working-class autobiographies, *Subjectivities*
(1991), simply repeats the basic tenets of the Williams–Kettle–
Lucas line of argument. She suggests that the account of social
problems given by Victorian realist novelists is deficient because
it is limited by its middle-class or bourgeois ideology; however,
she attempts to give a new authority to this familiar case by
framing it within that she calls the 'technical terms of structuralism and narratology':

> In middle-class fiction, when a crisis of irreconcilability occurs
> between two classes (e.g., 'masters and men' find their interests
> irreconcilable), and the plot logically threatens violent conflict, it
> is redirected from class conflict to romantic love and Christian
> charity. This plot redirection is concomitant with a narratological
> event called *suture* – when the viewpoints of the implied author,
> the characters, and the intended readership gradually converge
> at the point of closure ... The implied author's views are sutured
> with (or become 'seamlessly' indistinguishable from) model
> characters', and that identification sutures with the interpellated
> reader's, to create an ideological view of 'reality'. In the fiction I

have been discussing, the convergent viewpoints of author, character, and reader hold that social conflict can be resolved by acceptance of hierarchy and philanthropy rather than economic restructuring, or that the human spirit can survive any amount of material deprivation.[41]

The unproblematic use Gagnier makes of categories such as 'middle-class fiction', 'class conflict' (which later shifts to 'social conflict'), 'acceptance of hierarchy', 'economic structuring' and 'material deprivation' is typical of the approach established by Williams, Kettle and Lucas. Once again, it makes no distinction between those concepts which are exclusive to twentieth-century literary critics (and which have been derived from a specific twentieth-century interpretation of Marxism), and those which were available to, but for some reason not used by, nineteenth-century novelists. For Gagnier's criticisms to make both historical *and* political sense we need to know whether the nineteenth-century novelists in question analysed their society in the same (or analogous) terms as their twentieth-century critics: that is, *did* writers such as Gaskell, Dickens, Disraeli, Kingsley and Eliot define deprivation exclusively in terms of material wants? Did they see social conflict and class conflict as synonymous terms? Did they share a certain twentieth-century view of the primacy of the economic, and the conviction that problems in society should be resolved by reference to social structures. If the answer to any of these questions is 'no' – that is, if there is no simple conceptual continuity between nineteenth-century novelists and late twentieth-century Marxist literary critics – then the critical accounts of this group are telling us nothing more profound than the fact that nineteenth-century social-problem novelists did not analyse society in the same way as a modern Marxist might. Hence the contradictions and confusions perceived in their works may simply be the result of assuming the novelists were answering questions which they never actually posed. The Marxist claim that to offer 'philanthropy' or 'Christian brotherhood' rather than 'economic structuring' as a solution to social problems is politically reactionary *only* has force if mid-nineteenth-century writers can be shown to have understood but rejected the concept of 'economic structuring'. If the whole idea of economic structuring was simply alien or unavailable because of the way in which economics and economic policy was understood at that time, then it is difficult to see how the absence of any reference to it can constitute a political, or indeed, an ideological move on behalf of the writer.

II

I have suggested that both ahistorical and political accounts of the social-problem novels depend upon various kinds of anachronism, and that their accounts of these works tell us more about the values of modern critics than they do about the Victorian novelists. I have also argued that in placing the social-problem novels within history, the process of historical explanation must be much more sensitive to the specificities of the intellectual world within which Victorian writers themselves operated. In particular, it is necessary to appreciate that the 'reality' addressed by Victorian novelists was not necessarily the same as the 'reality' which modern critics describe; consequently, the problems which the Victorians perceived may not coincide exactly with the problems which modern critics identify in nineteenth-century society. There have been two further kinds of accounts of the novels which at first sight seem to use the sort of methodology I am advocating in the sense that they both appear to place a much stronger emphasis on historical contingency. The first kind I loosely described in Chapter 1 as 'contextualist', including in it the work of critics such as Louis Cazamian, Kathleen Tillotson, Sheila Smith and John Holloway. The accounts by the first three all have strong affinities with each other: so Cazamian is cited by Tillotson, and Tillotson and Cazamian are, in turn, cited and used by Smith. What marks them out is their attempt to explain a distinctive period of nineteenth-century literary history which is best exemplified by the social-problem novels. So all three accounts define their work chronologically: Cazamian's interest is the period which he defines as '1830–1850', for Tillotson, it is the '1840s', and for Smith, 'the 1840s and 1850s'. (It is worth observing that the tidiness of these dates might make us suspicious of their historiography, for historical causation rarely arranges itself so neatly.) Raymond Williams's *Culture and Society* was also an attempt to describe the social-problem novels in terms of a larger literary history; however Cazamian, Tillotson and Smith distinguish themselves from Williams by the scope and detail of their work. All devote book-length studies to their subject; and all make use of a number and variety of historical documents in order to substantiate their arguments. Cazamian's, Tillotson's and Smith's accounts can also be read as forming a historical narrative in themselves – a narrative about how contextualist literary history should be written, for although there are important continuities between all three accounts, there are also important differences. As we shall see, Tillotson attempts to modify Cazamian, and Smith to revise both of them. By contrast, John Holloway is not part of this narrative; his interest is not in describing a period of literary history, but rather in accounting for a single novel, *Hard Times*. However, I have chosen to discuss Holloway at the end of this section because he shares many of the historiographical principles of contextualist critics, and he also provides an important commentary on them.

Cazamian's study *Le Roman social en Angleterre: 1830–1850* was the first work of literary history to identify the social-problem novel (or to use Cazamian's terms, the 'social novel with a purpose' or *'roman-à-thèse'*) as a special sub-genre in Victorian fiction, one produced by 'a new emotional and intellectual response to the subject of social relations on the part of English society in general, and the middle class in particular'.[42] First published in France in 1903, Cazamian's work remained highly regarded for a number of years; in 1954 Kathleen Tillotson referred to it as the 'standard survey of the field'. In 1980 Sheila Smith also acknowledged its importance as a 'pioneering' study, although she had reservations about some of the details of its argument.[43] To continue to take seriously a work now almost a century old (and itself almost Victorian) may strike the modern reader as odd. After all the ways in which we 'do' history and 'do' literary criticism have changed almost beyond recognition since 1903. As I have indicated, modern historians (whether literary or otherwise) will hardly ever mark off historical periods (such as 1830–1850) with such adroitness or finality; indeed social historians tend to see the phenomenon with which the social-problem novels allegedly engage – industrialisation – as a group of much more complex and more contradictory processes than Cazamian allows. For example, rather than Cazamian's 'Industrial Revolution',[44] modern historians tend to talk of a variety of industrial changes as part of a process of industrial development which continues to affect Western industrial societies and which predates the nineteenth century by a considerable time. Moreover, within this large account, the details of local history are now given much more significance: so the industrial history of Manchester is seen to be quite different from that of, say, Birmingham. Finally, the work of social historians such as Dorothy Thompson has led us to revalue in dramatic ways the politics of the middle years of the nineteenth century.[45] In simple terms, the 'documentary' qualities which Cazamian finds in social-problem novels will be quite different from those which a modern historian might consider to be relevant to understanding industrialisation. Why, then, treat a work from 1903 as anything other than a historical curiosity – that is, as a document which demonstrates the limits of early twentieth-century thought?

Part of the answer lies in the publication history of Cazamian's work. In 1973 – that is, some seventy years after its first appearance in France, and seven years after Lucas's and Lodge's essays – Martin Fido produced an English translation of *Le Roman social en Angleterre* under the title of *The Social Novel in England: 1830–1850.*[46] Interestingly, the case which Fido made for his translation was not that Cazamian's work was an important historical document, but rather that it had a continuing significance as criticism. Indeed Fido hoped his translation would make the work available to a wide English-speaking audience. In his Foreword, he acknowledged that Cazamian's account was undoubtedly dated, and he suggested that its critical limitations 'to some extent, set it back in the period when it was written'. Fido had reservations not only about Cazamian's 'sources', but also about his approach to his subject, describing it as 'sufficiently un-English to present us with some difficulties'. In particular those difficulties related to Cazamian's interest in 'grasping broad movements and sweeping intellectual trends' – a mode of enquiry which, Fido suggested, resulted in some unreliable critical judgements. These caveats notwithstanding, Fido went on to argue that the book's 'essential meaning' was still valuable, and that as a whole it 'remains a work of great importance, the standard study of its subject, and one whose view of Victorian fiction could well be allowed more influence than it has normally been granted in England'. 'Our understanding of Dickens, Disraeli, Mrs Gaskell and Kingsley', Fido argued, 'is enhanced' by Cazamian's 'terms'.[47] As I suggested above, it is important to realise that Fido was making this claim for the significance of Cazamian's work seven years *after* Kettle's, Williams's, and Lucas's accounts of the social-problem novels. In fact Fido refers to this Marxist tradition, but he does so in ambiguous terms, praising its description and assessment of individual novels as 'cogent', but suggesting that it offered no overall thesis about their historical determination – about, that is, the 'thought of the society that produced [them]'. It is on these grounds that, according to Fido, Cazamian 'comes into his own' for he describes the 'intellectual movement linking one book to another'.[48] At this point it might be objected that Fido's criticism of Williams, Kettle and Lucas was misplaced in that it misunderstood Marxist historiography; more specifically, Fido perhaps failed to realise that Marxism understands 'intellectual trends' in terms of 'ideology' rather than 'ideas' – that is, in Marxism, the concept of ideology presupposes a notion of historical causation which Fido implies is missing from Williams's, Kettle's and Lucas's accounts. However, such a qualification, while it may be perfectly correct, does not necessarily invalidate Cazamian's thesis, nor indeed Fido's claims for it. A more appropriate question to ask would be whether the kind of historical determination which Cazamian describes is a more useful one than that offered by Marxist critics.

Given the limitations of Marxist historiography which I described earlier, and my suggestion that a useful account of the social-problem novels needs to attend to the specificities of the intellectual world within which the Victorians operated, Cazamian's emphasis on 'intellectual trends' may seem to promise much. Unfortunately, in practice it promises much more than it delivers. His argument is that the period between 1830 and 1850 saw the development of a new kind of response to social problems, one which he terms (rather clumsily perhaps) 'the idealist and interventionist reaction'. Opposed to this new response was the (equally clumsily named) 'rationalist movement and individualism'.[49] Cazamian argues that the fiction of the period can be explained (and should be judged) in terms of this opposition. So, on the one hand, there are novels which are characterised by their rationalist intellectual trend – 'utilitarian novels'; and on the other, there are works which endorse interventionism – the 'interventionist novels'. Within this framework 'utilitarian novels' are criticised as 'feeble' while 'interventionist novels' are described as 'rich'. Cazamian goes on to define interventionism as 'a positive attempt by the individual or the community to improve social relations'; for a novel to be 'truly a part of the interventionist movement, then its author must expressively have demanded positive action, either from the State, or organised institutions, or private persons'.[50] An informed reader would immediately guess (as Fido fails to do) that

the principal agents identified by Cazamian (the State and organised institutions) and the criteria judging their efficacy (interventionism) belong more to the social history of France at the turn of
the twentieth century than to Britain in the 1840s. Indeed the very
opposition which Cazamian isolates is more appropriate to French
than to British history.

In nineteenth-century Britain individualism and interventionism
were not mutually opposed categories; rather the opposite. As I
shall argue in more detail in the next chapter, a kind of social
atomism underwrote nearly every British response to social problems, regardless of whether they were radical or reactionary, interventionist or *laissez-faire*. More particularly, 'Christian socialism',
the doctrine which Cazamian categorises as interventionist and
therefore anti-individualist, quite openly depended upon an
atomistic model of society, one in which the agency for social
change was *individual* moral responsibility. Interestingly, Cazamian
traces the origins of 'interventionism' to English Romanticism and
the growth of philanthropy: the first he describes as helping define
a notion of 'conscious human brotherhood' and the latter is para-
phrased as meaning 'social duty'.[51] Once again, however, Cazamian
fails to understand that both Romanticism and philanthropy placed
great emphasis on the autonomy and agency of the individual: that
is, neither endorsed a sociological understanding of society which
is a characteristic of French social thought, one where the 'social' is
considered to be something more than the sum of the individuals in
society, and where social change involves structural changes, rather
than changes in the individual conscience. In simple terms,
Cazamian fails to see that the intellectual culture of Victorian
Britain was profoundly different from that of nineteenth-century
France; and that the essential point of difference was the virtual
absence in Britain (until the late decades of the century) of any
tradition of sociological thought. Hence in Britain, unlike France,
the definition of social responsibility (or intervention) was completely compatible with (and in many cases defined by) an emphasis on individual responsibility. Cazamian's failure to recognise this
connection is illustrated most dramatically by his description of
Thomas Carlyle as offering a 'sort of aristocratic, Christian, State
socialism'.[52] In fact the most dominant feature of Carlyle's thought
is an extreme authoritarianism underwritten by a Puritan individualism which advocates an unwavering attention to the individual
'moral self'. Carlyle's work is the paradigmatic example of a British

thinker who combines both a hostility towards *laissez-faire* politics and a deep distrust of the whole conception of the state with a determined emphasis on individual moral responsibility. It is an odd sort of intellectual history which sees Carlyle's criticism of society possessing more in common with 'State socialism' than it does with 'individualism'. Like so many of the other critics I have discussed, Cazamian's fundamental error is his failure to realise that the very terms which he uses to describe the past – 'individualism' and 'interventionism' – are themselves historically determined: they meant one thing to Cazamian, and quite another to the Victorians.

Having identified the intellectual trends which he alleges are characteristic of mid-Victorian Britain, Cazamian proceeds to discuss what he calls the 'literary essence' of the works, defining 'literary' in terms of the accuracy of their representation of social matters. Hence successful literary works are those which produce a 'convincing demonstration of the social conditions which they offer'.[53] At this point any number of questions spring to mind. So we might ask: what is the criterion for determining whether or not a demonstration is 'convincing'? Cazamian's answer is confusing, for he appears to adopt contradictory positions. At one point he states that this judgement is to be based on a modern (political) understanding of what would count as a proper response to Victorian social problems: good novels are novels which convince 'us' – the modern (in his case early twentieth-century) reader. So, for example, Cazamian notes that the 'literary merit of the works [social novels] is in proportion to the special interest they have *for us*'.[54] By contrast, in a later passage he argues that our concern should be with the Victorians' own judgements about literary value, suggesting that the aim of the study is 'to find the information on social problems and proposals for their solutions with which social novels persuaded *their readers*'.[55] Moreover this confusion reappears in the critical methodology which Cazamian adopts.

He outlines four areas of historical enquiry: first, 'the psychological make-up of the novelist' which (a little implausibly, we might think) Cazamian suggests 'offers us a key to the state of public feeling'; second, an examination of 'fictional characters in light of the fact that they were drawn from reality, and were accepted as realistic by the public'. Third, there is the study of 'the public who gave the book its success'; here, Cazamian argues, 'novels are as valuable as any external evidence in our assessment of these people'. Fourth and finally, the critic should take 'a quick glance at writings which are "social" in the same sense, and whose consequences were parallel and similar'.[56] In each of these four areas what is to count as evidence for the understanding of a particular historical event is determined by modern judgements, whether they are about 'psychology', about what comprises 'reality', or about what defines an appropriate definition of the 'social'. Cazamian is unaware of this confusion in his work, mainly, one suspects, because he does not allow for the possibility of historical relativism – in other words, he does not see that there is a difference between the way a modern historian might understand the past and the way that the past was understood by those who lived at the time. Hence those multiple distinctions between modern modes of thought and Victorian modes of thought which I have been insisting upon are simply elided or ignored in Cazamian's work. We can see this process of elision most clearly in his assumption that there is a realm of absolute moral value which defines the key concepts of his history: so the 'interventionist' or 'idealist' approach just *is* 'right'; and the 'individualist' or 'rationalist' approach just *is* 'wrong':

> [Social science] offered an exceptionally clear and lucid exposition of society, and of the necessary principles and consequences of individualism. But its field of vision was narrow, and excluded the truths of sensitivity, organic social relations, human sympathy, charity, and moral or religious responsibilities. On the other hand, we find social consciousness ... Here the perception of reality was clouded by compassion, yet for all its vagueness it was more complete, and marked by a sympathy for suffering which found an echo in the observer, and led to individual or collective relief work.[57]

Ironically Cazamian's explanation of the concepts which he uses makes it abundantly clear that his principles of evaluation are historically contingent, rather than absolute. The criteria which determine his judgements are manifestly derived from contemporary (that is, 1903) French social science. As I suggested earlier, a contrast between the individual good and the communal good is neither self-evident nor inevitable; but it is revealing that such a contrast was in fact made much more consistently in French social science in the last decades of the nineteenth century than it was (or has been since) in Britain. In mid-Victorian Britain, the common good tended to be defined in terms of the sum of individuals' good – or rather, as with modern Conservative thought, there was seen to be a continuity between the individual's good and what was good for society as a whole. More importantly, this was true for virtually all shades of social thought in mid-Victorian Britain, for Christian Socialists as much as for Utilitarians. Cazamian, then, like the Marxist critics I have described, offers anachronisms in the place of history; he too judges the success of the social-problem novels by reference to his *own* understanding of Victorian social problems. The only substantive difference between them is that his explanatory paradigms are derived from French social thinking of the early twentieth century whereas those of Williams, Kettle and Lucas come from British socialism of the 1960s.

As I have suggested, Fido's claim that he was rescuing *Le Roman social en Angleterre* from obscurity was exaggerated. Literary critics interested in the social-problem novels had continued to keep Cazamian's work in mind; and Tillotson's attempt in *Novels of the Eighteen-Forties* to write the literary history of the period acknowledged the importance of Cazamian's work. But like any historian, Tillotson was also keen to define the distinctiveness of her project, and this required that she also show distance between Cazamian's work and her own. The way in which she managed to walk this tight-rope is instructive. Rather than engage with the details of Cazamian's research, or with the substance of his thesis, she chose instead to contrast the nature of his project with her own. The key distinction she makes is between the work of the 'literary historian' and that of the historian 'of society or of ideas'.[58] As a literary historian, Tillotson is interested in describing changes in the forms of literary representation; in this particular instance, her subject is the development which she alleges took place in the English novel in the 1840s. In this decade, she suggests, the novel became the 'dominant' literary medium largely because it began to embrace more serious and socially engaged subjects – topics of contemporary public concern. This process in turn led to an 'extension' of the novel's field, particularly into the realms of geography and class, and to a formal preoccupation with factual documentary detail – with what Tillotson calls 'exactness'.[59] Interest in working- and lower-middle-class lives, seriousness of purpose, settings in the unfamiliar geography of the industrial northern towns and a preference for the techniques of realism – for Tillotson all these features appear to make social-problem novels paradigmatic examples of these changes. Indeed she singles out *Mary Barton* as one of four novels which best illustrate this transitional moment in the history of the novel.

At this point it is worth while bearing in mind that Tillotson's literary history depends upon a larger knowledge of social and intellectual history, for without it she would be unable to recognise the interest in contemporary social issues which allegedly distinguishes the novels of the 1840s from those of the 1820s or 1830s. In her view, social or intellectual history provides the 'context' by which changes in the form of fiction can be measured and explained. It would seem, then, that Tillotson is invoking a necessary relationship between literary history and social or intellectual history. However, as I suggested above, perversely Tillotson wants to see the work of literary historians (that is, of those like herself) and the work of social historians (in her view, of a critic such as Cazamian) as separate activities, involving distinct skills and ambitions:

> Whatever the problems for the novel as an art, there is no doubt that the novel gains something in prestige, is redeemed from mere entertainment, when it reflects the urgent preoccupations of its time. The accuracy and value of this reflection, the particular relevance of the 'topics' of *Sybil, Yeast,* and *Mary Barton,* to their 'day' of 1845 to 1858 and their immediate influence, are questions too large to be considered here, and are perhaps more appropriate to the historian of society or of ideas. To the historian it would also be important to explain why the rapid emergence and multiplication of such novels should belong to the forties and not to the thirties; he might see them as delayed fruits of Reform, as arising directly from the Commission Reports, as part of the instinctive barricade against revolution; he could perhaps relate them to the impulse towards revelation, exposure, prophecy; to the more articulate or more fearful conscience of the time. The literary historian must be content simply to range them alongside other works of their decade as *Past and Present,* Elizabeth Barrett's 'Cry of the Children', and Hood's 'The Song of the Shirt' and 'A spade, a hoe, a bill'; yes, and alongside 'Locksley Hall', *The Princess,* and *The Bothie.*[60]

Tillotson is suggesting that literary historians are concerned with *evaluations* of the forms which literary works take, while social historians are concerned with *why* works take the particular forms which they *do* take. In order to maintain this separation, Tillotson has to assume that evaluation has no necessary relationship to explanation. So, in terms of the social-problem novels, the determination of their literary value (achieved by 'ranging' them alongside other contemporary works) has to be quite unrelated to the question of the accuracy of their historical reference. The difficulty here is that Tillotson's argument appears to undermine the kind of literary history which she sets out to write. If it is really the case that an assessment of the accuracy of a novel's representation bears no relation to an assessment of its literary value, then it is difficult to see the reasons for a literary history which defines a group of novels precisely in terms of their commitment to what Tillotson had earlier called 'exactness', for the concept of exactness requires a knowledge of how a work is produced – of its historical circumstances. The confusion arises because Tillotson assumes that the relationship between literary history on the one hand, and the identification of its subject-matter, literary works, on the other, is entirely unproblematic: in her view, historical enquiry merely 'contextualises' a group of works already identified and valued. The function of historical knowledge is only to explain the forms and features of these works, and it has no bearing upon judgements about their literary value. In the terms I used earlier, historical knowledge can tell us why a work came to be the way it did; but it cannot tell us how we should value it. Unfortunately this view of the relationship between historical knowledge and literary judgments is self-defeating. If literary history is to matter – if it is to be an area of enquiry distinct from history proper – then it *must connect* historical knowledge with literary value. We can see the limitations of Tillotson's position very clearly in the extended discussion of *Mary Barton* in Part II of *Novels of the Eighteen-Forties*.

Tillotson's evaluation of the novel is based upon a judgement about its 'artistic integrity', which is in turn defined by reference to what she calls a 'unity of theme and tone'. She identifies as the 'true theme' (the solution to social problems) 'the persistence, against all odds, of humanheartedness', and she sees in the story of John Barton a successful (because unified) presentation of this theme. Where (for Tillotson) the novel is less convincing is in

Mary Barton's story which dominates the second half of the novel, but whose relation to the general theme is 'too weakly developed'. In Tillotson's eyes, Mary's story possesses new 'thematic possibilities' but they are only 'roughly suggested'; they are improperly incorporated into the novel's overall design, thereby compromising its unity.[61] She implies, then, that the value of *Mary Barton* lies not in the validity of the idea of 'humanheartedness' itself, nor in its appropriateness to the particular problems in society Gaskell identifies.[62] Rather, it is merely the way this notion is presented which is important. So *Mary Barton* would (and could) have been a better novel (nearer the 'scale and quality' of the other works Tillotson selects) if Gaskell had only been able to maintain the narrative focus on John Barton. Tillotson's separation of literary judgement from historical knowledge commits her to understanding thematic unity solely as a formal issue, where decisions about form (the ability to achieve a 'thematic unity') are not related to the specific subject-matter of the novel and therefore not contingent on historical circumstance. Indeed it is for this reason that she can claim that the 'greater artistic integrity' of *Mary Barton* (as opposed to *Sybil*, *Yeast* and *Alton Locke*) 'raise[s] this novel beyond the conditions and problems that give rise to it'.[63] The unfortunate result, though, is to force a separation between the particular way Gaskell thinks about problems in society (her arrival at the notion of 'humanheartedness') and how these thoughts are expressed in her novel. The shortcoming of Tillotson's literary history is that she does not (and cannot) see that there might be a necessary connection between the forms of literary representation and the historically contingent ways a mid-nineteenth-century novelist could have understood problems in society. More importantly, Tillotson cannot therefore either explain why literary representation (as opposed to government Blue Books or the arguments of statisticians or political economists) might have been particularly useful for exploring contemporary problems in society. In simple terms, she cannot convincingly explain why *Mary Barton* came to be written at all, and why therefore the sub-genre of social-problem novels (or the 'social' novels of the 1840s) ever appeared.

A similar situation occurs in Sheila Smith's work, but for slightly different reasons. Smith's *The Other Nation* (1980) is perhaps the most thorough and detailed of the 'contextualist' accounts of the social-problem novels. The title refers to what Smith terms 'the poor', and her subject-matter is in fact rather broader than in other accounts, for her book is about the representation of the poor in a selection of novels taken from the mid-nineteenth century, only some of which are the social-problem novels. Smith does not directly claim that novels about the poor themselves constitute a distinct sub-genre of Victorian fiction; indeed she has no interest in the kinds of issues which had been raised by Williams, Kettle and Lucas in their debate about the usefulness of terms such as 'social novel', 'industrial novel' and 'social-problem novel'. In this sense a defining feature of Smith's work is that its affinities lie not with Marxists and structuralists whose work dominated critical thinking in the 1960s and 1970s, but rather with an older generation of critics. As I suggested, it is Tillotson's *Novels of the Eighteen-Forties* (whose influence is acknowledged in the Introduction) which is closest to Smith's work in conception and tone; and it is Cazamian, rather than Williams, Lucas and Kettle (who are hardly mentioned) with whom Smith engages.

At first glance, Smith's aims seem modest and straightforward: 'I am not trying to survey all the novels written about the poor during the period,' she claims, 'but to examine selected novels treating different aspects of poverty and with different degrees of aesthetic achievement.'[64] Later she comments that 'my subject is the extent to which the poor could be "known" ... by these novelists of the 1840s and 1850s, and the nature of their imaginative response to this persistent fact of Victorian society'.[65] My discussion of Tillotson's and Cazamian's work should have alerted the reader to the kinds of assumptions at work in Smith's project and the kinds of questions which it poses. On what grounds are novels to be 'selected'? On what grounds is 'poverty' to be interpreted? And on what grounds is 'aesthetic achievement' to be judged? The way these questions are answered in its turn determines what Smith means by the phrases 'could be known' and 'imaginative response'.

The main strategy of Smith's book is to compare fictional representations of poverty in selected novels with what she calls 'reality' or, in the terms of one of the chapter headings, 'Naked Fact'. Indeed, the most striking aspect of Smith's book is the sheer number and variety of documents which she draws upon to reveal the 'reality' or 'facts' of Victorian poverty: they include periodicals, contemporary photographs, drawings and paintings, government reports and commissions, and broadside ballad-sheets. In this respect Smith's history is very different from those of Tillotson and Cazamian in that it is much more broadly based and much more strongly supported by evidence. It has the feeling of immediacy and authenticity, and the reader has the impression of being given access to the same social world as that inhabited by the Victorians. Like other critics, though, Smith also finds that most of the novels she discusses, despite their commitment to factual detail, consistently fail to express what she terms the 'essential reality' of Victorian poverty.[66] The phrase 'essential reality' is important and should alert us to the possibility that simple *quantity* of information is not the issue; rather it is the interpretation of the facts – their 'essence' – which matters. It might be the case that Smith's interpretation of contemporary documents is not the same as that of the Victorians – her interpretation of the 'facts' may not have been the same as the Victorians' interpretation of them. (Indeed the Victorians themselves may have had competing interpretations of the facts.) Smith's failure to appreciate this distinction between the identification of information and its interpretation leads her to search for a reason why, despite their obsession with facts, the novelists fail to get at the 'truth'. And so she has to explain why they do not interpret the evidence – why they do not see 'the essential reality' – as she does. The reason she gives is a strangely familiar one, for like John Lucas, she attributes the shortcomings of these mid-Victorian novels to a failure of 'imagination' – or more specifically, to a failure of the 'Romantic imagination':

> But often, in the novels I have been discussing, the appearance and environment of the Other Nation are recorded with detailed accuracy yet fail to create symbols expressive of the elusive essential reality. Quentin Bell, discussing Holman Hunt, comments on the disturbing effect of his fidelity to detail combined with his lack of imagination. Of 'The Triumph of the Innocents' he writes, 'the very sincerity of Holman Hunt's desire to believe and the ruthlessness with which he does in fact observe, makes the failure more painful and more obvious' ... The same is true, in varying degrees, of all the novels under discussion, apart from *Hard Times*.[67]

Smith, like Tillotson, resorts to a non-historical explanation for the discrepancy between her views and those of the Victorian novelists. Ironically that explanation once again turns out to be derived from a Romantic ideology, for it assumes that the novelist (or more precisely, literary art) has access to a privileged perspective on the world. The difficulty with this concept (as we also saw in Lucas's work) is that the faculty of the 'imagination' has to be conceived in ahistorical and transcendental terms. In other words, the very feature which turns out to distinguish the novelist (from what Smith calls the 'man of science') is itself not amenable to historical explanation: indeed it is not even subject to the contingencies of history. Such a situation leaves the literary historian with a real dilemma; if history cannot explain the very feature which distinguishes Smith's subject-matter – literary works – then what do we need such literary history for? The enormous amount of documentary evidence which Smith assembles is certainly valuable in providing details about elements of Victorian social life; what is missing, however, is an accompanying intellectual history – that is, an account of the concepts or ideas by means of which the Victorians interpreted or understood those social complexities, those 'naked facts'. As the next chapter will indicate, the 'facts' about poverty or unemployment, or whatever, were not in dispute. The difficulty for the Victorians lay in their inability to convert those facts into a coherent story or narrative. Importantly, that difficulty in turn was not the result of any personal or imaginative failing, but rather a consequence of the particular ways in which the Victorians understood their world – of what I call their 'conceptual set'.

The dilemma exhibited in Smith's and Tillotson's work, that of the relationship between social and intellectual history, and therefore between historical or 'contextual' knowledge and literary judgements, was the concern of an essay written earlier in the 1960s by John Holloway. Holloway was not concerned with the social-problem novels as a sub-genre of Victorian fiction. His interest (as was the case with Lodge and Leavis) was confined to explaining only one work, *Hard Times*.[68] Nonetheless it is because Holloway shares some of the historiographical principles of the contextualist critics that I have grouped him with them. However, his understanding of literary history, apparent from the opening paragraph of his essay, is subtly but significantly different from that of Cazamian, Tillotson or Smith.

Writing in 1962 (that is, after Tillotson but before Smith), Holloway begins by making an important observation about the social reference of the novel. Noting what he terms the 'now familiar knowledge' that *Hard Times* is a novel concerned with 'Utilitarianism', he goes on to suggest that:

> the ideas and attitudes which that word [i.e. Utilitarianism] most readily calls up today prove not to be those which were most prominent in Dickens's own mind or own time; and to trace the exact contour of significance which ran for Dickens himself, as he wrote the book, through the material he handled, will turn out to be a more than merely historical accumulation of knowledge: it determines the critical position which one must finally take with regard to the novel.[69]

At first sight such a statement seems to go to the heart of the matter, for it recognises the importance of precisely the issues consistently ignored or misunderstood in the work of the other contextualist critics: Holloway, that is, realises in the first place that the meaning of certain terms is historically contingent. So in the instance which he cites, Dickens's understanding of 'Utilitarianism' cannot be assumed to be the same as that of a twentieth-century critic. Second, and perhaps more significantly, Holloway also argues that a knowledge of historical contingency – in this case, a knowledge of Dickens's understanding of Utilitarianism – is a necessary prerequisite of an evaluation of the novel. Indeed at this point his meaning could not be clearer: in direct contrast to Tillotson, Holloway states that such knowledge, far from being 'merely historical accumulation' (the stuff of Tillotson's 'historian of society or ideas') actually *'determines* the critical position which one must finally take'. Here, then, we seem at last to have an acknowledgement of the interrelationship between literary judgements and historical knowledge; we seem, that is, to have a rationale for literary history.

Holloway argues that the 'Utilitarianism' which Dickens has in mind, and which is the target of his satire, is not the large-scale theory of 'social welfare and reform' associated with writers such as James Mill and his son, John Stuart Mill, but rather 'something less far-reaching, and much more mundane and common-place'. 'In *Hard Times,*' Holloway claims, 'Utilitarianism largely means "Manchester School" political economy', the chief characteristic of which, according to Holloway, is a 'naïve enthusiasm' for 'facts' and 'statistics'. The contrast which Holloway draws is between what he calls 'Utilitarianism' seen 'philosophically' (i.e., that proposed by Mill senior and junior), and 'Utilitarianism' reduced to 'arithmetic' (i.e., that proposed by the Manchester School).[70] Holloway identifies figures such as J. R. McCulloch and Charles Knight, today considered to be of 'minor' significance, as representatives of 'arithmetic Utilitarianism'; and in the portrait of Gradgrind and his school Holloway sees explicit and pointed references to them. For example, he argues that in books such as McCulloch's *Principles* and his *Descriptive and Statistical Account of the British Empire*, 'one may find both what sets the scene for Dickens's novel, and what brings one back to some of the attitudes ... depicted in it'.[71] The importance of this alleged distinction between Dickens's understanding of 'Utilitarianism' (based on McCulloch) and that of (say) John Stuart Mill, is revealed in Holloway's surprising claim that the morality of *Hard Times*, far from representing values of enlightenment and imagination (as earlier critics had argued), is in fact rather 'Philistine', and at times even 'vulgar'. In this respect the limitation of the novel, in Holloway's eyes, derives not only from the narrowness of its interest in the impoverished and naïve arithmetical Utilitarianism, but also, and more damningly, from its endorsement of some of the attitudes of those 'middle-class Philistines' which it is supposed to be attacking. 'All in all', Holloway concludes:

> Dickens stood much too near to what he criticized in the novel, for his criticism to reach a fundamental level. This is not a matter of his having a balanced view of the whole situation as between manufacture, labour and capital; but of his sharing the somewhat naïve enthusiasms, and with them to some extent the brusque middle-class hostilities and presumptions, of those whom he thought he was criticizing.[72]

In general terms, then, Holloway accuses Dickens of being anti-intellectual and of having a limited and rather reductive grasp of what were very complex moral issues – issues which were ironically addressed more profoundly and more seriously, and with greater integrity, by those writers whom modern critics had traditionally (but mistakenly) believed to be the object of Dickens's satire – that is, the philosophical Utilitarians such as James Mill. Holloway uses terms such as 'shallow', 'vulgar' and 'Philistine' to characterise what he terms Dickens's 'quality and development of mind'; and he goes on to explain how these intellectual weaknesses are revealed in various aspects of the novel's plot and structure. Finally, and unsurprisingly, Holloway attributes Dickens's alleged lack of 'insight' to his class position.

Holloway's account of *Hard Times* uses a wealth of historical detail, much of it about minor and now forgotten works (such as McCulloch's *Encyclopaedia*), to challenge our modern assumptions about this novel. Moreover, Holloway goes on to use that detail in order to revalue it; for him (and here he differs from Tillotson and Smith) the literary historian and social historian are one and the same. Is it the case, then, that Holloway provides us with a historical method which overcomes the shortcomings which I have located in the work of the other contextualist critics? Despite the promise of Holloway's research, the answer has to be equivocal. In recovering the historical context of *Hard Times*, in his attempt to 'trace the exact contour of significance which ran for Dickens himself', Holloway omits one important consideration. He tells us which ideas may have been available to Dickens, but he tells us next to nothing about the status of those ideas. As a consequence he cannot tell us with any certainty the significance of Dickens's use of them. So we encounter a shortcoming similar to that of Smith's book. Holloway is either unable (or unwilling) to extend his understanding of historical contingency to cover ideas of status and authority: put bluntly, he does not adequately distinguish between the *status* of ideas, concepts, or ideologies. Of course at one level, Holloway has a great deal to say about the status of ideas about Utilitarianism which were current in Dickens's time: his essay is full of evaluative words such as 'naïve' (to describe a reliance of statistics) and 'enlightened', 'emancipated' and 'comprehensive' (to describe 'philosophical' Utilitarianism). Importantly, however, these terms are *interpretations* and not descriptions; we do not know whether they reflect Holloway's views or those of the Victorians. Whether or not his identification of two kinds of Utilitarianism is correct, it is possible to imagine a situation in which they had very different values placed upon them. So, for example, in the eyes of the Victorians, there may not have been any contradiction between valuing the writing of John Stuart Mill and the work of McCulloch; alternatively, their work may have been valued quite differently from the ways suggested by Holloway. Holloway may judge McCulloch's work to be 'vulgar' and 'naïve', but it is not self-evident that McCulloch was considered so by many Victorians. At one point Holloway seems aware of the problem and comments that McCulloch's *Principles* was 'the standard work until Mill's book of the same name replaced it'.[73] One is tempted to observe that if McCulloch's writings were indeed so highly valued by middle-class Victorians, and (more importantly) if a reliance on statistics was not at that time considered 'naïve', then Dickens's satire would have had a rather different significance for Victorian readers than it does for Holloway. It may for that matter have indicated the very opposite of what Holloway sees as Dickens's Philistinism or reactionary, middle-class complacency. To put this observation in more general terms, it is difficult to see how both the satire and its target can be normative.

This question of status, considered in historical (rather than modern) terms is important, for a failure to take account of it leaves Holloway (in spite of his explicit acknowledgement of the problems inherent in writing history) in a position which is really quite similar to that of Tillotson and Smith. In the end, the impressive historical information which he marshals lacks significance, for if Holloway cannot tell us what it meant in the 1850s for Dickens to allude to this or that contemporary work, then he will not be able to persuade us why we need to know about it now. In fact a judgement that the morality of *Hard Times* is shallow, vulgar or Philistine does not necessarily depend upon knowing that Dickens was satirising the work of a minor political economist rather than that of Mill. On the contrary, we can judge the work in such a way for a much more basic reason. We are perfectly capable of seeing Dickens's conception of moral dilemmas in terms of an opposition between facts (a reliance on statistics and arithmetic) and fancy (a reliance on the creative imagination) to be a crude one. The question of the exact identity of the target of satire – that is, with whom ideas about facts and statistics were to be associated – is not necessarily related to a *modern* appreciation of the work's moral validity. But it is wholly relevant to our understanding of the Victorians' appreciation of its moral worth. I suggested earlier that for Holloway the novel failed in two ways: in his modern, twentieth-century view, the satire did not go far enough and, second, the target of the satire was itself ill-chosen. We can now see more clearly the paradox which Holloway's use of history produces, for the failings which he identifies are in fact incompatible: if his first judgement is valid (that the satire does not go far enough) then the object of the satire must be considered important, otherwise the question of the degree of Dickens's criticism, and hence the significance of the novel itself, would not be a matter of any critical interest whatsoever.

III

The final kind of account of the social-problem novels is represented by Catherine Gallagher's *The Industrial Reformation of English Fiction* (1985), a work which, as I suggested in Chapter 1, can be loosely described as 'new historicist' in character. Gallagher's book is easily the most detailed, complex and ambitious account of the subject yet written. Her point of departure, like that of the contextualist critics whose conclusions she attempts to contest, is a group of novels which are defined in terms of their response to a particular historical phenomenon which she refers to as 'industrialism'. However Gallagher does not simply take as her subject-matter the accuracy of the various representations of industrialism in narrative fiction; instead she is concerned with the relationship between what she calls 'the discourse over industrialism' and the novel form. This distinction between 'industrialism' and 'the discourse over industrialism' is far-reaching, for it has to do with the difference between the ideas and ideologies which the processes of industrialism generated and the actual processes themselves. About the latter Gallagher has little to say; she claims that an 'attempt to specify the ultimate sources or purposes of the discourse in either a history of material production or an account of a unitary, bourgeois class consciousness would be either futile or distorting'.[74] This strategy might strike 'contextualist' critics as inevitably leading to vagueness, for one of its consequences is to threaten to inflate her subject-matter to the point of intractability. Certainly her book contains very little of the kind of historical detail marshalled by Sheila Smith. Instead she discusses works by writers who in her view established or represented important intellectual paradigms for the understanding of industrialism (although, as I have noted, Gallagher never tells us in any detail what the phenomenon of industrialism actually amounted to).

Briefly, Gallagher's argument is that the 'state of the novel' underwent significant changes between the first (1832) and second (1867) Reform Bills and these changes can only be understood when viewed in relation to the 'discourse over industrialism'. Importantly, and in keeping with the general trends of new historicism, the relationship which Gallagher envisages between this discourse and the formal properties of narrative fiction is a 'reciprocal' rather than a determining one:

> The discourse over industrialism led novelists to examine the assumptions of their literary form. Reciprocally, the formal analyses in this study enable a new understanding of the discourse itself, for the formal structures and ruptures of these novels starkly reveal a series of paradoxes at the heart of the Condition of England Debate.[75]

It is worth noting that the distinction between text (the novel) and context (historical background) which underwrites contextual accounts of the social-problem novels is completely dissolved in such an argument. For Gallagher, novels are not explained by history; rather, they are a part of it. The distinction is easier to see once it is understood that Gallagher is using the term 'discourse' in a special sense, one which distinguishes it from the realm of ideas or from the realm of ideology:

> I assume there is normally some sort of tension between ideology and literary forms, but that forms are nevertheless also historical phenomena, parts of those transideological structures that are here called discourses. I am using 'discourse' to designate both what is said on a particular subject (for example, the actual contents of the Condition of England Debate) and the largely unstated rules that govern what can and cannot be said. Discourse exists between and within ideologies, thereby creating the coherence and legibility of ideological conflict. Literary forms often disrupt the tidy formulations and reveal the inherent paradoxes of their ostensible ideologies. However, I try to demonstrate the [sic] the ruptures thus created are neither the automatically subversive result of all truly literary treatment nor the timeless effect of all textuality. Rather, the formal and ideological transgressions and deviations described here are elicited by and recontained within the logic of the larger historical discourse.[76]

As my description of 'political' and 'contextualist' accounts has shown, historicising the social-problem novels tends to produce two mutually opposed explanations of literary forms: either they are seen to be ideologically determined, or they are understood to exist beyond the contingencies of history. Gallagher's historical method appears to be designed to avoid this dichotomy, for she implies that the concept of 'discourse' allows her to explain literary forms as historically contingent but (at the same time) not ideologically determined. Such a proposal might sound winning. It certainly has its advocates among modern new-historicist critics, and it may seem to present a more systematic connection between literary value and historical knowledge. But what exactly is 'discourse'? In the passage which I have just quoted, it designates both 'what is said on a particular subject' ('the actual contents of the Condition of England Debate') and 'the largely unstated rules that govern what can and cannot be said'. However, this explanation is rather disingenuous, for it raises more questions than it answers. We might, for example, object that 'what is said' will not be self-evident. 'What is said' literally means every utterance (written and oral) about industrialism (whatever that is). Of course, most of this information is recoverable, but some is not. Moreover, of those utterances which we can recover, only some matter. 'What is said', then, turns out to be anything but what was actually said; it turns out to be a selection made by time and by the historian. 'What is said', in other words, in effect means those things which the historian notices and finds interesting and significant. We can then go further and ask: what values define 'significant' and 'interesting'? Is the hierarchy which defines these terms derived from the values of the Victorians or from those of the modern historian? Because it tries to dissolve the whole idea of hierarchy, the concept of discourse does not permit these questions to be broached in any straightforward way. However, it may seem that Gallagher has precisely this issue in mind when she speaks of 'the largely unstated rules that govern what can and cannot be said'. But what sort of rules exactly does she mean? (And how do we know them if they are 'unstated'?) Are they conceptual, ideological or political? For example, were debates about industrialism in the mid-nineteenth century restricted because certain ideas or concepts (such as, say, Keynesian economics) had not yet been formulated or invented – in other words, because they were simply unavailable? Or, were debates about industrialism restricted by political interests so that the operation of power materially prevented certain ideas being expressed (by, for example, the various formal or informal mechanisms of censorship which were in place in

Victorian Britain)? Or, were debates about industrialism restricted by ideological interests; that is, was the hegemony of a particular way of thinking about industrialisation associated with (and restricted by) a particular interest group? These categories are not mutually incompatible, but they are certainly not identical, and in order to understand the relationships between them we need to employ the two further concepts, those of status and authority, which I have already alluded to in the context of Holloway's work. Gallagher's notion of discourse tends to elide these sorts of distinction; more importantly she omits to acknowledge that what she calls discourse will be composed of ways of thinking which posses a quite different status, and so a quite different social authority. The relevance and real purchase of these questions will become clearer when we look at the details of Gallagher's research.

Gallagher maps the 'discourse over industrialism' via what she terms three intellectual 'controversies': 'the nature and possibility of human freedom', the 'sources of social cohesion' and 'the nature of representation'.[77] In her view the first of these controversies is focused by a conflict between 'determinism' and 'free will', the rhetoric of which Gallagher locates in debates about slavery. Her argument concerns what she terms the 'worker–slave' metaphor where discussion of the rights and freedoms of slaves was extended to include the industrial working class. Gallagher locates her second controversy, the 'sources of social cohesion', in a debate about the relationship between the public and the private; this relationship, she suggests, provided an alternative arena in which to resolve the conflict between determinism and free will. Gallagher suggests that if free will could not be exercised in the public (and so socially determined) industrial work-place, then perhaps it could operate within the private and protected world of the family, and the family in turn might then act as the catalyst for social change. Gallagher's third controversy is less easy to explain succinctly, for her argument is often subtle and sometimes difficult to follow. It concerns aspects of the nineteenth-century debate about political representation which took the form of what she calls a 'discontinuity between facts and values' where the domain of 'facts' represents 'what is', and the domain of 'values' represents what 'ought to be'.[78] Moreover this opposition between facts and values maps on to the opposition between the public, market-orientated industrial world (facts, or 'what is') and the private domain of the family (the repository of values, or of 'what ought to be'). Hence in Gallagher's view, the debate about the 'right relationship' between facts and values represents yet another kind of critique of industrialism. Each of these three intellectual controversies is characterised by what Gallagher calls 'ideological disjunctions' which in turn are exhibited or mirrored in the novels in terms of certain 'formal disjunctions', that is, in inconsistencies or contradictions in characterisation and plotting. Moreover, Gallagher sees each controversy as appropriate to a different group of novels: so the first controversy 'explains' *Helen Fleetwood, Mary Barton* and *Alton Locke*; the second, *North and South* and *Hard Times*; and the third, *Sybil* and *Felix Holt*.

Gallagher's argument is difficult to summarise easily, and the complexity of her book might leave the reader perplexed as to why there is such a disjunction between the apparent simplicity of the novels themselves (few readers – then or now – have difficulty in understanding them) and the detail and intricacy of the information required to appreciate them. The main reason for the complexity relates to Gallagher's use of the concept of discourse, for it allows her to discuss and yoke together a range of heterogeneous ideas and texts without considering the relationships (of status and authority) between them. So we might ask, for example, why are the controversies which Gallagher isolates – about the nature and possibility of human freedom, the sources of social cohesion and the nature of representation – the most important ones? To the British reader, these concerns seem to belong more to mid-nineteenth-century America than they do to mid-nineteenth-century British culture.[79] Moreover, they seem no more particularly concerned with mid-nineteenth-century industrialisation than, say, with late eighteenth-century industrialisation (in fact, most of the terms of political debates in the nineteenth century were derived from the work of eighteenth-century political philosophers). These cautions suggest that there may have been other controversies about industrialism and politics – that is, other aspects of the 'discourse over industrialism' – which Gallagher has excluded from her study. There is a further reservation concerning the imprecision of Gallagher's account. Gallagher maps her three controversies in a broadly chronological order. The implication is that the relationship between them is successive. Moreover she wants to see a particular controversy answering to a particular group of novels; however, as she herself admits, the novels do not answer to such a simple chronology. Gallagher's explanation for this discrepancy is revealing. For example, she justifies grouping together *Sybil* and *Felix*

Holt, novels 'widely separated in time', on the grounds that 'they participate in one debate, the debate over the franchise, and they draw on a single tradition of thought about representation that persists throughout the nineteenth century ... [T]hese two political novels will be analyzed here as parts of a continuous discourse'.[80] However, if this discourse *was* continuous throughout the century, then why did other social-problem novels not engage with it? And why, if the discourse is continuous, do we not find similar kinds of novels being written in the 1870s and 1880s? Why was the facts/values debate appropriate to Disraeli's understanding of industrialism, but not to Kingsley's? Why did Disraeli not formulate his politics in terms of the 'slave–worker' metaphor, or the public– private, family–society dichotomy? A more general way of stating this difficulty would be to ask what exactly *is* the relationship between the intellectual controversies Gallagher identifies and the processes (that is, industrialism) which she alleges they explain? The failure to address this question in turn prevents her from providing a convincing account of the *nature* of the relationship between the way a problem in society is articulated and the kind of solution offered to it. Of course Gallagher will claim that these are not issues which interest her; unfortunately, though, her failure to attend to them leaves us with a history emptied of causality, and therefore not really a history at all – or at least not a history that is of much use.

Throughout this chapter I have argued that the fundamental problem for literary history is the articulation of a *dynamic* relationship between historical knowledge and literary judgements. In the end Gallagher's historicism turns out to be no more helpful in this task than any of the other accounts I have considered. By collapsing the categories of literary and documentary identity into the all-encompassing term 'discourse' she denies us the possibility of understanding how exactly the two might be related. Nowhere is this clearer than in the large claim Gallagher makes for her thesis: that the 'antitheses encountered as formal paradoxes in the industrial novels are finally, at the supersession of the entire discourse, transformed into a much more general antithesis between society and its literary representations'.[81] For this information to be of use, the *literary* historian needs to know not only why the 'entire discourse' was superseded, but also the role which literary representation played in it. Unfortunately it is just this kind of explanation which the premises of Gallagher's thesis prevent her from providing.

Part Two
The Social-Problem Novel

3

Society, the Social and the Individual

In Chapter 1, I suggested that social-problem novels have been defined as a group or sub-genre by their interest in large-scale social concerns, and that judging them involves an understanding of the nature of that social reference. However, as I indicated in Chapter 2, this task is not as simple or as straightforward as it seems. Indeed what might have struck the reader as an over-detailed survey of past criticism was intended to show that accounts of the social-problem novels, despite their wide theoretical and methodological differences, all possess the same limitation: they identify their sub-genre historically, but they nevertheless judge the individual novels by reference to concepts or criteria to which the Victorians would have had little or no access. The main reason for this state of affairs is, I have suggested, that the subject-matter which defines the sub-genre – those large-scale social issues which the novels address – is understood from the vantage-point of the twentieth-century critic.

Nearly all the accounts I discussed agreed that the social-problem novels are in some way flawed works. The reasons were various – they range from an alleged political prejudice, to a lack of conviction, or a failure of the imagination. Nonetheless they come together in an implication that there was another (and much better) novel about problems in mid-nineteenth-century society which Dickens, Eliot, Gaskell, Kingsley or Disraeli *could* have written, but for some reason failed to do so. By contrast, my argument will be to suggest that in the mid-nineteenth century there were limitations to the ways in which social problems could have been identified and discussed. By the term 'limitation' I do not mean political or ideological constraints, which suggest that other ways of thinking were available, but for some reason (the particular political prejudices of the author, for example, or the informal censorship of a publisher or periodical editor) were rejected. The kind of limitations which this chapter will outline are intellectual limitations. Specifically I want to examine those basic concepts which allowed the Victorians to 'see' problems in their society, and then identify them as *social* problems. It is these concepts which determined the mid-Victorians' understanding of contemporary social life. Outlining such an intellectual framework will permit us to see more clearly the connection between the kinds of problems mid-Victorian novelists identified in their society and the particular literary devices which they used to explore them. In other words, it will help to explain why fiction was seen as an appropriate medium for investigating contemporary social issues. In addition it will give us a new perspective on the radicalism of the social-problem novels, for once we understand the intellectual constraints within which writers operated, it becomes possible to acknowledge their novelty.

I

It is a truism that Victorian novels – and perhaps all novels – are concerned with the relationship between the individual and society. Indeed the main way in which society is made known to the reader is through the interaction of character with a social milieu. The plots of many novels work by placing a character in conflict with a social environment, and a theme of much early Victorian fiction is the process of education whereby transgressive individuals are made aware of the wrongness of their deeds or attitudes and are integrated back into society through a companion recognition of the rightness or appropriateness of its values. Although the extent and nature of a novel's social milieu obviously varies – it may range from the nation to a country estate, a village, a district of a town, and so on – it is usually presented as the fundamental given of a character's environment. That is to say, the social milieu is fixed, and the novelist's focus of attention is on the potential for change within the individual, rather than within society. When the sub-genre of the social-problem novels was identified, the possibility of a departure from this pattern was detected. It was suggested that conflicts between the individual and society invited the reader to consider the social environment rather than the behaviour of the individual within it. In this sense it was implied that the novels had a new subject-matter – a *social* problem, rather than a dissident individual. But what exactly does the term 'social problem' mean?

At this point it is important to stress a simple distinction which is common in sociology: that there is a difference between seeing a problem *in society* – that is, a problem which occurs in some aspect of the social environment – and seeing a problem *as social* – that is, identifying a conflict, dilemma, tension, or whatever, as one which has social causes. An example which I have used before may make the distinction clearer. Drunkenness among groups of young men may be seen as a problem in society in the sense that it may result in violent and destructive behaviour which destroys the social environment. However, if such drunkenness is attributed to the irresponsibility of individuals in failing to control alcohol abuse, then its causes are not seen to be social ones. Alternatively, if such behaviour is explained in terms of the alienation produced by (say) structural unemployment, then its causes would (at least in part) be social, and one way of preventing such behaviour would be to bring about changes in the structure of society. This distinction between identifying problems in society and problems which have social causes is of central importance for understanding the social-problem novels. The weaknesses or failings commonly attributed to them centre on the perceived discrepancy between the problems in society which the novelists identity (the conflicts, inequalities and hardships associated with the processes of industrialism) and – to the modern eye – the disappointing solutions by which they are resolved (for example, the resort to Christian brotherhood or various forms of individual moral redemption). However, these sorts of solutions only seem inconsistent or inappropriate if they are applied to problems which are identified as having social causes. If problems identified in society are seen to be caused by individuals' misconduct, then solutions which advocate changes in individual behaviour are entirely logical. So before we judge the social-problem novels, a central question needs to be settled: did the mid-Victorian mind typically see the problems associated with industrialisation as problems which possessed social causes? To put this question more precisely, we need to know whether solutions which work by recommending modifications of individual behaviour were the result of a conscious rejection of social solutions; or, alternatively, whether social solutions were not even considered because at that time problems themselves were not seen (and could not have been seen) as having social causes. In practice this amounts to trying to understand what concepts of 'society' and of the 'social' were available in mid-nineteenth-century Britain, for that information will allow us to assess the relevance (for the Victorians) of the criticism of society offered by the social-problem novelists.

One way of approaching this question is to look at other areas of Victorian intellectual life in order to discover whether there were some underlying conceptual continuities which determined the ways in which the Victorians understood the world around them. Today we are accustomed to specialised explanations of our environment: so we recognise distinctions between, say, the explanations offered by the social sciences and those by the natural sciences. Indeed a common way of explaining the development of knowledge in the twentieth century is in terms of an accelerating process of specialisation in which areas of knowledge become increasingly differentiated. In the mid-nineteenth century, however, this 'knowledge-explosion', as some modern commentators have called it, was barely under way. Its effects became increasingly apparent by the end of the century, but between the 1840s and 1860s there was much less differentiation between areas of knowledge, and it was common for individuals to feel accomplished enough (and to be considered accomplished enough) to extend themselves across a broad range of knowledge. Economics, history, art and politics – all these areas could quite easily be the province of one individual. The *oeuvre* of John Stuart Mill, one of the most prominent figures in nineteenth-century intellectual life, is a good indication of the character of the mid-Victorian intellectual: Mill felt at ease in writing about politics, economics and literature.[1] So did contemporaries such as John Ruskin or Thomas Carlyle. A further consequence of the twentieth-century tendency towards the specialisation of knowledge is that explanations provided by one group of specialists may seem to be conceptually incompatible with explanations offered by another group. So today, for example, there are many conceptual incompatibilities between modern physics and modern biology, even though the explanatory criteria of each of those disciplines are by themselves conceptually coherent. By contrast, in the mid-nineteenth century we find a substantial overlap in what today are considered to be very different areas of thought. These overlaps in their turn both indicate and enable a set of broad conceptual continuities in mid-Victorian intellectual culture. If one individual felt capable of theorising about economics, politics and literature, we should not be surprised to find consistency of explanation in that individual's work; we should, that is, expect to find a shared conceptual framework (or conceptual set) underlying the Victorians' explanations of the various aspects of their environment.

Of course none of this is to suggest that any particular Victorian novelist – here Dickens, Gaskell, Disraeli, Kingsley or Eliot – read a particular work by a particular economist, social scientist or philosopher; nor is it to imply that they assiduously followed the intricacies of the intellectual debates which took place in other areas of contemporary thought. Such a notion of influence – where one writer is said to be affected by another if it can be proved that he or she read a particular work, or alluded to a particular argument – is not the issue. Rather, I am trying to outline what might be termed the conceptual 'givens' of a particular intellectual climate – that part of an individual's way of thinking which is taken for granted in the sense that it is only rarely available to be questioned. Popular terms for such givens are 'a world-view' or 'a mind-set'. By definition, evidence for such a conceptual set cannot be derived from any one writer or from the influence which any writer has on any other. A conceptual set is that way of thinking which is implicit to members of a particular culture; it is that part of intellectual activity which is taken for granted because it is largely assumed to be correct. This idea has similarities with what historians of knowledge, particularly Michel Foucault, have called the epistemic foundations of a society, where the term 'episteme' is used to define the intellectual boundaries or categories within which it was possible to think, and where unravelling the episteme amounts to an archaeology of knowledge.[2] A more accessible formulation of the kind of intellectual archaeology which I have in mind is given by Stefan Collini, who describes the recovery of an intellectual context as 'trying to identify the forensic resources' at a given writer's disposal, where the term 'forensic resources' means discovering 'the overriding force of certain arguments, the emotional resonances of key terms, [and] the exploitable tensions within accepted beliefs'.[3] Collini's emphasis on the importance of attending to the contemporary (rather than modern) status of ideas in the past reinforces one of the key concerns of this book. Of course conceptual sets change; there will always be individuals or groups of individuals who suggest new ways to look at things, and when their explanations convince enough other individuals, a new set of concepts will gradually replace the old set, in time becoming the conceptual givens of a new period. The mechanisms of such a process are highly complex, but a good modern example of the kind of developments which I have in mind is to be found in the emergence of 'neo-Darwinism', a successful attempt in the 1930s to accommodate Darwinian theories of evolution with Mendelian genetics. The result of this synthesis was the modern theory of evolution which, since the 1930s, has been an intrinsic part of how we understand the world, so much so that it is no longer really questioned.[4] Neo-Darwinism is the foundation on which any modern theorising about the natural world must be located, and it is in this sense that we can say that neo-Darwinism represents a conceptual set within which a whole variety of opinions and theories about adaptation, selection, genes, and so forth, are now articulated. In studying mid-nineteenth-century Victorian intellectual life we should be concerned with finding an analogous phenomenon, a basic set of concepts for which there were no substantive alternative ways of understanding.

To anticipate the argument of this chapter, I will suggest that a factor common to many areas of mid-nineteenth-century thought – to psychology, aesthetics, history, economics, social science and evolutionary biology – was an emphasis on the individual as the unit of analysis. Such an emphasis is perhaps to be expected in the first two areas of thought (psychology and aesthetics); in the third, the reader is likely to be familiar already with the 'great man' theory of history – that is, with the stress placed on the role of individual agency in historical causation. Nineteenth-century historiography, as practised by figures such as Thomas Babington Macaulay or Charles Kingsley, was typically conceived of as a 'species of drama with the major figures of the past characterized as either heroes or villains'.[5] The materialist history of the maverick historian, Thomas Henry Buckle, is the exception which in many ways proves the rule.[6] What is arresting, however, is to find a similar reliance on the individual in those areas of nineteenth-century thought obviously related to an understanding of *social* life. So, as I demonstrate below, whether the Victorians took as their explicit subject economic activity, the principles of justice, or the development of species, in every case they started from the premise that agency is defined in terms of the actions, desires and needs of individuals. I shall argue that the concept of what I shall term 'atomistic' agency was so pervasive and unexamined that it constituted the key element of the mid-Victorians' mental set. Importantly, it informed their understanding of the social, ensuring that the problems which they identified in their society were invariably seen to have *individual* causes, and that the solutions which they subsequently advocated invariably recommended changes in the actions and beliefs of *individuals* (rather than changes in social structures).

II

In the preface to *Mary Barton*, Elizabeth Gaskell made one of the best-known confessions of ignorance in literary history: 'I know nothing of Political Economy, or the theories of trade'. And towards the end of the book, one of the characters, Job Legh, echoes her ignorance when he confesses to the mill-owner, Mr Carson, 'I'm not given to Political Economy, I know that much. I'm wanting in learning'. The reference to political economy is perhaps to be expected; in so far as it theorised the conditions of a market economy and the nature of industrial labour relations, this body of thought directly engaged with the very aspects of contemporary social life which were so troubling to the social-problem novelists. The modern reader, however, alert to the similarity between the *laissez-faire* politics associated with classical political economy and the apparent unwillingness of the social-problem novelists to advocate any form of state intervention to resolve social problems, may find Gaskell's disclaimer – her attempt to distance herself from political economy – rather disingenuous. It may appear little more than an excuse for the non-interventionist and non-economic solution to social problems which *Mary Barton* proposes, and therefore a justification for the idea of Christian brotherhood. However, in the context of mid-nineteenth-century intellectual culture, Gaskell's apparent reluctance to engage with complex arguments about economic theory is perfectly understandable. As I will argue below, at the time there was no intellectually coherent alternative to political economy which she could have drawn upon, and it is hardly surprising that she might have felt unequal to the task. Moreover, Gaskell may also have been making an artistic decision: she may simply have judged that this kind of intellectual seriousness was out of place in a novel which drew heavily on elements of melodrama and romance. Nevertheless it is still interesting that Gaskell felt required to defend the omission, for its immediate effect is to draw attention to the importance of what she had left out. Moreover it also implies that in some way political economy was part of the general knowledge of her readership, its premises part of their intellectual set. Those readers, like Gaskell herself, may not have been in command of all the details of classical political economy, and thus probably would have been no more competent to analyse it than she was, but they presumably would have known what she was referring to. We need, then, to be careful about how we interpret Gaskell's disclaimer: while she may not have understood the complexities and details of all its doctrines, she was certainly not ignorant of what political economy at some basic level 'meant', and of the intellectual prestige which still attached to it. In this respect it might indeed have been the case that what was 'known' about political economy by Gaskell (and her implied readers) was not really open to question or analysis, and that Gaskell's apparent confession of ignorance was much more to do with her consciousness of being unable to present an alternative economic analysis.

What follows is no more than a skeletal account of nineteenth-century economic thought, for I want to describe only the general way of thinking – the general intellectual orientation – which underwrote classical political economy and which classical political economy in turn helped to normalise. It will be noticed that I have used the phrase 'classical political economy' where Gaskell uses 'Political Economy'. The term 'political economy' was first introduced by Adam Smith in his *Wealth of Nations* (1776) to describe a new way of understanding the relationship between the political and economic affairs of the state, and therefore, by implication, a new way of conceptualising social life.[7] The systematic body of theory which was subsequently developed from Smith's arguments, principally by early nineteenth-century writers such as David Ricardo and later by John Stuart Mill, is referred to by modern economic historians as 'classical political economy' or 'classical theory' in order to distinguish it from developments in thinking about the relationships between the political and the economic which they term 'neoclassical political economy' or 'neoclassical theory' and which are associated with a different generation of economists working later in the nineteenth century, principally William Stanley Jevons, Léon Walras and Carl Menger. 'Classical political economy' and 'neoclassical political economy' are there-

fore modern terms coined to describe developments in the history
of economic thought. The exact limits of these periods, and the
nature of the relationships between them, are disputed, for they
depend upon how the particular historian understands intellectual
history.[8] For the purposes of this book, however, this kind of detail
is largely irrelevant, for I am only concerned with the dominance of
the intellectual paradigms which were articulated via classical
political economy (or Political Economy) during the first half of the
nineteenth century – a matter which is not in dispute.[9]

The term 'political economy', then, was coined to describe a new
way of understanding the relationship between politics and
economics. At the heart of that understanding, which underlies all
classical political economy, were two propositions, one of which
concerns the separability of the economic sphere, and the other
which argues for its primacy in human conduct. These propositions
in turn led to a new way of thinking about the relationship between
the individual and society. Two recent historians of political
economy, James A. Caporaso and David P. Levine, describe this
change as follows:

> The founders of political economy perceive a change in the rela-
> tionship between political life and the nonpolitical activities
> loosely termed the satisfaction of private wants. This perception
> leads to a redefinition and realignment of terms used to talk
> about the social order, terms such as political society and civil
> society; private and public; economy and state. This realignment
> involves a shift of emphasis toward the idea that society organ-
> izes itself and develops according to its own laws, processes, and
> imperatives. The vitally important social institutions do not
> develop according to plans articulated and instituted by political
> decisions, but according to underlying and unintended impera-
> tives of group life. If this is true, then history becomes less an
> account of political processes, conflicts, or deliberations, more an
> account of the unintended consequences of private activities.[10]

The impetus behind classical political economy was a desire to
minimise the role of politics (and politicians) in social life, and this
in turn led to rethinking the relationship between society and the
state. The result was an attempt to explain the origins of modern
civilised society in non-political terms in the sense that the particular nature of modern social life was understood to have

arisen 'unintentionally' from the multitude (or aggregation) of individuals' private actions, rather than to have been determined by the decisions of political bodies – that is, by the exercise of the power of the state. In simple terms, classical political economy proposed that modern society was 'the result of profit-seeking behaviour rather than of any plan known to and instituted by a political process or public authority ... it was the unintended consequence of a multitude of actions taken for purely private purposes'.[11]

The important point to notice is that classical political economy displaced the concept of the social from the political on to the economic sphere: it was only within (and because of) economic transactions – that is, profit-seeking behaviour – that modern forms of sociability were possible. Moreover, the economic sphere in its turn was defined as a 'system of private want satisfaction made up of independent private agents'.[12] In this view the social was understood to be the *result* of the aggregation of individual actions, but at the same time it was not *intended* as such by any one individual or group. The theoretical project of classical political economy was therefore an attempt to understand the nature or structure of this system for satisfying private wants. Although this system was identified by a number of terms, including 'civil society', the 'market economy' and 'bourgeois capitalism', it was always seen to be motivated by individual egoism or self-interest, and one of the central issues in classical political economy was the relationship between private self-interest (the satisfaction of individual wants as exercised in the market) and the public good.[13] In classical political economy it was argued that the laws by which the market works, although a consequence of individual actions, operate independently of the wills or desires of people; and that the pursuit of self-interest will lead to public good in a market economy which is competitive and unregulated – that is, in a market where there is no attempt by politics (or the state) to regulate economic activity. The general reasoning behind this position is summarised by Caporaso and Levine as follows:

> Under its normal workings, and in the absence of regulation from outside, the market will assure the full utilization of society's capital stock. Given the overall amount of capital and labour available to society, the proportions devoted to different industries should depend on profitability because profitability measures the contribution each industry can make to the size of

the social revenue and to the growth of social wealth. The only way to assure that profit directs investment is to place that investment into private hands and subject it to decisions based on self-interest. This works because self-interest is best served by the pursuit of profit. Given that profit seeking is a private rather than public motive, this approach argues against public guidance of investment. Public regulation means ... that something other than profitability will determine investment. The unregulated but self-ordering market will encourage the growth of society's capital stock and achieve the public good.[14]

The advocacy of *laissez-faire* politics popularly associated with classical political economy inevitably followed from such propositions. More generally, such an argument also implied that the conditions for social life could not be legislated for.[15] It is worth noting in passing that, in practice, classical political economists often did not advocate or pursue 'pure' or consistent *laissez-faire* policies. Indeed the early and mid-nineteenth century was characterised by a considerable amount of government legislation.[16] At the time, however, such legislation was not seen to be incompatible with a belief in non-interventionist policies, nor was it enacted via a concept of the 'social good', or from a 'collectivist' perspective. Indeed much of the legislation concerned 'developments of administrative practice' and therefore did not implicate changes in social structures.[17] More significantly, the rationale for such legislation was that individuals needed to be persuaded into pursuing their 'true' self-interests. Describing classical political economy's reaction to problems in society, Philip Abrams has argued that 'situations of overt conflict were problematic not because one had to take sides but because one had to determine how men had come to mistake their real interests. Conflict had to spring from ignorance or unreason, since it could not spring from real incompatibilities.'[18] Such a view in turn permitted 'systematic intervention to enable or force men to square their lives with the natural laws of society where these were known but not working freely; and nonintervention where these laws, unencumbered by the remnants of an older, less enlightened society, were already working well'.[19] In this line of argument, intervention (here government legislation) was perfectly compatible with the principle of *laissez-faire* to the extent that it did not function to change social structures, nor did it determine new laws or principles of social life.

My brief account of the basic arguments of classical political economy simplifies what was a complex body of ideas. However, the kind of material which is of interest to the economic historian – the detailed arguments about how the market operates, and the importance of concepts such as the division of labour, accumulation of capital, distribution of wealth, and so forth – are, for my purposes, largely irrelevant. My interest is confined to the observation that in classical political economy explanation of the social derives from the concept of the autonomous, self-interested individual, for the market exists only in so far as it is a mechanism by which *individuals* are able to satisfy their private wants. As Caporaso and Levine point out, the market is 'a social mechanism to assure satisfaction of private wants. It is also a passive mechanism because it does not affect the property or the wants satisfied by it'.[20] In this view, agency originates in individuals who act independently and according to their selfish desires; the market is nothing more than 'an unintended consequence of [individual] self-seeking'.[21] The distinction to emphasise is that between the theoretical starting-point of classical political economy with the self-interested individual and the subsequent concern with understanding the 'objective' laws of the market economy which arise in an unintended way from the aggregation of individual behaviours. Of course classical political economy had nothing to say about specific elements of individual behaviour. It was not concerned with subjectivity; that is, it was not concerned with the details of human action and motivation, for these kinds of differences cannot by definition affect the laws by which the market operates. Adam Smith's famous metaphor of the 'Invisible Hand' directed attention to the independence of the market and, in theorising about how the market works, the initial presumption of individual agency was displaced by an interest in the abstract 'laws, processes and imperatives' which governed the market's operation. In this respect it may seem paradoxical to attribute to classical political economy an individualistic approach to social issues. However, classical political economy only *arrived* at its abstract theory of market mechanisms because it began with an acknowledgement of the primacy and autonomy of the individual as an agent. In this sense there was no contradiction between classical political economy's lack of concern with the individual as such (that is, with subjectivity) and the foundation of its theory in individual behaviour (whereby people are assumed to be motivated by their human nature rather than by social forces).

Later John Stuart Mill was quite clear about the compatibility of these two positions. He insisted that 'the laws of the phenomena of society are, and can be, nothing but the laws of the actions and passions of human beings united together in the social state', and he then explained than 'men ... in the state of society, are still men; their actions and passions are obedient to the laws of individual human nature'. Mill thus defined the subject-matter of political economy as 'the science which treats the production and distribution of wealth, so far as they depend upon the laws of human nature'.[22] Samuel Hollander suggests that for Mill, 'political economy was thus a social science precluding interest in man, the individual, as such'. It was to be distinguished from what Mill termed the science of *social economy* which 'embraces every part of man's nature, insofar as influencing the conduct or condition of man in society'. Political economy, by contrast, was 'more narrowly conceived'; as Mill argued:

> It does not treat of the whole of man's nature as modified by the social state, nor of the whole conduct of man in society. It is concerned with him solely as a being who desires wealth, and who is capable of judging of the comparative efficacy of means for obtaining that end. It predicts only such of the phenomena of the social state as take place in consequence of the pursuit of wealth.[23]

Mill's ambition was to counter the reductivism held to be inherent in classical political economy by some of his contemporaries. He argued that the profit-seeking individual postulated by classical political economy did not exhaust human nature. Rather it was just one attribute of humanity, but it was the *only* attribute which political economy needed to take any account of. Other aspects of human nature were relevant to explanations of other social phenomena. As Hollander argues, Mill was proposing a series of 'disciplinary boundaries' by which 'different classes of social fact' would be seen to have different 'causes'. The important point to bear in mind, however, is that for Mill, whatever the social phenomenon happens to be, its causes are always explained by reference to individual behaviour which in turn is rooted in the 'laws of human nature'. In this sense the basic method of social science was to '*analyse* the existing state of society into its elements' and this was followed by 'referring to the experience of individual man to learn the *law* of each of these elements, that is, to learn what are its natural effects'.[24] Indeed Mill's explanation of political economy made this point very clearly: he argued that 'the immediately determining causes [of political economy] are principally those which act through the desire of wealth; and in which the psychological law mainly concerned is the familiar one, that a greater gain is preferred to a smaller'.[25]

Despite the abstraction of classical political economy, and despite its view of society as following its own laws, processes and imperatives, implicit in its general view of things was nevertheless an individualist paradigm, for the origin of the social was traced back to the behaviour of the individual, and this in turn was determined by the dictates of 'human nature'. In this sense, classical political economy generated a theory of sociability (either in the market or in civil society) from a set of assumptions about human nature, that individuals were – at least in part – selfish and thus profit-seeking. It was the 'laws' or 'principles' of human nature which permitted an understanding of the social, rather than the other way round. This kind of theoretical orientation was very different from what for convenience I shall term a 'sociological' perspective whereby the postulate or concept of the social is used to explain the activities and nature of the individual. It was not until much later in the century, when the work of Karl Marx was discovered by British intellectuals, that serious attention was given to this latter kind of explanation.[26] As I have already suggested, in early and mid-Victorian Britain, the dominance of political economy's explanation of social life was partly due to the absence of any sustained alternative account of the way in which social conditions were determined (particularly an account of the operations of the market and industrial labour relations). This does not mean that political economy was uncontested; but it does go some way towards explaining why those (including the social-problem novelists) who were unhappy with its conclusions continued to theorise about the social by means of a set of assumptions about the behaviour of the individual. Of particular significance in this respect was the suggestion in classical political economy that the social was the *unintended* consequence of human nature – simply of the way humans were. It is also worth recalling the argument that conflicts in society were seen to derive not from 'real incompatibilities' but rather from 'ignorance or unreason' – that is, from circumstances where individuals had mistaken 'their real interests' or had acted against their 'nature'.

Resolving such conflicts therefore required not changes in social structures, but merely the education of individuals in order that they learn to square their lives with 'natural law'. As we shall see, this emphasis on human nature, rather than on social structures, is exactly the resolution imagined by the social-problem novelists; however, their challenge to political economy lies in their attention not simply to the re-education of individuals, but rather to redefining what is meant by human nature (and therefore to redefining the form of social life which will arise 'unintended' from individual behaviours). Articulating a disquiet about social conditions by focusing not on what individuals might *do* to change society, but rather on what constituted *human nature* – such a strategy is perfectly logical for a writer who had 'internalised' the individualist paradigm. My argument is simply that we need to be alert to the potential in such a strategy to subvert or challenge existing descriptions of social life.

III

Classical political economy construed the social in terms of the behaviour of autonomous individuals. Behind such a view there was an underlying assumption about individuality: that individual agency was to be understood in relation to certain givens of human nature. In other words, the paradox of classical political economy was that the focus on the individual did not necessarily imply an attention to individual difference, simply because human nature – what united individuals – was held to be a constant. This proposition in turn ensured that classical political economy did not link individual agency to social change. This contrast between the individual and individuality is crucially important for an understanding of early and mid-Victorian intellectual culture. The distinction between the two concepts tends to become blurred to the extent that when we think of the individual we automatically register individuality in terms of uniqueness or difference. Indeed modern debates about the relationship between the individual and society (at least in Western liberal democracies) often centre on the political and legal rights of individuals to articulate and act upon their difference within a social context. The obvious examples in modern Britain are equal opportunity legislation, and political agitation for, say, gay rights. By contrast, in early and mid-Victorian

Britain (certainly until the late 1850s and early 1860s), implicit in any reference to the individual was generally a notion of sameness.[27] At that time individual behaviour was typically understood in relation to the 'laws' of human nature or to specific attributes of humanity which predicated identity rather than difference between individuals. And it was for this reason that the mid-Victorians found it unproblematic to theorise about the social from the behaviour of the individual. The possible conflicts or tensions which we see today between an individual's good and the social good were simply not apparent within a Victorian frame of reference.[28] An interesting example of this tendency is to be found in Utilitarianism, a body of thought which was very closely linked to political economy.

The origins of Utilitarian thought are generally traced to the middle of the eighteenth century and in particular to the work of philosophers such as Thomas Hobbes and David Hume, and (on the Continent) Helvétius and Beccaria. However, it was Jeremy Bentham who was largely responsible for bringing Utilitarian thought to prominence. As John Plamenatz argues, Bentham was both 'the most typical Utilitarian' and also the first 'to have disciples, and to create something that deserves to be a school of thought'.[29] Bentham first coined the famous Utilitarian formula 'the greatest happiness of the greatest number' in 1768; however the systematic theory of utility which he developed from it did not come to general public attention until the beginning of the nineteenth century. Bentham's first published work was his *Fragment on Government* (1776); it was, however, the later *An Introduction to the Principles of Morals and Legislation* (published in 1789) which earned him a reputation. The work's first edition, though, received only scant attention, and in this sense the *Introduction* was like many other works which proved to be important in the nineteenth century. A second edition, with minor corrections, appeared in 1823, and a third edition, incorporating additional material, was published posthumously in 1838 as the first volume in Bowring's edition of Bentham's *Works*. However, Bentham only became well-known through the agency of the French scholar Etienne Dumont, who published in 1802 his *Traités de législation civile et pénale*. Compiled from Bentham's manuscripts, it corresponded in substance to the first six chapters of *An Introduction to the Principles of Morals and Legislation*. This form of Bentham's thesis was, according to H. L. A. Hart, 'more widely read than Bentham's original work'. The subsequent translations of

Dumont's *Traités* served to establish Bentham's reputation not only in England but also in America and on the Continent.[30]

The principle of utility – that of 'the greatest happiness for the greatest number' – sounds deceptively simple. Bentham outlined the assumptions underlying it in the opening paragraph of the *Introduction*:

> Nature has placed mankind under the governance of two sovereign masters, *pain* and *pleasure*. It is for them alone to point out what we ought to do, as well as to determine what we shall do ... They govern us in all we do, in all we say, in all we think ... The *principle of utility* recognises this subjection, and assumes it for the foundation of that system, the object of which is to rear the fabric of felicity by the hands of reason and law.[31]

Bentham went on to explain that the 'principle of utility' meant 'the principle which approves or disapproves of every action whatsoever, according to the tendency which it appears to have to augment or diminish the happiness of the party whose interest is in question'. And 'utility' referred to 'that property in any object, whereby it tends to produce benefit, advantage, pleasure, good, or happiness' for either the 'community' or the 'individual'.[32] The main concern of Utilitarianism was of course 'the greatest happiness of the greatest number', and so Bentham had to devise an argument which allowed him to identify the interests of the community with the interests of the individual. In so doing he invoked an atomistic conception of society similar to that which underlay political economy:

> The interest of the community is one of the most general expressions that can occur in the phraseology of morals: no wonder that the meaning of it is often lost. When it has a meaning, it is this. The community is a fictitious *body*, composed of the individual persons who are considered as constituting as it were its *members*. The interest of the community then is, what? – the sum of the interest of the several members who compose it ... It is in vain to talk of the interest of the community, without understanding what is the interest of the individual. A thing is said to promote the interest, or to be *for* the interest, of an individual, when it tends to add to the sum total of his pleasures ... An action then

may be said to be comfortable to the principle of utility ...
(meaning to the community at large) when the tendency it has to
augment the happiness of the community is greater than any it
has to diminish it.[33]

It is worth remembering that Bentham's work was primarily concerned with legislation, and the rationale for the 'principle of
utility' was that it would provide logical and objective rules to
guide legislators in their attempts to create the conditions for a fair
and harmonious society. The style of the *Introduction*, therefore,
was not so much philosophical as scientific, where the term
'scientific' was understood by Bentham to mean not the furnishing
of laws or generalisations from empirical observation but rather, in
John Stuart Mill's paraphrase, 'treating wholes by separating them
into their parts, abstractions by resolving them into Things, –
classes and generalities by distinguishing them into the individuals
of which they are made up'.[34] This kind of methodology produced
a book which was preoccupied with facts and how to classify them.
It also illuminates Bentham's conception of the social, for it implies
that society itself must be understood not as a 'whole' or 'body',
but rather in terms of the totality of its smallest constituent parts –
which are, of course, individuals. The exposition and justification of
the 'principle of utility' which begins the *Introduction* was thus
followed by detailed descriptions of the sources of pleasure and
pain. Indeed a long chapter of the *Introduction* was devoted to discussing the various circumstances (thirty-two in all) which
Bentham thought determined the experience of pain and pleasure.
He argued that the 'quantity' of pleasures and pain was not based
directly on the characteristics of external 'causes' or 'forces', but
depended also upon an individual's 'disposition' – upon the 'circumstances influencing sensibility'.[35] The circumstances included
'health', 'strength', 'hardiness', 'bodily imperfection', 'firmness of
mind', 'sex', 'age' and so on. Succeeding chapters of Bentham's
work specified rules for measuring the quantity (and so value) of
pleasure and pain in order to determine actions to secure an
increase in happiness. The main kind of action was the establishment of laws or sanctions. They were to be upheld by a system of
punishment, and the rest of the *Introduction* was concerned with
analysing the actions, consequences, motives and intentions of individuals in order to allow a legislator to decide the nature and extent

of the punishment necessary to achieve a general conformity to the principle of utility.[36]

There are some obvious problems with Bentham's theory. For example, the basic premise of his argument – that 'Nature has placed mankind under the governance of two sovereign masters, *pain* and *pleasure*' – is only ever asserted, and many commentators have noted that there are profound difficulties with the terms which Bentham uses. As John Plamenatz wryly points out: 'Bentham was not primarily a philosopher. He was anxious to have done with first principles as quickly as possible.'[37] So here the question of what is meant by 'pleasure and pain', of what the phrase 'sovereign mastery' actually entails, and so on, are all left unanswered. Plamenatz concludes that at one level it is just 'not possible to make sense of what Bentham is saying. Nothing can be done except to indicate the more important ambiguities'.[38] One of these ambiguities, however, is worth exploring in some detail, for it is pertinent to the argument of this book. It concerns Bentham's attempt to combine two incompatible doctrines: 'egoistic hedonism' – the Hobbesian view that man is a selfish animal, acting only to secure or promote his own interests – and Utilitarianism, or the greatest happiness principle.

One might suppose that the principle of the greatest happiness for the greatest number requires as a precondition the concession that human nature is fundamentally altruistic, and that individuals are guided in their actions by benevolence. However, it is clear that Bentham, like the classical political economists, tended to view individuals as inherently selfish and egoistical. Indeed the opening paragraph of the *Introduction* announced a form of 'psychological hedonism' in which it was held to be an axiom – a 'natural constitution of the human frame' – that the only thing which individuals desired and acted upon for its own sake was their own pleasure or happiness. Moreover, in Bentham's view it was precisely this attribute of humanity which led individuals to accept the greatest happiness principle as the standard of right and wrong. Although it might be the case that calculations would show that one individual's happiness would have to be sacrificed for the sake of the greatest happiness, nevertheless, as Hart argues, all individuals could be confident that 'in making all such calculations each individual's pleasures are considered and given equal weight'.[39] In Bentham's terms, 'Each is to count for one and nobody for more than one'.[40] The practical difficulty with an egalitarianism of this sort is that it can be almost guaranteed to produce profound inequalities between individuals, and it is therefore susceptible to the criticism that 'it treats individuals as mere receptacles with no intrinsic value for the experiences of pleasure and pain'.[41] In such a case individuals would indeed be justified in preferring a very different kind of felicific calculus. There is a further problem: if individuals are constituted by their nature to desire only what they believe will conduce to their own happiness, then what happens when this self-interest diverges from what is needed to secure general welfare? In such a situation, how can the individual comply with the utility principle and accept it as the *natural* standard of right and wrong? Bentham argues that in such cases individuals 'ought' to comply, but it is far from clear what is meant by the term 'ought'.

Modern critics of Bentham have resorted to a variety of interpretations of his work in order to try to resolve this contradiction.[42] For the purposes of my argument, what matters is simply the *existence* of such an ambiguity, for it is an inevitable consequence of Bentham's initial (and unexamined) frame of reference. Like classical political economists, Bentham starts from the premise that the social could be understood only in terms of the autonomous individual agents who compose society, and his theory of utility in turn requires that the behaviour of individuals can be understood (at least in part) in terms of identity rather than difference. Indeed, in procuring or promoting the greatest happiness for the greatest number, the legislator was entitled to ignore all the differences between individuals – in, for example, their income, living conditions, employment prospects and so on – which were irrelevant or immaterial to realising this larger ambition. In the same way, while they acknowledged that the operations of the market would necessarily produce large inequalities (of wealth, living standards and so on) between individuals, classical political economists did not see proposals to resolve such inequity as part of their brief. As far as their understanding of the social was concerned, then, Bentham and Smith shared the same basic individualist conceptual set, and this common ground in turn made it easy for subsequent thinkers to assimilate Benthamite Utilitarianism to political economy.

One work which well illustrates the intellectual continuities between political economy and Utilitarian modes of thought is Thomas Malthus's *An Essay on the Principles of Population*. Malthus

was an obscure country clergyman when his thesis about population growth first appeared in an anonymous pamphlet published in
1798. However – and in stark contrast to Bentham's fortunes – it
achieved an immediate popularity, and was followed by a revised
and greatly extended second edition published in 1803. Seven
further editions (with relatively few changes) followed. Malthus
also published a book on political economy, *Principles of Political
Economy* (1820) together with several works about related issues
such as the Corn Laws and free trade. Indeed, from the very start
Malthus acknowledged his debt to Adam Smith, and he later
formed a lasting friendship with David Ricardo. His population
thesis had a formative influence on Ricardo and, through Ricardo's
work, Malthus influenced a whole generation of political economists. Particularly significant (for the purposes of my argument)
was Malthus's redescription of the role of politics in social life.
According to the radical interpretation of the science of politics
associated with French writers such as Condorcet, 'politics con-
noted the activity of human reasoning operating directly through
positive laws and via the remodelling of political institutions to
improve the lives of individuals and nations'. As Donald Winch
argues, Malthus 'stood this proposition on its head'; he rather
argued that 'misery and vice were attributable to a fundamental
law of nature that was impervious to institutional change and
legislative contrivance'.[43] The continuities here with the way political economy minimised the role of politics in social life is striking;
at the same time, though, it is worth noting that there were some
aspects of Malthus's argument which ran counter to political
economy, particularly (and perhaps paradoxically) Malthus's
qualified endorsement of the principles of *laissez-faire*.[44]

In contrast to Bentham's *Introduction*, the argument of Malthus's
Essay can be simply summarised. His theme was human progress;
he argued that the possibility of progress was constrained by the
fact that a population tended to increase faster than the supply of
food needed to maintain it. He illustrated this argument by the use
of two ratios. According to Malthus, a population increased
geometrically (or exponentially, roughly doubling every twenty-
five years), but the supply of food increased only by an arithmetic
progression. The disparity between these ratios was in turn derived
from two axioms: that food was necessary for survival, and that
sexual desire was an unchanging attribute of humanity. The result
of these uneven rates of progression was poverty, misery and

eventual starvation. In the first edition of the *Essay* Malthus suggested two kinds of 'checks' which slowed down population growth: the 'positive' and the 'preventative'. The positive check was death through famine, warfare, disease (plagues and epidemics), poor childcare, and so on; a preventive check was one which tried to lower the birth rate, principally through the postponement of marriage. Actually Malthus was pessimistic about the effectiveness of any sort of preventive check, believing that the sexual instinct was so strong that delayed marriage would simply be replaced by illicit, pre-marital sexual relations. The result would not only be poverty and starvation, but vice and degradation as well. Malthus suggested that selfish human instincts would always thwart attempts to persuade individuals to put aside their selfish desires and act for the good of society as a whole. He concluded pessimistically that attempts to control the population by changing institutional structures would be futile so long as individuals had to eat and so long as sexual drives were strong – in other words, permanently.

The first edition of the *Essay* was a polemical piece; its thesis was unsupported by any empirical evidence and its tone was deeply pessimistic. In the 1803 edition, Malthus attempted to rectify these weaknesses by incorporating extensive historical examples to illustrate his principle of population growth, and by describing a new kind of population check, moral restraint. The result was a much longer and more authoritative work which was this time supported by copious statistical data and which used a more inductive methodology. One of the criticisms made of the first edition of the *Essay* concerned the disjunction between its pessimism – its view of the world as evil and depressing – and the Christian values which Malthus, as a clergyman, was assumed to endorse. His suggestion for a new kind of check on population growth, that of moral restraint, can be seen as a direct response to such criticism. In the original *Essay* Malthus had argued that certain attributes of human nature – the desire for food and sex – were responsible for population increase. In the second edition of the *Essay* the argument about human nature was modified in order to reconcile it with the assumed existence of a beneficent deity. Malthus claimed that the tension between the rate of population growth and the rate of food production was necessary for the successful 'replenishment of the earth' which he saw as the 'Creator's object': if population and food supply were 'exactly balanced', he argued, 'I do not see what motive there would be sufficiently strong to overcome the acknowledged indolence of man, and make him proceed in the cultivation of the soil'. 'The population of any large territory, however fertile', he went on, 'would be as likely to stop at five hundred, or five thousand, as at five millions, or fifty millions. Such a balance, therefore, would clearly defeat one great purpose of creation.'[45] The necessity for potentially destructive desires in turn explained why these desires gave individuals so much pleasure. Adopting the language of Utilitarianism, Malthus acknowledged that the pursuit of our desires was 'the materials of all our pleasures, as well as of our pains; of all our happiness, as well as of our misery; of all our virtues, as well as of our vices'.[46]

The issue at stake, then, was not the 'diminution or extinction' of desire, but its proper 'regulation and direction' where such control was understood in relation to those circumstances which produced 'the greatest sum of human happiness'.[47] While it was held to be part of a divine plan, this regulatory law (that is, moral restraint) also operated at the level of individual behaviour. Malthus argued that when desires were pursued to excess individuals naturally experienced painful consequences, and in order to avoid that pain they learn the importance of keeping their desires in check. According to Malthus 'natural and moral evil' were 'the instruments employed by the Deity in admonishing us to avoid any mode of conduct which is not suited to our being, and will consequently injure our happiness'. He gave some examples of how such 'instruments' worked:

If we be intemperate in eating and drinking, we are disordered; if we indulge the transports of anger, we seldom fail to commit acts of which we afterwards repent; if we multiply too fast, we die miserably of poverty and contagious diseases. The laws of nature in all these cases are similar and uniform. They indicate to us that we have followed these impulses too far, so as to trench upon some other law which equally demands attention. The uneasiness we feel from repletion, the injuries that we inflict upon ourselves or others in anger, and the inconveniences we suffer on the approach of poverty, are all admonitions to us to regulate these impulses better; and if we heed not this admonition, we justly incur the penalty of our disobedience, and our sufferings operate as a warning to others.[48]

When it was applied to the specific issue of sexual desire (and the consequent dangerous growth in population) Malthus's line of argument suggested that sexual continence and delayed marriage were in the best interests of both the individual and society, for they alleviated both the individual's pain (that is the poverty brought on by supporting too many children) and the pain of other individuals (that is, society) who became pauperised through having to help that individual:

> There are perhaps few actions that tend so directly to diminish the general happiness as to marry without the means of support-ing children. He who commits this act, therefore, clearly offends against the will of God; and having become a burden on the society in which he lives, and plunged himself and family into a situation in which virtuous habits are preserved with more difficulty that any other, he appears to have violated his duty to his neighbours and to himself, and thus to have listened to the voice of passion in opposition to his higher obligations.... [I]t is in the power of each individual to avoid all the evil consequences to himself and society resulting from the principle of population, by the practice of a virtue clearly dictated to him by the light of nature, and expressly enjoined in revealed religion; and as ... the exercise of this virtue to a certain degree would rather tend to increase than diminish individual happiness ... [,] we can have no reason to impeach the justice of the Deity.[49]

The Utilitarian framework of Malthus's argument permitted him to move seamlessly from the happiness of the individual to the happiness of society. Because pain and pleasure derive from the laws of nature they are experienced by all individuals. So Malthus could assume that an appeal to individual self-interest (the avoid-ance of pain by the exercise of moral restraint) is sufficient to bring about the social good (which he understands as the greatest happi-ness for the greatest number). Any improvement in society, he argued, will always be 'effected in the way in which we have been in the habit of seeing all the greatest improvements effected, by a direct application to the interest and happiness of each individual'. Malthus explicitly rejected the possibility of consciously acting in accordance with an idea of a 'general good'. Rather the 'happiness of the whole is to be the result of the happiness of individuals', and it was therefore necessary always 'to begin first with them. No cooperation is required'.[50] It is perhaps worth noting that much of Malthus's argument invoked what he admitted was an 'ideal society'; in reality he was not optimistic about the effectiveness of moral restraint, acknowledging at the end of the *Essay* that historically the 'duty' of moral restraint had been very 'incompletely fulfilled', and that it would therefore 'certainly be visionary to expect any very material change for the better in future'.[51] Significantly, though, this realism did not in any way weaken Malthus's basic premise that problems in society (poverty and the vice and degradation which accompanied it) could be resolved by an appeal to changes in *individual* behaviour which in turn were dictated by the laws of nature: 'It is less the object of the present work to propose new plans of improving society,' he suggested, 'than to inculcate the necessity of resting contented with that mode of improvement which is dictated by the course of nature, and of not obstructing the advances which would otherwise by made in this way.'[52]

There are a number of difficulties with Malthus's thesis, and they have been acknowledged by modern critics for some time. For example, there was little evidence for the existence of the arithmetic and geometric ratios which he proposed (and in the case of the geometric ratio, it was unclear whether Malthus was referring to actual increases in population, a tendency of the population to increase or its power to increase).[53] Malthus also took no account of the potential of agricultural technology to increase food production and distribution, and he failed to distinguish between sexual desire and the desire to have children. Finally, his theological background led him to dismiss the most obvious practical solution to sexual 'incontinence' – contraception. Some of these criticisms were made at the time and his work, although popular, was always controversial. However, my argument does not rest on the currency of Malthus's thought in the 1840s (or principally on its status) but rather on the fact that he exemplified a way of thinking which came to dominate the early and middle decades of the nineteenth century. Like Adam Smith and Jeremy Bentham, Malthus's fundamental idea was conceived nearly half a century before some of the social-problem novels were written, and it is inherently unlikely that his work held the same significance in, say, 1853 as it had in 1803. The importance of Malthus for my argument lies in the intellectual continuity which existed between his understanding of social problems and the concept of the social assumed by political economy and

Utilitarianism. All these ways of thinking about society take individual behaviour, defined by reference to the 'laws of human nature', as the basic unit for understanding the social environment. In order to suggest improved social conditions, early and mid-Victorian thinkers hardly ever appealed to fundamental changes in social institutions. Indeed, a notion of the *social or communal good* is rarely invoked. Rather, it is the self-interested actions of individuals which are the focus of attention. And individual interests are in turn understood not in terms of their variety and difference, but rather in terms of their identity, and this is in turn predicated on a particular view of human nature. My argument is that this paradigm, established at the beginning of the century, dominated Victorian intellectual life for several decades. Malthus's work was much criticised by his contemporaries but his continuing popularity (evident in the frequent reissues of the *Essay*) is at least partly explained by the fact that his basic conceptual apparatus – that society was an aggregation of individuals acting according to the dictates of human nature – rang 'true' for the early Victorians, and continued to ring true in some sense for their descendants.

Why was this so? Why did this way of thinking about the social and society, developed in the late eighteenth and early nineteenth centuries, come to be such a normative attribute of British intellectual life? There are in fact two elements to this question. The first concerns the specific history of Utilitarianism and classical political economy; and the second concerns other areas of thought which sustained the individualist paradigm which Utilitarianism and classical political economy helped to introduce and to normalise. It is important to note that although these two areas of intellectual activity were related to each other, that relationship was not necessarily causal or determining. In practice this means that we should not overestimate the influence of either system; specifically it means that the authority of classical political economy and Utilitarianism was not alone responsible for the dominance of an individualist paradigm in mid-Victorian thought about the social. However, it is true to claim that the dominance of individualist conceptions of the social was one of the reasons why those novelists who were dissatisfied with classical political economy's and Utilitarianism's explanation of social problems were unable to formulate a fully social or sociological alternative. Indeed it is exactly this circumstance which explains why, in 1848, Mrs Gaskell could refer to political economy as an area of knowledge which she (and her readers) simultaneously knew about, were deeply unhappy with, and yet were unable satisfactorily to oppose. Mrs Gaskell's dilemma (like that of the other social-problem novelists) was that she shared far too many assumptions (about the nature of the social) with the very body of ideas which she wanted to criticise.

IV

Malthus's work is one example of the ease with which Smith's and Bentham's ideas could be accommodated to each other. One reason for the influence of the individualist paradigm throughout the early decades of the nineteenth century was precisely because classical political economy was so successful (in the eyes of many Victorians) in forging a theoretical link between the principle of utility and the economics of the market.[54] It might be thought that social conditions in the 1820s and 1830s would have very quickly undermined the authority of this synthesis by posing a challenge to its basic proposition of a society which worked by consent. After all, these decades were marked by varying degrees of social unrest and consequent repressive legislation: they saw, for example, popular agitation over policy decisions made under the influence of political economy (particularly the new Poor Law), and they also saw the growth of working-class agitation which culminated in the Chartist movement. However – and perhaps surprisingly to modern eyes – classical political economy (and its explanation of social life) nevertheless proved to be remarkably resilient to criticism and its intellectual authority remained more or less intact until the 1860s. Although there were many *local* criticisms of classical political economy, and although there were many profound disagreements among classical political economists, no sustained alternative economic theory was elaborated until the last quarter of the century.[55] This is not to say, however, that classical political economy and the individualist paradigm which made it possible constituted an ideology in the sense proposed by Louis Althusser – that is, it did not constitute a totalising and unquestioned way of viewing the world.[56] As I hinted earlier, there was in practice a consistent (and vocal) opposition to the use of ideas associated with political economy and Utilitarianism, particularly at the level of policy decisions. There were also attempts to formulate different ways of understanding society and social relations. But, as the remainder of this chapter will make clear, these alternatives were always marginal, and they never properly escaped the dominance of the individualist episteme.

In general terms it is accurate to say that the language and conceptual framework of political economy continued to dominate intellectual culture long after specific elements or details of its doctrines had been brought into question. The reasons for this are complex, but two points are worth emphasising because (as we shall see in the next chapter) they have a specific relevance to the social-problem novels. One reason concerns the role of empirical evidence in confirming the propositions of classical political economy and Utilitarianism; another concerns the institutionalisation of these doctrines, particularly in the handling of social problems. Both of these issues are discussed by Philip Abrams in his study, *The Origins of British Sociology: 1834–1914* (1968). Abrams's interests seem at first sight to be far removed from those of the literary historian; however if we recall that in the eyes of some modern critics the chief weakness of the social-problem novels was their failure to develop a sociological critique of society, then the relevance of Abrams's work becomes obvious. His history suggests that the absence of such a sociological critique was not the result of an imaginative failure, or of political imperatives, but derived from the fact that a sociological paradigm – a systematic theory of social causation – was absent from nineteenth-century British thought.

In the early decades of the nineteenth century classical political economy developed into a highly abstract body of thought, working from deductive principles with scant regard for empirical investigation. In 1836 the political economist, Nassau Senior, gave an account of his subject which is worthy of attention for the representative qualities of its arguments. In his *An Outline of the Science of Political Economy* Senior argued that the task of political economists was to ensure that their reasoning developed logically and consistently from a given set of principles which themselves were not open to question. Significantly one of those unexamined principles was the notion that individuals were rational and calculating, and that they were motivated by a desire for wealth. In general terms, Senior argued that:

> [the] premises [of the economist] consist of a very few general propositions, the result of observation, or consciousness, and scarcely requiring proof, or even formal statement, which almost

every man, as soon as he hears them, admits as familiar to his thoughts, or at least as included in his previous knowledge; and his inferences are nearly as general, and if he has reasoned correctly, as certain, as his premises.[57]

An interesting consequence of this bias was that when empirical observations seemed directly to contradict the tenets of political economy, it was the dogma of first principles which was upheld, and uncomfortable evidence simply ignored. As Harry Landreth and David Colander argue, this situation continued despite the fact that 'by the middle of the 1830s, enough historical evidence had been accumulated to completely discredit ... the [distribution] theory, and along with it Ricardian economics'.[58] Another modern critic, Mark Blaug, has gone so far as to suggest that 'the divorce between theory and facts was probably never more complete than in the heyday of Ricardian economics', and that the main reason for this situation was 'embedded' in Ricardian methodology.[59] The consequence of this discrepancy between evidence and explanation was that the theoretical premises of classical political economy continued to have authority long after the usefulness of its explanations of specific economic issues – such as wages, labour, profit and rent – had all but disappeared. Indeed John Stuart Mill, perhaps political economy's most articulate and authoritative spokesman, published as late as 1848 his *Principles of Political Economy*, a work which remained standard for the rest of the century (and which ran to seven editions).

Although, as I hinted earlier, there were many significant differences between Mill's book and the work of his predecessors, the *Principles of Political Economy* has been described as 'simultaneously the most mature statement of the classical position and the start of a new period in the development of economic thinking'.[60] Mill's methods differed from those of his predecessors in his willingness to take account of empirical evidence and in his attempt to incorporate economics within larger philosophical concerns. As we have already seen, for Mill the profit-seeking abstraction of 'economic man' was merely that – an abstraction. Although necessary to the political economist, it represented only one element of human nature, and a fuller understanding of the social domain required a more comprehensive view of human social activities. Mill was particularly disturbed by the assumption of Bentham's followers, the 'philosophical radicals', that the pleasure–pain calculus could be used to understand *all* human behaviour.[61] Mill's most distinctive theoretical contribution lay in his attempt to make the theoretical models of classical political economy more flexible; in particular, while subscribing to the orthodoxy that the 'laws of production ... are laws of nature ... which cannot be changed by human will or institutional arrangement', he nevertheless suggested that the 'laws of distribution' were not fixed. Rather they were the result of social arrangements. The distribution of wealth, Mill argued, 'is a matter of human institution solely. The things once there, mankind, individually, or collectively, can do with them as they like'.[62] Such a view in turn cleared the way for proposals for wider state intervention than classical political economy had hitherto been prepared to countenance.

Appearing as it did in 1848 – that is, virtually simultaneously with the social-problem novels – Mill's work represents a particularly interesting account of political economy, precisely because it demonstrates a dissatisfaction with some of its implications at the same time as acknowledging the pervasiveness of some of its axioms. Unlike his predecessors, who had tended to see poverty as an unavoidable consequence of market operations, Mill viewed contemporary treatment of the poor as wholly inadequate. He recognised that at the heart of the problem was the unequal relationship which the market enjoined for employer and employee (which was, of course, precisely the concern of the social-problem novelists). In so doing, Mill had sympathy with some elements of contemporary French socialist thought, particularly the notion that employees should have a share or 'interest' in the profits of labour. Indeed one general way to characterise the distinctiveness of Mill's interpretation of classical political economy is in terms of its 'socialist flavour'. Ultimately, though, Mill's faith in political economy's central tenet – the competitive market – led him to reject socialist criticism of private property and competition. While Mill claimed to agree with 'the Socialist writers in their conception of the form which industrial operations tend to assume in the advance of improvement', he nevertheless also stated: 'I utterly dissent from the most conspicuous and vehement part of their teaching, their declamations against competition ... They [the socialists] forget that wherever competition is not, monopoly is; and that monopoly, in all its forms, is the taxation of the industrious for the support of indolence, if not plunder.'[63] There are in such statements echoes of Malthus and Ricardo, and it is perhaps not surprising that Mill recalled Malthus when he recommended how some of the more baneful effects of capitalism might be ameliorated by 'a due limitation of the number of the community'.[64] Specifically, in envisaging ways to resolve conflicts between masters and men, Mill looked first to the realm of private action, and only second to the role of the state (in so far as it might secure the freedom of private individuals to act more profitably). Importantly, though, Mill remained uncomfortable with the general idea of state intervention, believing (as Robert Lekachman argues) that 'individual action was superior not alone because of government's defects, but also because individual action developed individual character'.[65] Lekachman goes on to suggest that 'there was a tension between ... [Mill's] urge to ameliorate the condition of the poor and his distrust of state action'.[66] In his more famous work, *On Liberty* (1859), and in his rewriting of Bentham in *Utilitarianism* (1861), Mill went on to elaborate the proper role of the state in securing individual freedom.[67] Moreover, it is important to remember that this point in Mill's intellectual career was reached some time after the first of the social-problem novels was written. It is necessary to bear in mind, then, that although Mill's *Principles* was, in many ways, a critique of classical political economy and Utilitarianism, the more 'social' aspects of his thought are most fully developed only *after* the period with which I am concerned. But even then Mill's liberal doctrines were always theorised *within* the general individualist framework of classical political economy and Utilitarianism, and although influenced by more 'social' thinkers (such as Auguste Comte) Mill remained (and always saw himself) as the intellectual heir to the Smith–Malthus–Ricardo tradition. Hence Mill, despite reservations, maintained a commitment to the notion of the autonomous individual as the basic unit of society; he assumed that the ways in which the individual could change the laws of social life were limited, and he believed that there were fundamental laws or regularities of human nature underlying human behaviour. In this sense Mill is a particularly significant figure, for his work demonstrates the pervasiveness of the individualist paradigm, even for those writers (including the social-problem novelists) who perceived faults in the ways in which political economy and Utilitarianism operated.

Although in principle political economy was considered to be a deductive science, and although few political economists were willing to test its axioms against empirical evidence, it was nonetheless true that political economy was a prime mover behind one of the most famous elements of Victorian institutional life, the phenomenon of the Blue Book. To a modern reader, it may seem that the Blue Books, which were compilations of government statistics about poverty, crime, disease and so on, would have posed a challenge to the complacency of political economists. Indeed some modern critics have commented on the use made of government statistics by Victorian novelists, particularly Disraeli. Certainly there seems to be an opposition between the 'facts' which these publications documented and contemporary explanations of problems in society. However, as Philip Abrams has argued, one kind of reaction to the troubling mismatch between facts and explanation was ironically a demand for more 'information' – that is, for *more* 'facts'. Rather than revise their axiom of a rational social order, political economists argued that more information would eventually serve to prove them right, and would dispel the mounting disagreements among their ranks. Indeed Abrams suggests that there was a mutually reinforcing relationship between the failure of political economy to predict events and the search for new information to prop up its central tenets:

> The broad consensual boundaries of political economy left room for disagreements on a wide range of particular issues: the whole problem of the basis of value; the concrete meaning of the all-important idea of enlightened self-interest; the proper role of the state; and above all, the meaning of the increasingly disturbing phenomenon of social disorganization known as 'the condition of the people question.' By 1830 a whole chain of controversies had become explicit inside the encompassing consensus. And as disagreements accumulated so did the appetite for facts, the belief that information would dispel the clouds of controversy. The alternative was to recognize the diminishing usefulness of Adam Smith's paradigm.[68]

Returning to Nassau Senior, it is interesting to note that he was both a vociferous advocate of Ricardo and a member of the Poor Law Commission of 1832. In that role he was responsible (as Abrams notes) for transforming 'a routine inquire-and-report enterprise into one of the most sweeping and meticulous official fact-finding investigations ever conducted'. Senior (along with Malthus) was also a member of the Statistical Society of London. If this cohabitation between empirical fact-finding and deductive *laissez-faire* reasoning strikes the modern reader as odd, it is worth recalling Bentham's obsession with 'facts' and the synthesis of Utilitarianism with political economy. At any rate, the relationship is less surprising if we remember that 'facts' were not being tested against theory; rather, they were simply being sought as evidence to *prove* that the theory was fundamentally correct. In this sense it is important to realise that 'facts' were being selected, identified and interpreted within a framework already established by classical political economy. In practice this resulted in a focus on facts about *individuals*: after all, as Abrams argues, 'What facts could there be for the political economist but aggregated data about the circumstances and behaviour of individuals?'[69] A representative example of this way of thinking is provided by a report of an investigation into strikes printed in the journal of the London Statistical Society in 1838. The aim of the enquiry was set out in the following terms:

> to collect a statistical account of the various strikes and combinations which have existed in different parts of the United Kingdom for the purpose of altering the rate of wages, and of introducing new regulations between masters and men ... to exhibit the condition of the workmen at the time of the commencement of the strike or combination, and the terms and conditions on which they resumed work; showing also, as far as the same can be statistically stated, the permanent effects of the several disputes upon the character and condition of the workmen.[70]

In glossing this quotation, Abrams points out that the facts which such an exercise would discover were predetermined by a certain frame of reference – in this case, by a preconception of what causes a strike. Moreover it was a preconception based on a proposition fully in line with the tenets of classical political economy – that 'whatever the ostensible cause of strikes, the real causes are to found in the economic self-interest of the workmen'.[71] It is important to note here that facts were *not* interpreted 'socially'; that is to say, the accumulation of facts in Victorian Blue Books did not lead to an awareness of the *social* causes of individual behaviour. Rather, the central concern was 'to find an explanation for the incidence and distribution of poverty that squared with a self-regulating and optimistic conception of society'.[72] It was not until the pioneering work of William Booth and B. S. Rowntree towards the end of the century that an interpretation of facts in relation to social (rather than individual) causation began to be articulated. Booth and Rowntree used statistics to argue that poverty was structural, and should be understood in terms of unemployment, housing and wages, rather than in terms of character flaws or intemperance. In so doing they challenged the central dogma of a century of political economy. However we should remember that they were able to do so precisely because the central propositions of political economy had in their turn already been revised by marginal utility theorists. By contrast, in the period in which the social-problem novelists were writing, the kind of interpretation proposed by Booth and Rowntree was wholly absent, and the search for factual detail was nearly always motivated by an attempt to understand the behaviour of individuals *as individuals*.[73]

This interest in marshalling factual information had important ramifications for social policy. Fact-finding became institutionalised with the setting up of the Statistical Society of London in 1834. Philip Abrams singles out three main circumstances which contributed to the Society's influence and prestige in the early and middle decades of the nineteenth century: there was 'its direct engagement with social policy, its orientation to the gathering and evaluation of facts as an alternative to the radical reconstruction of theory, and its close involvement with government'.[74] The Society was notable for the range of people which it brought together, both 'party politicians' and 'a very distinguished group of private intellectuals'. It was a powerful and wealthy institution, and it had a formative influence on government social policy. Its members always included significant numbers of government officials and Henry Goulburn (himself Chancellor of the Exchequer from 1841 to 1846) described it as 'an object of great national importance'.[75] The closeness of statistician to statesman was a direct consequences of what Abrams calls 'the diffusion of political economy' which made it 'easy and instinctive for such men in both roles to see eye to eye'.[76]

Most of the practical work of the Society was in complete accord with the theoretical paradigms established by political economy. Typically attention was directed towards tabulating the links between 'economic and social indicators' or 'market variables and life-chances'. Abrams describes how members tried to map 'relationships for different classes between, say, price fluctuations or entrepreneurial expansion on the one hand and sanitary conditions or occupational mobility, income or education on the other'.[77] It might be thought that such concerns would sooner or later have led to a sociological understanding of the social data being examined, but the idea that social structures determined individual behaviour was never made explicit. Furthermore, despite the existence of 'fieldwork' in areas such as Soho and Westminster, and rural parishes in counties such as Essex and Hertfordshire, there was nevertheless a strong bias towards using materials gathered from official or semi-official sources, such as employers or the police. Abrams describes this bias forcefully when he observes that statisticians were interested in 'aggregate data on conditions or behaviour not ... experimental data'[78] – another legacy from the theoretical premises of classical political economy. In evaluating the contribution of the Statistical Society towards understanding social problems, Abrams concludes that empirical 'investigation of social conditions did not of itself produce a new understanding of society – only a greater concern and a greater sense of urgency of administrative and legislative action to bring society into line with what was essentially still Adam Smith's blueprint'. He goes on to suggest that by 'focusing persistently on the distribution of individual circumstances, the statisticians found it hard to break through to a perception of poverty as a product of social structure'.[79] Although the Society's papers reveal frequent and vociferous discussions about the problematic relationship between 'facts' and 'theory', it was not until the 1880s, under the joint stimulus of socialism and translations of classical German writings on statistical methods, that some members of the Society suggested that inadequate theories, rather than insufficient facts, were the root of divisions within it.[80]

In the early and middle decades of the nineteenth century there was resistance to the pervasiveness of statistical explanation, for not everyone (Charles Dickens included) was convinced of its powers. Typically, though, this reaction did not engage with the *economic* basis of those statistics; rather, it was articulated by an appeal to morality. Moreover (and perhaps more importantly) this reaction to the dominant interpretation of statistics was framed within the self-same individualist paradigm as that which underwrote the arguments both of the political economists and statisticians. It is not surprising, then, that this 'moralizing perspective' (as Abrams terms it) was at the same time both removed from the statistical 'impulse' and quite compatible with it. Indeed, one of the features of early and mid-nineteenth-century debates about social problems is that differences of opinion do not form themselves into sharp antitheses – rather they are two sides of the same coin. And this congruence of thinking in turn is the result of the dominance of a basic individualistic conceptual set which both sets the terms of *and* the limits to intellectual debate.

There was a widely held concern that statistical findings, useful and necessary as they might have been, offered only an unreliable or limited programme for action. One response to this dilemma was to use statistics as a guide for philanthropy. The tradition of philanthropic activities in Victorian life is a butt of recurring jokes in nineteenth-century literature, from Dickens's Mrs Jellyby in *Bleak House* to Dr Daubeny in Wilde's *A Woman of No Importance*. Less well-known, perhaps, is its institutionalisation under an 'umbrella organisation', the National Association for the Promotion of Social Science. Founded in the winter of 1856, this institution was the product of a growing feeling of dissatisfaction with statistically-based research. The Association brought together a number of reform groups and voluntary bodies, all of whom were united by a desire, in Carlyle's terms, to see something 'done'. The Association's membership is described by Abrams as 'both brilliant and representative', and over its history of thirty-odd years it numbered peers of the realm, Members of Parliament, members of the Bar, fellows of the Royal Society, baronets, knights, ministers of the Church of England, professors, and fellows of the Statistical Society. One of the earliest products of this organisation was a journal called *Meliora*, which in the first year achieved a circulation of about seven thousand issues per quarter. The journal voiced a general dissatisfaction with statistics, and in one issue statisticians were satirised as 'men with yellowed wizened bodies, lean and withered souls ... whose whole existence was spent in the endless practices of the four rules of arithmetic'.[81] An alternative approach to social problems was argued for, one based on philanthropic principles which would be compatible with 'Utilitarian Christianity'.

Translated into the larger arena of social problems, this perspective tended to view issues such as poverty and crime as a direct result of the lack of moral rectitude in particular individuals. In practice it led to an obsession with disease, understood as referring to 'ignorance, spiritual destitution, impurity, bad sanitation, pauperism, crime and intemperance – above all intemperance'.[82]

Significantly, if all these states were disease, then they were discussed in terms of pathology and not in terms of epidemiology; hence once more remedies for them required not changes in social structures or institutions, but the moral re-education of individuals. Abrams's summary of the priorities of this 'moralizing perspective' illustrates very well its intellectual continuity, with both the statisticians (which many ameliorists were ambivalent towards) and with classical political economy and Utilitarianism:

> As the moralizing perspective took hold, we find a clearer focus on individuals instead of social organization as the relevant unit of analysis for all social problems ... We find a distinctive interest within social research on the collection of what are called 'moral depravities' – essentially the mapping of depravity. We find social policy debates clustering around the issues of crime and criminal law, prison reform and prison administration, temperance, sexual conduct, schools, and public health – all those issues that were seen as directly relevant to the central problem of setting the individual free or equipping him to be thrifty, self-reliant, orderly, clean, and in a word, moral.[83]

There are strong similarities here with John Stuart Mill's emphasis on the importance of individual 'character'. Indeed such a view explains why for ameliorists drunkenness was the most commonly invoked explanation for social problems – it was, as Stephen Blackpool's wife demonstrated, 'the great subverter of character'. Abrams suggests that even a figure of the stature and experience of Lord Shaftsbury could resort to the 'great undeniable truth' – that 'seven-tenths' of the 'causes of moral mischief ... are attributable to that which is the greatest curse of the county – that which destroys their [the working classes'] physical and moral existence, cuts through their domestic ties, and reduces them to pauperism, with all its various degradation – habits of drinking and systems of intoxication'.[84] The quotation is taken from a volume of *Meliora* published in 1859, just five years after *Hard Times* was first published and four years after *North and South*. The Association was moved by exactly the same dilemma which the social-problem novelists wished to confront. There was a manifest concern with problems in society and an accompanying distrust of contemporary attempts to resolve them; yet at the same time there was an inability to develop any radically new understanding which might break away from the conceptual boundaries of current individualistic modes of thought and develop instead a sociological perspective by means of which problems in society were understood in terms of social rather than individual causation.

The individualist paradigm was not of course the only way of thinking about society in early and mid-nineteenth-century Britain, but it was the dominant one. Why was this so? More specifically, why did it prove so resistant to incursions from what we now think of as the major nineteenth-century contribution to political philosophy, the invention of socialism? Stefan Collini has remarked that in Victorian Britain socialism did not figure 'seriously in the mainstream of political controversy until the 1880s'. Up to that time, he argues, 'Englishmen were wont to compliment themselves on its comparative absence from British politics'.[85] In early Victorian Britain, the term 'socialism' was generally equated with 'Owenism' – with, that is, the body of social thought developed by Robert Owen and his followers. Initially, Owenites had used phrases such as the 'new view of society', 'the social system', and 'cooperation' to describe their distinctive approach to social issues; by the 1840s they adopted the relatively new term 'socialism' in order to draw attention to their emphasis on 'a social, as opposed to an individual, approach in all fields of human endeavour – including, though not limited to economic organization'.[86]

Owen's early career has been described by J. F. C. Harrison as 'one of the big success stories of the early industrial revolution'.[87] Owen's business was the cotton-spinning industry, and as manager and partner of the New Lanark Mills in Scotland – at the time the largest cotton-spinning business in Britain – he made himself a large fortune at a relatively early age. Owen attempted to turn New Lanark into a model factory, and in the process became keenly interested in the education and social welfare of the factory's employees. Around 1812, he began to extend his ideas to the organisation of society in general, and in 1813 he published the first essay in *A New View of Society; or, Essay on the Principle of the Formation of Human Character*. A second essay was also published in 1813, and a third and a fourth in 1814. They were followed by a whole series of lectures, letters, addresses and books in which he developed a radical social theory arguing for the reconstruction of contemporary society. The core of Owen's thought was the idea of community. He believed that the absence of a proper sense of community was the chief cause of contemporary social evils, for it produced a society which was both fragmented and fractious. In Owen's view, this sense of community was necessary for the establishment of satisfactory human relationships; moreover, it could only be fostered under a different kind of social system – what he called a 'communional system' in which there was common ownership of property. This new kind of society would be brought into being, Owen believed, not by class conflict, revolution, or government legislation, but rather by practical example – by the setting up of experimental communities which would eventually transform the whole of society. The rationale of Owen's communitarian concept of social life was Utilitarian; agreeing with the Benthamite dogma of the 'greatest happiness principle', Owen nonetheless proposed that the principle of utility could only be achieved in a 'system of general cooperation and community of property'.[88] Owen was also a firm believer in social determinants of character. His most mature expression of this conviction is to be found in his *Book of the New Moral World* (1836–44) where he argued that man was 'a compound being, whose character is formed of his constitution or organisation at birth, and of the effects of external circumstances upon it from birth to death; such original organisation and external influences continually acting and reacting upon each other'.[89] In Owen's view there was an important distinction between a person's individual character and his or her social character. As J. F. C. Harrison explains, 'because of the large number of variables involved in the combination of original constitution and external circumstances, the individual characters of men will be infinitely diverse; but their social character, which is less specific, will be determined by their basic life experiences as members of a particular group in a particular type of society'.[90]

It might seem, then, that Owen's way of thinking offered the basis of what I have described earlier as a sociological understanding of society, in the sense that it was concerned with the idea of social rather than individual causation, approaching problems in society by advocating a wholesale restructuring of social institutions rather than changes in the behaviour of individuals. As one Owenite, William Thompson, starkly put it: 'wherever we turn our eyes over the machinery of society ... the irresistible effects of institutions ... arrest the attention'.[91] The important question then becomes: if such a perspective on social problems existed in early nineteenth-century Britain, why is it so conspicuously absent from the social-problem novels? Was the rejection of this sort of solution the result of straightforward political prejudice on behalf of middle-class writers? Or were there other reasons why Owen's concept of the social failed to recommend itself to them? One answer to these questions lies in the nature of Owen's theory, which was far from convincing or coherent in its notion of social causation – particularly with regard to character formation. A second answer lies in the status which Owen's theory achieved.

Conventional accounts of Owenism locate the collapse of its popularity around 1846 with the disintegration of the Owenite movement. Although Owen continued to publish until his death in 1858, there was no institutional dissemination of his ideas, and his followers tended to be isolated. However, Owenite theories had fallen into disrepute long before his death. There had been a brief moment of celebrity between 1829 and 1834 when Owen became involved in working-class movements, setting himself up in 1834 as the head of a national federation of trades unions, the Grand National Consolidated Trades Unions, only for it suddenly to collapse eight months later. This episode apart, Owenism never threatened to enter mainstream intellectual culture, and its communal model of society never proposed itself as a serious alternative to the dominance of the individualist paradigm. The most significant weakness of Owen's thought lay in his assumption that the changes brought about by the processes of industrialisation were only temporary. This led him to argue that the existing social system did not need to be destroyed in order to set up new kinds of social structures. In distinction to later socialists, most obviously Karl Marx, he envisaged a process of gradual and evolutionary change whereby model communities would peacefully replace existing social institutions. While this kind of analysis might have seemed plausible in the early decades of the century, by the 1840s (when the social-problem novelists were writing) it was clearly inadequate, for by that time it had become obvious that the institutions of industrialism were far too firmly established to be dislodged by the 'small-scale' experiments which Owen's model communities represented. As Harrison argues, 'what had earlier been regarded as the special virtues of communitarism – its voluntary, small-scale, self-contained nature and its non-political, antistatist approach – became its defects. The basic characteristics of communitarism no longer appeared relevant to the main problems of society'.[92] Moreover matters were not helped by the fact that all such communities established in both Britain and America collapsed within two or three years, and that their impact on society was virtually 'negligible'.[93] A related problem concerned the agrarian bias within Owen's thought. Despite his early success in the cotton industry, his model society was one where the 'whole population [was] engaged in agriculture, with manufacturing as an appendage'.[94] Indeed at late as 1842, he claimed that Britain 'must now become essentially agricultural', for 'the substantial wealth of the world is only obtained from the land'.[95] Once again this kind of comment seemed both far-fetched and irrelevant. Social and economic change simply dated Owen's work and it is not surprising that Owen's socialism was disparagingly referred to as 'Utopian'.[96] The paradox of Owen's reputation, then, was that as industrialism became more firmly established, and its consequences for social life more obviously problematic, the only sustained social critique of it became more and more dated, and so more and more irrelevant to the sorts of problems being exposed by the evidence of the Blue Books. Put simply, Owenism did not seem to offer an answer to the kinds of questions which the social-problem novelists posed.[97]

More fundamentally, perhaps, Owen and his followers failed to construct a coherent economic theory to support their communitarian model of society, and this in turn made it difficult for them to refute the criticisms made by political economists. We can appreciate the significance of this shortcoming when we recall the role of political economy in redefining social life, together with its claim to address directly the very conditions of an industrialised economy which were then seen as the sources of contemporary social problems. After the publication in 1819 in the *Edinburgh Review* of an authoritative attack on Owenism by Robert Torrens, political economists ignored the body of thought associated with his name.[98] The mainstay of the Owenite criticism of capitalism was a form of Ricardo's labour theory of value in which it was argued that workers should retain the full value of their labour, and that economic exchanges should be equal rather than competitive. Accompanying this was the proposition, in direct opposition to Malthus, that contemporary society was characterised by material abundance: that is, more goods were being produced than were needed to sustain the population. In Owen's view the task was not, as Adam Smith had argued, to increase the wealth of the nation, but rather to cope with an excess of wealth which was injuring all classes. Basic to the Owenite view, Harrison suggests, was the 'contradiction between a vast increase in productive capacity and the distress of 1810, 1815–16, 1818–19 and 1825'.[99] And this contradiction was in turn seen as a consequence of the use of machinery within a competitive economic system. Instead of reducing hours of work, or relieving individuals of unpleasant tasks, machinery, in Owen's view, simply devalued labour.[100] It is easy to see how attractive Owen's views would have been to working-class movements, for they drew heavily on the rhetoric of exploitation and injustice. Unfortunately, though, a tone of moral indignation was too often used as a substitute for coherent economic argument. As Harrison argues, 'sophisticated economic theory was not a strong point of Owenites, and they were usually content with a labour theory of value which was vaguely felt to be derived from juridical right'. He goes on:

> A large part of the difficulty which Owenites had in challenging classical political economy was caused by their refusal to be limited by its declared boundaries. The economy of cooperation ... was both more and less than a theory of economics: more in that it was an attempt to reassert the values of an older, pre-capitalist concept of 'moral economy' which was felt to be threatened: less in that it was not a coherent and complete theory of the functioning of an economy. The concerns of Owenism were not those which were primary or central in classical political economy, so that a dialogue between the champions of the two philosophies was not particularly fruitful.[101]

This inability to engage with the basic tenets of political economy was a serious weakness, for much of the impetus behind Owenite communitarism was a hostility to political economy's atomistic, individualistic model of society. However, criticism of the model was always articulated in moral rather than theoretical terms. Had it been the case that Owenism itself represented an epitome of moral rectitude, then perhaps this would not have mattered. Unfortunately, though, the morality of Owen and his followers was viewed with deep suspicion. The main problem was the secular nature of Owen's thought, particularly as it was manifest in his attacks on those sacrosanct Victorian institutions, marriage and the family. Owen located the competitiveness of modern society within the nuclear family which he saw a divisive force, encouraging isolation and self-centredness. In its place he proposed 'scientific associations of men, women and children, in their usual proportions, from about four or five hundred to about two thousand, arranged to be as one family'.[102] Owen blamed the privacy and isolation of the conventional family on Christian marriage. He singled out Christianity's inflexible attitude towards sexual relationships, arguing instead for a freer and (allegedly) more natural expression of love and desire, and for a system of divorce. Regarding celibacy as unnatural, Owen was also a strong advocate of birth control. None of these views endeared Owen to the Christian community, and Owenite polemic all too easily became associated with slurs of immorality. This was particularly true of the controversies surrounding his emphasis on the social determinants of character. In the eyes of many Victorians (including some of Owen's supporters) it was impossible to reconcile his arguments with the Christian emphasis on duty and moral responsibility.[103] To make matters even worse, through the 1820s and 1830s, Owenism became inextricably bound up with the marginal religious beliefs of Millenarianism and, according to Harrison, by 1840 it tended to be viewed as 'a rapidly growing sect which challenged established religion and encouraged immoral practices'.[104] It is little wonder, then, that Owen's understanding of society failed to pose a significant threat to the dominance of the individualist paradigm. Owen was unable to argue his position theoretically, and the moral authority which he believed underwrote his way of thinking became increasingly vulnerable. Owenism could too easily be dismissed as irrelevant, theoretically flawed and deeply immoral.

Despite seeming to confront the individualist paradigm, then, Owen's theories were too unsystematic to represent a serious critique of it. Most importantly he was unable to extend his ideas of social causation to precisely those areas, the political and economic, which had been so successfully appropriated by political economy, and which were the focus of so much attention by the social-problem novelists. In simple terms his social understanding was far too limited; the concept of social life (agrarian communities) which his theories expounded had no relevance to the problematic social world which confronted the Victorians in the 1840s and 1850s. Social problems for the mid-Victorians (particularly the social-problem novelists) were problems arising from an industrial economy, but it was precisely this form of social life which Owen (unlike later socialist thinkers) could not satisfactorily address.[105]

V

As I suggested earlier, sustained evidence for the dominance of an individualist conceptual set can be found in the variety of disciplines or areas of thought which it underwrote. In this respect an arresting instance is to be found in what at first sight seems to be an unlikely source, an anecdote about Charles Darwin. The source is unlikely precisely because there is no immediate connection between Darwin's interests and the issues discussed in mid-Victorian fiction. Indeed, with the exception of *Felix Holt*, the social-problem novels all appeared before any of Darwin's writing was published (his first major work, *On The Origin of Species by Means of Natural Selection*, did not appear until 1859). More pointedly, Darwin does not seem to have been at all concerned with either industrialisation or with those problems in contemporary society which mid-nineteenth-century novelists had identified. In a very obvious way, Darwin had much larger concerns than the immediate particularities of contemporary British society: his subject-matter was the origin of life itself, and the materials he drew on were gathered on a five-year trip around the world as a passenger on the *Beagle*. It is, however, the very absence of any obvious topicality or contemporary reference which makes the comparison between his work and the social-problem novels so impressive, for Darwin arrived at his controversial theory of the evolution of species by means of exactly the same conceptual set as that which informed the understanding of society which we find in the social-problem novels: his theory of nature was coterminous with their theory of the social.

On 18 September 1838 Darwin made what historians have come to see as an important jotting in a private notebook:

Take Europe on an average every species must have the same number killed year with year by hawks, by cold etc. – even one species of hawk decreasing in number must affect instantaneously all the rest. – The final cause of all this wedging, must be to sort out proper structure, and adapt it to changes – to do that for form, which Malthus shows is the final effect (by means however of volition) of this populousness of the energy of man. One may say there is a force like a hundred thousand wedges trying [to] force every kind of adapted structure into the gaps in the economy of nature, or rather forming gaps by thrusting out the weaker ones.[106]

Historians have seen in this entry the first fumbling formulation of Darwin's theory of natural selection, which would not be presented to the general public in anything approaching a finished form for another twenty years. In his *Autobiography*, written in 1876 when he was an old man, Darwin described how he had arrived at this moment of enlightenment:

> Fifteen months after I had begun my systematic enquiry, I happened to read for amusement Malthus on Population, and being well prepared to appreciate the struggle for existence which everywhere goes on, from long-continued observation of the habits of animals and plants, it at once struck me that under these circumstances favourable variations would tend to be preserved, and unfavourable ones to be destroyed. The result of this would be the formation of new species. Here, then, I had at last got a theory by which to work.[107]

Darwin's brief account is a rather modest oversimplification, although one which is perhaps understandable given that he was recalling events which had taken place forty years earlier. What is relevant to my subject is the formative role which Darwin attributes to the work of Malthus and his theory of population growth. There is considerable debate among historians of evolutionary biology about how precisely Darwin's thought developed over the crucial months between July and September 1838 when the outline of a theory of natural selection was first conceived. Some argue that the most important influence was his understanding of the practices of animal-breeders which provided evidence of a process of 'artificial selection' which he later adapted to form the basis of a theory of natural selection. Other historians have taken a broader view, emphasising the continuity between the intellectual paradigms underlying Darwin's thought and those which dominated mid-nineteenth-century intellectual culture in general. So, for example, they see parallels between the theory of natural selection and nineteenth-century accounts of the processes of industrial capitalism. Indeed, Darwin's own repeated reference to Malthus seems to lend support to this argument.[108]

The theory of natural selection was in fact only one aspect of Darwin's thought, although history has judged it to be the most important.[109] In simple terms it describes the mechanism of the processes of evolution. The idea of evolution itself was not

Darwin's invention. The notion that the world was neither constant, nor a recent 'on-off' creation, nor in a process of perpetual cycle, had in fact been mooted since the eighteenth century; it was stated most explicitly in J. B. Lamarck's *Philosophie zoologique* (1809) and in a different context in Charles Lyell's *Principles of Geology* (1830–3). Darwin departed from his predecessors in his formulation of a non-teleological and mechanistic explanation of evolutionary change, one which could account for the diversity and apparent harmony of natural life-forms in non-supernatural terms. As I have suggested, his interest in the variety and origins of natural phenomena was first stimulated by his five-year voyage around the Pacific and South America. On his return to England he spent a great deal of time studying and classifying his findings, and it was through this work that he came to the conclusion that the natural world was evolving rather than static. His difficulty, though, was finding an explanation of precisely how evolution worked – how the wonderful variety of life, until then explained in terms of a divine plan or grand 'design' (in which species were fixed), could have come about. The entry in his notebook in September 1838 presents both his solution to this problem and a brief explanation of how he arrived at it – by means of the work of Malthus.

Historians are as divided in their interpretations of Darwin's reading of Malthus as they are about the origins of the theory of natural selection. The basic point of controversy is whether Malthus was merely the catalyst for ideas which Darwin had already been developing, or whether his role was more formative, providing Darwin with a completely new way of thinking which broke dramatically with his thought up to that moment.[110] What is not disputed, though, is that the most important feature of Malthus's work to find a place in Darwin's theory of natural selection was the proposition that competition took place between individuals and not between social groups. This led Darwin to understand the evolutionary process in terms of what is now called 'population thinking' rather than typology or essentialism. The American biologist Ernst Mayr defines population thinking as a 'viewpoint which emphasizes the uniqueness of every individual in populations of a sexually reproducing species and therefore the real variability of populations'. It is the opposite of typology or essentialism – 'the belief, going back to Plato, that the changing variety of nature can be sorted into a limited number of classes, each of which can be defined by its essence'.[111] The language of these definitions may seem unfamiliar, for the term 'population' is used in evolutionary biology in a specialised sense to refer to a group or community of 'interbreeding individuals, particularly at a given locality'.[112] However, if the term 'society' is substituted for the term 'population', then it becomes easy to see the concepts which Darwin and Malthus had in common and how both shared the individualist conception of the social which dominated early and mid-nineteenth-century intellectual culture. In both cases, contemporary Victorian society and breeding populations are understood atomistically – that is, they are seen as being composed of autonomous individuals. And it is these individuals rather than the group (understood in terms of an abstraction, as social laws, or as a species) which form the basic way of thinking. Two of Darwin's biographers, Adrian Desmond and James Moore, sum up his early formulation of the theory of natural selection as a 'new way of viewing nature [which] ... kept faith with the competitive, capitalist, Malthusian dynamics of a poor-law society'.[113]

The theory of natural selection describes the differential survival and reproductive capacities of individual members of a population. This differential in turn is the result of the abundant variation and competition between individuals in every generation. In simple terms, those individuals who are superior are those who are successful in reproduction: indeed, such success is precisely what defines the whole notion of 'superiority'. Significantly, nature itself is not a selecting agent, for nature does not select *for* anything. Like the concept of society invoked by political economy, nature has no agency, nor can it be described as goal-directed. It is only individuals, through their superior physiology – that is, their better adaptation to climate, resistance to disease, or ability to attract mates – who possess agency and goals (to survive and reproduce); and therefore it is *only* individuals upon whom selection acts. Mayr puts it succinctly when he states that in the theory of natural selection 'there is no external selection force';[114] there is also no direction, no teleology, and therefore no 'purpose' to natural selection. It should by now be clear that in all of this there is a marked similarity to the conceptual set underlying political economy and Utilitarianism. Indeed, the terms 'Nature' and 'Society' fit both explanations – so much so that they are virtually interchangeable. So in Darwin's view of nature, as in Malthus's view of human populations, the survival of the individual has nothing to do with the survival or success of the group; rather, the only way a group does survive is through the fitness of the individuals which constitute it. Such a view maps on to the central proposition of political economy – that problems in society can only be resolved by reference to the behaviours of individuals. Also similar to the tenets of political economy is Darwin's characterisation of nature as viciously competitive, rather than (as natural theology had argued) benign and consoling. Moreover, in nature as in society, it is competition which paradoxically produces the apparent harmony and order of the natural world. Darwin's nature was an 'unintended' entity in exactly the manner in which Malthus's or Smith's society was: that is, nature, like society, was not susceptible to any form of human control or intervention. The logic of Darwin's argument is not only that nature embodies the order or regularities of Malthus's or Smith's contemporary society, but also that contemporary society operates as a state of nature.

As I have noted, Darwin's work was not published during the period when most of the social-problem novels were being written, so there is clearly no direct line of influence. However, Darwin was thinking and writing in the late 1830s and 1840s, and despite its radical originality, *On the Origin of Species* nevertheless reveals the typicality of its concerns: that the starting-point of its enquiry was the individual, and that social or natural phenomena could be understood in terms of an aggregation of individual behaviours. As I suggested at the beginning of this chapter, the same pattern can be found in any number of areas of mid-nineteenth-century thought, and we should therefore not be surprised to find it also in the social-problem novels, where the theme of individuality takes the form of advocating 'changes of heart' rather than changes in social structures.

In addressing the social disorder increasingly evident in mid-Victorian Britain – the riots in the streets, the conflicts between masters and men at the factory gates, and the appalling suffering from poverty and disease – the primary task of the social-problem novelists was to define a new principle of social cohesion, a new basis for social life. A contemporary reviewer put matters succinctly when he noted that the new kind of fiction was no longer 'content to exhibit society' by 'turning up little social problems illustrative of every-day experiences'. Instead the 'modern' writer was 'boldly invading those realms of politics and economy'.[115] To invade those realms inevitably meant to engage with the descriptions of social life in the areas of thought outlined in this chapter –

with Utilitarianism and political economy. As we have seen in earlier chapters, however, the results of the 'invasion', of the attempt to address 'large' issues, have tended to strike modern readers as disappointingly insubstantial. The reasons, though, are not primarily to do with a lack of 'imagination' (and the notion of personal failure which it implies). Nor can it be adequately explained by a simple political prejudice (a tacit desire to retain the status quo). The social-problem novels are 'conservative' in the sense that they do not advocate large-scale structural changes in society, and they exhibit a distrust of collective action, be it Chartist agitation or union activity. But the contradictions and inconsistencies noted in them are not fully explained by such attitudes. After all, a novel may be conservative in its politics, but still be logical, coherent and thematically unified. Furthermore, the proposition that the weaknesses of the works derive from constraints inherent in their narrative devices is also unhelpful. Whether or not a literary form embodies or articulates an intellectual contradiction does not on its own explain why that contradiction should exist (or remain unresolved) in the first instance.

The root source of the novels' limitations can be glimpsed in a much more fundamental paradox: the alternative model of social life which the social-problem novelists offer turns out to share many of the same assumptions (about the nature of the social and the role of the individual) as those of the doctrines which they criticise. As in Utilitarianism and political economy, so in the social-problem novels we find a focus on the individual as the basic unit of analysis. With the exception of Disraeli's work (which I explain later), we also find a distrust of politics and the general capacity of socio-political intervention to mould social life. Third, and most significantly, we find a belief in a form of human 'universalism' – that is, the location of the basis of social life in a changeless human nature. These similarities derive from the shared individualist conceptual set. Where the social-problem novelists differ is in their definition of what constitutes human nature. The claim that individuals are selfish egoists is replaced by the assertion that human nature is fundamentally moral and altruistic. For the social-problem novelists it is therefore a moral (as opposed to an economic) agency which holds out the prospect of a more cohesive society. The difficulty in such a position was to explain quite how such a moral agency might work – how *in practice* it could transform social life. Having redefined human nature, the problem was how to understand those elements of social life which political economy and Utilitarianism seemed to explain so fully and so authoritatively. The most important of these elements, because it directly affected conflicts between classes, was the role of the market in determining social relationships. Unfortunately, however, one consequence of opposing morality to political economy as a method of redefining social life was the virtual evacuation of economics as an explanatory category, for the social-problem novelists did not have, and could not conceivably have had, any coherent alternative economic theory. As a result the individualist view of social life which they proposed, one which assumed a fundamentally altruistic human nature, was simply unable to provide the basis for a way of theorising economic activity. More troublingly, their redefined human nature (the basis on which they remodelled social life) was by definition anti-economic; it was defined as 'other' to the profit-seeking agency postulated by political economy. We can glimpse the dimensions of the problem when we recall the willingness of the social-problem novelists (particularly Mrs Gaskell) to acknowledge a link between social unrest and economic circumstances – in, for example, the frequently reiterated references to the connections between trade cycles, unemployment and strikes. This tension between an acknowledgement of the importance of economic circumstances and a conception of social life which seems totally to exclude the economic goes some way to explaining the inconsistencies of the social-problem novels. They derive, I suggest, not so much from the 'refusal' of a theory of social or structural change (that omission is to be expected in the intellectual climate of the mid-nineteenth-century), but from the absence of a 'virtuous' theory of economic activity – one, that is, which was consonant with a belief in a fundamentally moral and altruistic human nature. As I shall suggest in the next chapter, it is precisely an *acknowledgement* of this tension – an awareness that the opposition between altruism and the market might indeed be problematic – which distinguishes the social-problem novelists from one other.

4

Morality, Economics and the Market

Hard Times, Mary Barton, North and South, Alton Locke, Sybil and *Felix Holt* were not the only works of mid-nineteenth-century fiction to address problems of social discontent or of disorder in contemporary industrial society.[1] This chapter will not attempt to provide a comprehensive survey of all the works which could be included in the sub-genre. What distinguishes the novels I have listed is the immediacy of their representation of social conditions and the degree of complexity and sophistication with which those conditions are both described and discussed. Most of the novels which I have listed are unshrinking in their vivid portrayals of urban poverty. In Mrs Gaskell's *Mary Barton* and *North and South* we are given striking portraits of working-class dwellings, ranging from the hygienic ordinariness of the sparsely furnished Barton home to the insanitary squalor of the Davenports' cellar. The opening chapters of Kingsley's *Alton Locke* contain some equally arresting descriptions of sordid London slums and sweat-shops, reminiscent of Friedrich Engels's account of the dwellings alongside Manchester's River Irk but more vivid in its evocation of the unfortunate individuals forced to eke out a living there. Disraeli's description in *Sybil* of the 'interior' of Marney with its squalid tenements and open drains is similar in detail and tone, and Dickens's archetypal industrial town, Coketown, although presented metaphorically, suggests the same overpowering sense of oppression and dismal decay. In contrast to this apparent commitment to verisimilitude, the plot structures which the novels use are anything but realistic; indeed they are invariably derived from the stock situations of melodrama and romance. In these parts of the novels, we could be in the world of Victorian popular theatre, and so we find traditional melodramatic devices such as mistaken identity, wrongly apportioned blame, *la voix du sang* and the twists and turns of a Victorian 'hue-and-cry'. We also find that predictable but potent Victorian combination of the themes of crime and thwarted love. The plots also tend to take the reader far beyond the original urban industrial setting – to an imaginary society, such as Sleary's circus, to a Liverpool courtroom, or to the decadent world of Alton Locke's Cambridge. I have suggested that such displacements are typically described as evasions, the result of imaginative failings or political expediency. Before acceding to such a judgement, though, it is worth asking *why* these features appear so consistently in novels which at other points and in other ways take their subject-matter so seriously.

The evidence from the previous chapter suggests a more prosaic explanation for the combination of realism and melodrama: that realistic description, or the enumeration of factual details, could not provide material for plots. As I have suggested, the characteristic ways in which the Victorians understood their society led to the accumulation of facts for their own sake. Generally speaking, factual detail did not generate new theoretical insights, nor did it lead to the development of new kinds of explanations. More fundamentally, contemporary commentators found it very difficult to form meaningful narratives from their accumulated facts – they simply could not make a coherent story (or explanation) from the data which they observed for themselves or which they took from the Blue Books. It should come as no surprise, then, that the social-problem novelists, like political economists and statisticians, were confused rather than galvanised by the aggregation of factual detail. Facts may have presented them with a clearer picture of social conditions (that is, with the settings for their novels), but facts alone could not lead to a better understanding of those conditions: they did not produce a new narrative. Facts alone, as the ameliorists had recognised, did not – and could not – produce a prescription for action. That the novelists should plot their novels using familiar literary resources, particularly those most readily at hand in popular traditions of romance and melodrama, is therefore to be expected; after all, even if it were possible to construct a coherent non-fictional narrative which explained 'the facts' it would not automatically have been part of the resources of the writer of fiction. Furthermore melodrama and romance were (and still are) the staples of popular fictional narratives because they are unequalled for holding the attention of an audience; indeed they were particularly suited to mid-Victorian publishing conditions, where serialisation and multi-volume novels were the norm. Less obvious, though, is an underlying epistemological continuity between the values which melodrama and romance encode and contemporary ways of defining social life. These narrative devices, despite their self-conscious fictionality, were surprisingly appropriate vehicles for exploring the kinds of problems which had been identified in mid-Victorian society.

Melodrama and romance embody a certain value-system which is not negotiable and which is therefore incapable of modification. So in melodrama villains are always villainous, heroes always heroic, and heroines invariably victims; a character cannot at the same time exhibit both heroic and villainous qualities. As the features which define right and wrong exist as constants, so they can simply be invoked by the writer. Today we would probably consider that these dichotomies offer too simple an answer to the complexities of experience; more locally it might be objected that they seem too rigid to encompass the range of group interests and social roles in mid-Victorians society. Such criticism may be true, but for the purposes of my argument it is also trivial. Of much more interest is the *dynamic* relationship between the stability of character types in melodrama and romance and the essentialist view of human nature which underlay mid-Victorian definitions of the social. The point is perhaps more clearly seen in relation to another common criticism of the social-problem novels – the alleged weaknesses of their characterisation. Here the difficulty once again centres on the resort to melodramatic caricature in, for example, figures such as Stephen Blackpool or Slackbridge in *Hard Times* who seem little more than the stock martyr and stage villain. The same limitation appears more subtly in figures such as Louisa, where the sexual and psychological complexities of her situation are obscured by their melodramatic framing, most obviously in her famous descent 'lower and lower' down the staircase of respectability. A similar situation occurs with Gaskell's John Barton, where the conflict in his character between working-class decency and potentially criminal resentment is removed when he resorts to murder. However, the most crude example is probably to be found in Kingsley's portrayal of Alton Locke's religious conversion at the hands of the saintly Eleanor; the plot demands that Locke be transformed, but there is no adequate psychological or social explanation for what appears to be a rather mysterious volte-face, the result of a feverish dream. These narrative manoeuvres are generally described as reductions or simplifications and they are usually explained in the same way as the alleged weaknesses of plot. They tend to be attributed either to ideology (say, to Dickens's hostility and fear of union agitators) or, more charitability, to simple ignorance (for example, how could middle-class writers have any real insight into working-class lives and personalities?). In this chapter I shall propose a different explanation, suggesting that methods of characterisation need to be seen in relation to the typically Victorian way in which social-problem novelists understood the relationship between individuality and human nature, and between individual agency and social forces; that is, those processes of reduction or simplification, far from being evasions or the result of ignorance, follow logically from the way in which problems in society were conceptualised.

As indicated in the previous chapter, a focus on the individual as the unit for analysing society did not necessarily entail an interest in subjectivity or individual difference. Rather, social atomism drew upon what was *similar* in individuals – on a (supposed) universal human nature – for the form of social life was a direct but 'unintended' consequence of what it meant to be human. From such a perspective, interest in the behaviour of individuals was confined to how it could be accommodated to the regularities or laws which where held to underlie human nature. Inner psychology, the exploration of the vagaries of the individual mind or of individual motives – all these issues would always be subordinate to a general explanation of human motivation. It was exactly this kind of general explanation which was assumed by the alleged 'simplifications' which we find in melodrama and romance. Importantly, though, the concept of human nature presupposed by those fictional narratives was in one respect significantly different from that which underwrote the dominant conceptualisations of the social in political economy or Utilitarianism: melodrama and romance assume a concept of humankind defined by a moral rather than by an economic agency. In using these simplifying fictional devices to redescribe human nature, the social-problem novels were able to suggest the possibility of a new form of social life – one which would arise 'unintended' (as political economy had suggested), but from the activities of moral, as opposed to economic, agents. It is in this context, then, that we can appreciate the significance of those scenes of emblematic reconciliation between characters (usually drawn from different classes) who have hitherto been hostile or opposed to each other. The tableaux in which John

Barton is reconciled with Carson, Nicholas Higgins with John Thornton, Louisa and Gradgrind with Stephen, Alton Locke with Eleanor – these are the main devices by which the social-problem novelists figure that community of interests which will bring about the restoration of social order. To the modern eye such scenes of course seem mawkish, sentimental and reactionary, precisely because they appear to reduce or simplify the very differences (of circumstance and personality) which marked out the individuality of the characters in question. But the primary function of these scenes is rather to exhibit the constancy and universality of human nature, for it is only from such a redescribed human nature (and not from individual difference) that a new form of social life will be possible.

This line of argument becomes easier to see in the novels themselves. The earliest of the novels which I shall discuss is *Sybil: or The Two Nations*, published in 1845. The others appeared in quick succession. *Mary Barton* was published in 1848, and its success led Dickens to invite Mrs Gaskell to contribute to his journal *Household Words*. It serialised her next novel, *North and South*, in twenty-two weekly parts between September 1854 and January 1855; *North and South* was published in book form later that year, and proved so popular that a second edition (with some corrections) followed in a matter of months. Meanwhile, Dickens also used *Household Words* to serialise his own novel *Hard Times*, which was published as a book in 1854. It is perhaps worth noting that during the serialisation of *Hard Times* the sales of *Household Words* first doubled and then quadrupled indicating, as David Craig suggests, a 'successful appeal to current interest in themes from industrial life'.[2] Kingsley's *Alton Locke* appeared anonymously in 1850, with a second, corrected edition following in 1851 and a third in 1852. There was also a cheaper popular edition published in 1855 (although it bears the date of 1856), and finally a revised edition in 1862 which constituted a substantial reworking of many of its elements. The anomaly in this history is George Eliot's *Felix Holt, the Radical*. Written between March 1865 and May 1866, it was published by Blackwoods in the following June, well over a decade after the main group of social-problem novels had appeared. By that time, the specific events which had stimulated Disraeli, Dickens, Kingsley and Gaskell were in the past; moreover the intellectual climate of the late 1860s was significantly different from that of the 1840s and early 1850s. For this reason *Felix Holt* is perhaps better viewed not as a member of the sub-genre of social-problem novels, but rather as a commentary on it. As I argue in the next chapter, Eliot's novel marks a boundary between a way of thinking about social conflict and social disorder which we find in mid-nineteenth-century fiction, and new ways of thinking about society which emerge in the changed intellectual climate of the late nineteenth century and which influence novels by late nineteenth-century writers such as Thomas Hardy and George Gissing.

I

Hard Times has received more critical attention than any other social-problem novel. Such a situation no doubt reflects Dickens's general standing among modern critics, but it needs to be seen in the light of two further considerations: that *Hard Times* is generally taken to be the least representative of Dickens's *oeuvre*, and that it is also judged one the most problematic or flawed of the social-problem novels. Dissatisfaction has typically centred on alleged weaknesses in the novel's characterisation (in particular its portrayal of working-class characters) and on the symbolic nature of the plot, which offers the Sleary circus as an alternative social environment to the corrupting world of Coketown. Most obviously, as I hinted earlier, there is the allegation that the novel's working-class characters – Stephen Blackpool, his drunken wife, Rachael, Slackbridge, Sissy Jupe and the 'Hands' – are simple caricatures which rely heavily on the crude devices of melodrama. So, for example, Stephen Blackpool, Rachael and Sissy are seen as archetypal heroes and heroines who embody goodness, stoicism and altruism; by contrast, Slackbridge and Stephen's drunken wife are stage villains who represent selfishness, immorality and evil. Indeed they are barely human: so at one point Slackbridge is memorably described as wearing 'mongrel dress' and elsewhere Stephen's nameless wife is a mere 'creature ... clawing of herself with the hand not necessary for support'. Furthermore, it is often taken to be significant that the villains of the piece are also those characters who try to upset or challenge the existing social order – particularly Slackbridge and his fellow union agitators. Of course there are also middle-class characters who are criticised in the novel – Bounderby and Mrs Sparsit are the most obvious examples. But they tend to be treated comically, and belong to the novel's satiric rather than melodramatic impulse. For many, particularly Marxist critics, these circumstances are taken to be indicative of the middle-class or bourgeois prejudices of Dickens and his intended audiences – a view perfectly captured in George Orwell's famous characterisation of the novel, that Dickens viewed the north of England with the prejudices of 'a slightly disgusted southern visitor'.[3] David Lodge has gone so far as to suggest that Dickens's hostility to working-class agitation can be glimpsed in the way he adapts revolutionary rhetoric, which in turn derived from the widespread and deep-seated fear that working-class agitation might turn into the lawless mob violence which contemporary British historians had dramatically condemned in their accounts of the French Revolution.[4] In all of this there is the suggestion that, despite his evident indignation at the conditions which modern industrial society inflicted on the working classes, Dickens's real sympathy was always with the interests of the middle class, and particularly with the interests of his middle-class readers. Such a view is typified by John Holloway's assertion that Dickens was fundamentally the middle-class 'Philistine' who dismissed the trade unions, in the words of Raymond Williams, 'by a stock Victorian reaction'.

Critics have exhibited the same sort of unease with the plot of *Hard Times*, and with the basic thematic opposition between Coketown and the circus. Disquiet has been expressed with the ways in which the assumed values of these societies are represented – that is, the extent to which the form of social life embodied in Sleary's circus is either admirable or capable of being realised, and the extent to which Coketown is representative of a 'real' or 'typical' northern industrial town. More fundamentally, there is criticism of the way in which the novel plots the relationship between these two social worlds. The circus, by definition, has to exist outside Coketown; then, as now, circus people were marginal, travellers who live on the periphery of society. In this sense, the circus and its values are seen to represent not a solution to contemporary problems in industrial society, but an escape from them, so much so that many critics emphasise the fact that Coketown at the end of the novel is much the same as Coketown at the beginning. As Raymond Williams noted, Dickens had 'to go outside the industrial situation to find any expression of his values'.[5] Those changes which do take place in the novel are not to social structures or institutions, but rather they are within individuals. So contact with the circus and its values leads to the moral re-education of Gradgrind, Louisa and (to a lesser extent) Tom; but the inequalities of class, gender and employment which characterise Coketown society are as present at the end of the novel as they are at the beginning. More pointedly, as the final chapter looks forward to the future, we are shown a world where the moral integrity of Sissy is rewarded with the Victorian prize for subservient women – a happy marriage and loving children; but in Coketown the 'Hands' dutifully remain, as obedient as ever to the 'ringing of the Factory bell'. Bounderby may have had his come-uppance, but in general terms, circus values do not seem to have impinged on the lives of the working class in any significant way. So, this line of argument goes, even within its own terms, the solution which the novel offers to problems in modern industrial society seems to be a wholly inadequate one.

This sort of dissatisfaction with the novel's plotting is exemplified in John Lucas's account of *Hard Times*. He suggests that at the heart of the 'weak' ending is an inconsistency in the treatment of individuality. He claims that the novel argues for a 'change of heart' in the individual while at the same time it indicates that no change of heart can happen '*unless* there is some social change, unless the worship of "fact" is abandoned'. The difficulty here, according to Lucas, is that 'social change is what Dickens won't allow'.[6] At the same time Lucas acknowledges that within Coketown there are some decent individuals (Blackpool and Rachael), as well as some individuals who become decent (Louisa and Gradgrind). For Lucas this leads to a troubling contradiction: Coketown seems to be a determining environment in some instances, but not in others – a circumstance which, he claims, 'shatters' the 'consistency' of the novel. Lucas offers little by way of explanation of this conundrum, except to hint at a political prejudice, that Dickens approached the topic of the industrial north with a 'predetermined' hostility which led him to reject 'everything about it, without bothering to enquire whether some things might be worth saving, let alone whether they might be saved only by change and not regress'.[7] The suggestion that the plotting of *Hard Times* is contradictory is repeated in Gallagher's account of the novel, although she gives a different description of it. In her view, *Hard Times* is informed by the contemporary ideology of 'social paternalism'. She claims that the 'structuring metaphor' of the novel is social paternalism's attempt 'to make social relations personal' and 'to advocate that the relations between classes become like the cooperative associations of family life'.[8] This metaphor, Gallagher argues, explains the relationship between the main plot and the sub-plot – the parallels, that is, between the experiences of Louisa and those of Stephen Blackpool which suggest that 'middle-class children and workers share a common oppression and a community of interest'.[9] But Gallagher also contends that the interrelated plots are full of 'ambiguities' which reveal what she terms the 'paradoxical logic' of social paternalism. Hence for Gallagher (as for Lucas) the model of social change offered in *Hard Times* is fundamentally inconsistent; in her terms, the novel subverts the ideology which it is supposed to endorse.

The areas of difficulty I have listed – the alleged class-biases in the melodramatic characterisation, the Coketown/circus opposition and the contradictions held to inhere in Dickens's conception of social change – all these assume a different significance when the novel is placed in the intellectual context described in Chapter 3. As I have mentioned, two aspects of that context are particularly significant: the understanding of problems in society in terms of individual rather than social causation, and the understanding of individual motivation and individual agency in terms of the constancy of human nature. Examining the novel in the light of these concerns has several advantages: in distinction to Gallagher it permits an explanation for the inconsistencies noted by modern critics; and in distinction to Lucas it allows us to distinguish between the contemporary politics of *Hard Times* and the political implications which it possesses for a late twentieth-century reader. That is, we can differentiate between the radicalism which nineteenth-century readers could have identified in *Hard Times*, and the reactionary qualities which modern critics have drawn attention to.

Arnold Kettle commented that for a novel purportedly about industrialisation, *Hard Times* describes only fleetingly the actual processes of industrial production. The reader is never shown the inside of the factory, nor told the exact details of the kind of work which goes on there. Lucas had objected that Coketown is not representative of a 'real' industrial town. This sort of criticism presupposes that Dickens attributed a causative role to the industrial environment in the fragmentation of social life. However, as Holloway reminds us, evidence from his non-fictional writings suggests that matters were not that simple; in his journalism, for example, Dickens can be found eulogising modern manufacturing processes, describing the Victorian factory as 'a grand a machine in its organization – the men, the fingers, and the iron and steel, all work together for one common end'.[10] The apparent contradiction between these views and some of the sentiments in *Hard Times* was not unique to Dickens. Indeed a combination of admiration and aversion were fairly typical of Victorian responses to technology.[11] Moreover, the relationship between mechanised production, wealth creation and unemployment were complex and contested issues (even among political economists), and it is perhaps not surprising that Dickens does not attempt to address them. *Hard Times* is not really 'about' industrial processes at all. As Herbert Sussman suggests, Dickens's interest in the machine is principally as a metaphor – it stands as a 'symbol' for 'the emotional and moral life of his time';[12] industrial production, in other words, is not registered by Dickens in economic terms (a point to which I shall return). Dickens's main concern in *Hard Times* is rather with a particular set of attitudes – a particular view of social life – which had been developed to explain (but which were not coterminous with) industrialisation: Utilitarianism and political economy. Coketown is a deliberately exaggerated embodiment of the kind of sociability predicated by the assumptions of these doctrines. And it is these assumptions (rather than industrialisation *per se*) which the novel attacks. We should therefore not look to *Hard Times* to provide a fully worked-out, practical solution to current problems in society; nor should we expect to find a particularly acute analysis of them. As I suggested, Dickens is primarily interested in what we might loosely call an 'ideology' of industrialism. Significantly, however, he does not assess the validity of that ideology by systematically testing it against the 'facts' or 'experience' (as the 'realism' of Gaskell attempted to do). Perhaps this is the reason for Dickens's failure to acknowledge the contradictions which Holloway notices – Dickens instead concentrates on undermining its basic premises.

The limitations of Dickens's subject are clearly marked out in the 'Key-Note' chapter. There the dominant feature of Coketown is indeed its uniformity. Uniformity characterises the buildings and the inhabitants. Its source, however, is not simply nor primarily mechanised production. Dickens does suggest links between the monotonous labour demanded by machinery and the regimentation of the workforce – 'so many hundred Hands, to the Mill; so many hundred horse Steam Power'; but, as I suggested earlier, the links remain metaphorical, and his critical energy seizes upon a different subject – the relentless assertion of 'fact'. Coketown's obsession with 'tabular statements', with quantitative rather than qualitative analyses, parodies the Utilitarian tendency to treat individuals as mere receptacles, denying the relevance of experience, of the role of temperament, emotion, sensibility, and so forth. Louisa, for example, only knows the Hands 'by hundreds and thousands' and by 'what results in work a given number of them would produce, in a given space of time'. In Coketown the primary problem with the 'relations between master and men' lies not in industrial labour practices, nor in the uncertainties of the market. Unlike Gaskell's work, these issues are not explored by Dickens in any detail. Instead he concentrates on the 'factual' or quantitative way in which those relations are computed. Coketown is also defined by a form of social atomism exhibited most dramatically in the town's geography. The 'labyrinth of narrow courts upon courts, and close streets upon streets' (similar to the backstreets of Disraeli's fictional Marney) are described as having 'come into existence piecemeal, every piece in a violent hurry for some *one man's purpose*, and the whole an unnatural family, shouldering and trampling, and pressing one another to death' (my emphasis). Here we have a material embodiment of the selfish egotism and ruthless competition which political economists suggested was a 'natural' feature of a market economy. Coketown, the narrator reminds us, was a place where you 'must take everything on political economy'. In one sense, of course, it is not saying anything new to identify these doctrines as the principal objects of Dickens's satire; what has not been sufficiently appreciated, though, are the relationships between this body of ideas, mid-nineteenth-century concepts of social change and the particular fictional forms which Dickens employs.

The substance of Dickens's attack on Utilitarianism and political economy is that they offer inadequate theories of social life, and are therefore inappropriate doctrines upon which to base decisions about social policy. The opening chapters of the novel are fundamental to setting out this basic political theme. There is much more to the portrait of Gradgrind's school than a specific attack on Utilitarian principles of education, or the Victorians' fascination with compendia and encyclopaedias.[13] The occasion for Bitzer's disquisition on a 'Quadruped' is a visit of the school inspectors in the company of Coketown's foremost 'banker, merchant [and] manufacturer' – Mr Bounderby. The power-base we see operating in Gradgrind's classroom is exactly the triad of interests described in the previous chapter: that is, the interconnections between government officialdom, Utilitarian ways of thinking and free-market enterprise. Dissatisfaction with government and distrust of its eminently corruptible agents is a common enough theme in mid-Victorian writing; it underlies the polemic of Thomas Carlyle (to whom *Hard Times* is dedicated) and, in a different way, it informs John Stuart Mill's preference for 'individual action ... because of government's defects'. Similarly criticism of materialism and of the contamination brought about by contact with the world of commerce and money is a common thread in Dickens's *oeuvre*. Where *Hard Times* differs from, say, *Our Mutual Friend* or *Little Dorrit* is that an obsession with commerce is used to trope not archetypal themes of greed and corruption, but a specific dissatisfaction with contemporary ways of thinking about social life. Dickens's principal concern in the opening chapters of *Hard Times* is with the way Utilitarianism and political economy were endorsed by the state. As the polemic of Carlyle had demonstrated, the model of social life which these doctrines articulated was popularly seen to be directly informing government responses to contemporary social problems – those fissures in society which coincided with the emergence of an industrial economy. The satire of *Hard Times* is directed against this 'established' view, and in its place Dickens offers not a 'real' alternative to industrial life, but simply a different set of assumptions upon which to model or theorise social relations.

In Chapter 3, I suggested that the foundation of Utilitarianism and political economy was 'economic man' – that is, a model of humanity understood principally as a selfish, profit-seeking agent, motivated only by a desire to increase his own wealth. Such a view, as John Stuart Mill realised, was a crude abstraction which did little justice to the variety and complexity of human feeling (although it was necessary to the work of the political economist). It is precisely such a crude abstraction which defines Bounderby; Bounderby is a caricature of the model of humanity which informs the accounts of social life to be found in the doctrines of Utilitarianism and political economy. Bounderby has no feelings or sentiments apart from those which lead him to increase profits; even his honeymoon, the 'nuptial trip to Lyons', is organised in order that 'Mr Bounderby might take the opportunity of seeing how the Hands got on in those parts, and whether they, too, required to be fed with gold spoons'. The grossness of this caricature becomes apparent when we remember that in the mid-nineteenth century industrial technology in

Britain was far in advance of any competitor, and a British manufacturer would be unlikely to learn anything from a French counterpart.[14] Bitzer, the star of Gradgrind's school, is a Bounderby in miniature; another parody of economic man, he proudly boasts to Mrs Sparsit of his independence from all those 'recreations' which get in the way of making money: 'wives and families', for example, make him 'nauseous'. In a comic but revealing scene towards the end of the novel, Gradgrind's attempt to spirit his criminal son overseas is suddenly thwarted by Bitzer's timely appearance. Having suspected Tom of the robbery, Bitzer has finally caught up with him, and attempts to apprehend the culprit. Gradgrind pleads with Bitzer to let his son escape, and when an appeal to Bitzer's compassion fails, he tries 'self-interest'. Bitzer replies:

> I beg your pardon for interrupting you, sir ... but I am sure that you know that the whole social system is a question of self-interest. What you must always appeal to, is a person's self-interest. It's your only hold. We are so constituted. I was brought up in that catechism when I was very young, sir, as you are aware.[15]

With the help of a trick involving Sleary's dog, Tom is able to escape, but not before the narrator reminds us that:

> It was a fundamental principle of the Gradgrind philosophy, that everything was to be paid for. Nobody was ever on any account to give anybody anything, or render anybody help without purchase. Gratitude was to be abolished, and the virtues springing from it were not to be. Every inch of the existence of mankind, from birth to death, was to be a bargain across a counter. And if we didn't get to Heaven that way, it was not a politico-economical place, and we had no business there.[16]

The passage is notable for the way it exhibits the encompassing nature of Gradgrind's philosophy: a Utilitarian attention to quantitative rather than qualitative analysis – what we might term an accountancy of value – has been seamlessly transposed into a vulgar materialism which in turn invokes the market values of political economy. What enables these doctrines to be so easily run together is precisely their shared interest in 'economic man' – in a form of human agency which collapses all questions of value into financial self-interest. It is this basic model of humanity, rather than any particular detail about, say, the 'laws of supply and demand', which is Dickens's principal target. In this sense his suggestion, as I hinted earlier, is that political economy and Utilitarianism can be dismissed out of hand because they are based on false premises about human nature.

The motivations of economic man (as well as, we should say, of economic woman) explain the behaviour of many characters in Coketown: not only of Bounderby and Bitzer, or Tom and Mrs Sparsit, but also of Slackbridge, the union leader. In his confrontation with the honest Stephen Blackpool, Dickens makes 'money' and its power to corrupt the bone of contention. So, for example, in response to Slackbridge's goading, Stephen explains that "'Tis this Delegate's trade for t'speak ... an he's paid for't, and he knows his work. Let him keep to't. Let him give no heed to what I ha had'n to bear. That's not for him. That's not for nobody but me.' The scene spells out the isolation of Stephen from his colleagues, and it is often read as evidence of Dickens's inability to conceive that working-class decency and working-class militancy could possibly coexist. The development among the working classes of a 'class consciousness' or 'class interest' may seem to be further undermined by being attributed to the manipulative activities of an unscrupulous individual; the narrator reminds us (in a rather patronising tone) of how 'particularly strange' and 'particularly affecting' it was to see 'the crowd of earnest faces, whose honesty in the main no competent observer free from bias could doubt, so agitated by such a leader'. (A similar example of this sort of treatment, discussed in the Conclusion, exists in Eliot's concern in *Felix Holt* with the inflammatory activities of election agents.) Dickens may also be alluding to the payment of Chartist activists, and the contentious issue of 'professional' agitators – he had, after all, witnessed one such 'professional' on his visit to Preston. These details notwithstanding, the scene also raises a larger, thematic issue which cuts across any simple class-bias: the commercial link between Slackbridge and Bounderby reminds us that the form of selfishness which dominates Coketown is not class-based. 'Economic man' is a possible condition of everyone (regard-less of class or sex). Indeed it is the dominance of 'economic man' in Coketown, the assumption that economic self-interest is 'normal', which leads to the false accusation endured by Stephen Blackpool – that he *must* be a thief.

The destructive nature of the values of economic man, as we have already seen in the description of Coketown, is troped by reference to the family, for the self-interest of economic man, as Bitzer well knows, must be antithetical to family life. In this respect, Catherine Gallagher is right to draw attention to the value Dickens places on family life. However, a form of social paternalism underwrites nearly all Dickens's work, in the sense that he often traces fractures in the social fabric – criminality and so forth – to imperfections in, or the absence of, proper familial relations (*Barnaby Rudge, Oliver Twist* and *Great Expectations* are all good examples of this concern, and so more generally is Dickens's interest in orphans). Social paternalism, for Dickens at least, is not specifically linked to industrialism, or its 'discourses'. Gallagher fails to see that in *Hard Times* the success or failure of families depend upon the kinds of individuals who comprise them. That is, it is the constitution of the individual (as an economic or a moral agent) which determines the nature of the family, and it is therefore the resources of the individual rather than the family which suggest the possibility for social change. In Coketown we see families destroyed by economic atomism, by, that is, self-interest: marriages, such as that of Stephen or Bounderby, break down; other characters – Bounderby, Louisa and Tom – disown filial ties. The epitome of this perversion of human relationships by economic self-interest exists in Gradgrind's desire to 'sell-off' his daughter to Bounderby and in Louisa's acquiescence in the arrangement. She believes that in marrying Bounderby she will be helping to promote the financial interests of her brother Tom. Here we see clearly how family feeling – Louisa's 'natural' sisterly concern for her brother – has been contaminated by economic interest.

The contrast to 'economic man' is what we might call 'moral man'. Moral agency is represented in the novel by Stephen, Sissy and Rachael. All these characters are guided in their actions by moral sympathy, not by money, and in consequence they are presented as being more sensitive and more imaginative – indeed more fully human – than the other residents of Coketown. Importantly, though, their humanity is not a product of their social or familial environment; it is part of their nature and of their identity. So Sissy remains uncorrupted by the education she receives in Gradgrind's school – she is literally invulnerable to it, in exactly the same way as Stephen is impervious to the rhetoric of Slackbridge. In this respect the consistency with which these particular characters are portrayed is significant. What many critics have taken to be melodramatic caricatures in fact serve to figure the givenness and permanence of moral values; the simplifications of melodrama, that is, are wholly appropriate to an essentialist understanding of human nature. The *kind* of person Sissy is, and the *kind* of person Stephen is, represent the possibility of moral value in a corrupted world. Or, more precisely, it suggests that the model of human nature which these characters represent is more fundamental – in some sense more 'true' or authentic – than the 'mask' of economic self-interest assumed by a Bitzer or Bounderby. Here we can appreciate the significance of the theme of education, for, as Bitzer testifies, individuals must be taught to act in their economic self-interest (the pupils at Gradgrind's school literally have to be indoctrinated with the tenets of political economy and Utilitarianism). By contrast, Sissy, Rachael and Stephen are 'naturally' moral. The moral re-education of, say, Louisa or Gradgrind is in turn only possible precisely because beneath the mask of self-interest there is an uncorrupted moral self which can be recovered. (We catch a glimpse of this 'self' early in the novel, when the young Louisa and Tom steal a visit to the circus: 'Louisa [was] peeping with all her might through a hole in a deal board, and ... Thomas abasing himself on the ground to catch but a hoof of the graceful equestrian Tyrolean flower-act!') This distinction between what is natural and what is taught – the belief that 'goodness' can transcend circumstance – goes to the heart of Dickens's polemic, for it suggests that the concept of human nature assumed by political economy and Utilitarianism, one which appeared to have proved so useful to government and officialdom, was what we might today term an 'ideology'.

Identifying these basic oppositions in the novel, between the economic and the moral, and between what is taught and what is natural, is helpful in understanding the function of the sexual sub-plots. As in so much Victorian fiction, the topic of sexual fidelity is used by Dickens to trope moral integrity. So the 'natural' goodness of Sissy and later the moral irresolution of Louisa are measured in terms of their ability to resist the temptation of illicit sexuality (on one occasion Harthouse is memorably described as 'the Devil'). In the same way Stephen's and Rachael's moral probity is indicated by their sexual continence. The issue of sexual ethics is connected to the themes in the main plot by the topic of divorce. The subject of a Royal Commission in 1853, and of a parliamentary debate while

Hard Times was being serialised, divorce was certainly a topical issue, and may also have recommended itself to Dickens for personal reasons.[17] In *Hard Times* the contrast between the ability of Louisa to gain a divorce from Bounderby and the inability of Stephen to be legally separated from his dissolute wife is an indication of the inequalities between the classes, as well as pointing to the class basis of sexual morality. Such a situation was of course as true in fact as much as it was in fiction. Divorce was a privilege for the rich, for those among the middle classes who could afford both the money and time necessary to prosecute a case successfully. In *Hard Times* the economic dimension of divorce explicitly associates it with the values and attitudes which attach to 'economic man', a connection which is reinforced by the relationship between the machinery of divorce and government bureaucracy: as Bounderby tells Stephen, 'you'd have to go to Doctors' Commons with a suit, and you'd have to go to the House of Lords with a suit, and you'd have to get an Act of Parliament to enable you to marry again, and it would cost you (if it was a case of plain sailing), I suppose from a thousand to fifteen hundred pounds'. Divorce, seen here, figures the material corruption of Coketown; it is another example of value computed as a form of accountancy, of the conflation of the emotional with the economic. So it is significant that it is Bounderby who eventually instigates divorce proceedings; and that once divorced Louisa is released not to remarry, but only to repent. It is implied that she is as much contaminated by the divorce as she was by her inappropriate marriage (and her equally inappropriate desire for Harthouse). That divorce is part of the corruption of Coketown is unfortunately not much help to Stephen, who can only shake his head and mutter "*tis* a muddle. 'Tis a muddle a'toogether, an the sooner I am dead, the better'. The words are prophetic, for in the melodramatic dénouement death does indeed release Stephen from the 'muddle' and from the dilemma of his situation. It also releases Dickens from having to confront the potential contradictions in his discussion of divorce – the tension, that is, between advocating more liberal divorce laws while simultaneously valorising marriage, sexual fidelity and family life. It is perhaps significant that Stephen, despite his drunken and debauched wife, and despite his evident 'feelings' for Rachael, is nevertheless still able to idealise his original marriage. So we are told that in a moment of reverie Stephen 'thought that he, and some one on whom his heart had long been set – but she was not

Rachael, and that surprised him, even in the midst of his imaginary happiness – stood in the church being married'.

Against the selfish, atomistic society of Coketown we are given the circus. As that form of social life which derives from the activities of moral as opposed to economic agents, the circus is a world defined by familial (rather than sexual) relationships. Dickens describes that communal life as 'two or three handsome young women ... with their two or three husbands, and their two three or mothers, and their eight or nine little children'. This notion of an 'extended' family prioritises filial and parental relationships over sexual ones; it is in the responsibilities of parents for children, rather than in the exclusive fidelity of lovers, that we find the possibility for a fully sociable life. The circus acts give a physical embodiment of this principle of community:

> The father of one of the families was in the habit of balancing the father of another of the families on the top of a great pole; the father of a third family often made a pyramid of both these fathers ... all the fathers could dance upon rolling casks, stand upon bottles, catch knives and balls, twirl hand-basins, ride upon anything, jump over everything, and stick at nothing. All the mothers could (and did) dance, upon the slack wire and the tight rope, and perform rapid acts on bare-backed steeds.[18]

The emphasis here is on a social life defined by altruism and mutual responsibility – the circus folk are described as possessing 'an untiring readiness to help and pity one another' – which at the same time respects a range of human feeling: the circus, in contrast to Coketown's uniformity, embodies and empowers extreme eccentricity. In the context of Dickens's *oeuvre*, this in itself is not at all unusual. For Dickens, the defining attribute of kindness is often eccentricity – particularly where the kindness of male characters is concerned.[19] In *Hard Times* we should observe that individual difference is only possible because of a fundamentally moral human nature; altruism is necessary for eccentricity to thrive. At the same time the careful modern reader will certainly notice that the circus is far from egalitarian. It is controlled by the ring-master (a benevolent patriarch, but a patriarch all the same), and it is organised via very strictly demarcated gender roles. So while the men are involved in acts of dangerous derring-do – knife-throwing, for example – female expertise is exhibited in dancing. The gendering of morality is also evident in the treatment of Louisa; as I hinted earlier, although stepping back from the 'brink of the abyss', in the end she is judged by Dickens to have descended too far down the moral stairwell to be fully redeemed: hence her new-found 'feeling', her 'gentler and humbler face' is only for 'children' – and other people's children at that. Simply put: the modern reader will recognise that Dickens's morality is far from 'natural', and far from transcending all the inequalities which oppressed human relationships in Coketown. That said, it is nevertheless important to keep in mind the distinction between, on the one hand, modern objections to Dickens's moral essentialism (which will no doubt be judged as reactionary), and on the other, the appropriateness of employing that essentialism to critique 'economic man' – to oppose the model of human nature which underwrote the descriptions of social life in Utilitarianism and political economy.

It is often objected that Dickens does not adequately explain how the values of the circus could transform the conditions in Coketown, and that the moral agency he champions seems curiously impotent. Although Sissy successfully remonstrates with Harthouse, Stephen dies, Rachael after a 'long illness' is left alone 'working, ever working' with the rest of the Hands, and Louisa and Gradgrind live out their lives in celibacy and loneliness. Sissy is rewarded with a family, but (as Gallagher notes) the family life of the Gradgrinds is not restored by their newly-found feeling. Part of our dissatisfaction with the novel's resolution relates to Dickens's decision to focus his attention on the 'ideology' of industrialism, rather than industry itself. More precisely, difficulties arise from his failure to see how the two might be related. In concentrating on undermining the premises of political economy and Utilitarianism by opposing economic man to moral man, Dickens ends up by marginalising economics altogether: the circus *is* an 'unreal' world to the extent that it is defined by a form of labour which is economically marginal. Moreover the notion of the circus as a self-contained community, separate from the world of markets, evades one of Bentham's real difficulties – that of defining the extent and *nature* of communities. The consequence of Dickens's critical method is thus the avoidance of any number of pertinent and vexed questions about the relationships between, say, market operations, mechanised production and working-class degradation. Dickens's initial premises prevent him from connecting the 'real' market with the theories deployed to explain it, and it is this limitation (rather than a 'refusal' of 'social change') which makes his notion of moral agency seem peculiarly vulnerable and insubstantial. So, for example, how altruism might transform the market is a question he never entertains. At the same time (and as I argued in Chapter 3), it is worth remembering that there was no alternative economic analysis which Dickens could have drawn upon to fill this gap. The workings of the market (and the role of machinery in it) were 'a muddle' to the extent that no serious or sustained opposition to political economy had been forthcoming. We should therefore not be too surprised at Dickens's method of criticism – if, like so many critics of political economy and Utilitarianism, he was more confident in exhibiting the defects of those doctrines than in offering viable alternatives.

If we consider the novel on its own terms, confining our attention to the notion of moral agency itself, there are still some difficulties with its argument. The conundrum is not (as Lucas suggests) whether individuals, as individuals, are *able* to change their ways; but whether they *want* to: that is, whether morality *is* fundamental to human nature, and therefore whether it does indeed exist in us all to be recovered. This particular dilemma is of a piece with the rest of the *oeuvre*. It has often been noted that in many of Dickens's novels (serious and comic) evil possesses an animus and a vigour which is denied to the 'good' characters. For example, figures such as the self-interested Steerforth and the avaricious Quilp seem much more potent than their opposites, David Copperfield or Little Nell. All of this seems to betray an anxiety at the heart of Dickens's Christian optimism. In *Hard Times*, too, there are traces of this anxiety – not only in the unrepentant Bounderby, the irrepressible Mrs Sparsit and the demoniac energy of Bitzer, but also (surprisingly) in the circus. That environment too cannot be wholly freed from the taint of commercialism; at the novel's close we are shown the figure of Mr Kidderminster who is too busy checking for 'base coins' to notice Sissy: 'he never saw anything but money'. Throughout the novel there are persistent and unsettling hints that 'economic man' might in fact have been more than an abstraction of political economists; that this view of human nature which had been used (or at least which was popularly seen to have been used) to justify the poverty and degradation which accompanied urban industrial life, might not have been simply an 'ideology'. The sense we have in reading *Hard Times* is of a qualified pessimism – that the moral basis of human nature is exceptionally vulnerable – and this pessimism may have derived from Dickens's reluctant suspicion that 'economic man' was in fact a permanent embodiment of the 'fallenness' of humanity. In a revealing moment early on in the novel the narrator comments, 'not all the calculators of the National Debt can tell me the capacity for good or evil, for love or hatred, for patriotism or discontent, for the decomposition of virtue into vice, or the reverse, at any single moment in the soul of one of these quiet servants'. The 'weakness' of *Hard Times* (or perhaps its strength) is that imagination or 'fancy' cannot settle this question either. Sleary's principal evidence that 'there ith a love in the world, not all Thelf-intereth after all' is, bathetically, the fidelity of 'Merrylegth' – Mr Jupe's abandoned dog.

II

Of all the social-problem novels, it is *Mary Barton* which has received the highest praise, although it ought to be added that generally praise has tended to be reserved for the novel's politics. Critics have conceded that the novel possesses certain formal weaknesses, once again principally inconsistencies in its plot and characterisation; but they have nevertheless commended what they perceive to be an unusually sympathetic and detailed exploration of working-class lives and culture. In short it is these elements of alleged 'realism' in *Mary Barton*, particularly the detail with which Gaskell documents working-class life, which has allowed the novel to be praised for its 'humanity', 'immediacy' and 'integrity' – epithets very different from those which have typically been applied to *Hard Times*.[20] It is indeed true that in *Mary Barton* working-class characters are portrayed as individuals with their own personalities, their own life histories and their own culture, all of which are recorded with abundant and affectionate detail. As Gaskell's most recent biographer, Jenny Uglow, has shown, this documentary style – with its obsession for domestic detail – was certainly very much a habit of mind for Gaskell and perhaps a pathological trait, for it informed her copious letter-writing as well as her fiction. Gaskell was always impatient to know what she termed 'every little, leetle, particular'.[21] For the modern critic, though, this habit seems to be the most significant tactic of her fiction, for it issued in an attempt to describe faithfully the habits of a class to all intents and purposes invisible in previous English novels. Indeed it is precisely the power of *Mary Barton*'s descriptive detail, in contrast to its argument or plot, which has earned Gaskell the admiration of modern critics. Commentaries on the novel typically praise the way in which Gaskell identifies and illustrates the 'problems' of mid-nineteenth-century society. Equally typically they censure the way the novel plots a solution to them.

However, as I hinted in earlier chapters, this kind of judgement brings with it some particularly thorny problems: most obviously, it forces a rather crude separation between 'form' and 'content'. In such a view it becomes necessary to explain the discrepancy between, on the one hand, Gaskell's ideology (her allegedly subversive sympathy with the plight of a disenfranchised working class) and on the other, the conservatism of her narrative devices (particularly those of melodrama and romance) which seemingly function to channel that sympathy into conventional and (for her middle-class readership) acceptable forms. To put matters simply, there appears to be a contradiction between the radicalism underlying the verisimilitude of the novel's descriptive detail and the conservatism of those plot devices which Gaskell uses to resolve the social tensions she describes in conventionally fictional, rather than explicitly political, terms. Since Kathleen Tillotson first drew attention to this dilemma in her *Novels of the Eighteen-Forties*, it has dominated discussion of *Mary Barton*. In short, the problem has been to explain how it was that an alleged 'truthfulness' could inform or cause some elements of the novel (the content), but not others (its form).

The usual way out of this dilemma was to offer a biographical explanation, one which accused Gaskell of personal failure – that at some point in writing her novel Gaskell lost her nerve, and that her reliance on the stock devices and moral certainties of melodrama and romance permitted her to avoid confronting the full implications of the awful 'truths' exposed in her portrait of working-class misery. This line of argument focuses on the shift of narrative attention in the second half of the book from John Barton to his daughter Mary, and the plot's subsequent concern with Mary's romantic attachment to Jem, rather than with the more fundamental conflict between Victorian classes. These developments are usually viewed as a simple evasion of the uncomfortable questions which the earlier part of the novel raised. In its closing chapters the conflict between masters and men does briefly come to the fore again; John Barton, a broken but repentant man, returns to confess his sin to Henry Carson just before dying. However for nearly every critic this emblematic reconciliation, made possible by a common experience of suffering (both Carson and Barton have lost an only son), is seen as an inadequate solution to the tensions described in the first half of the book, principally because it situates responsibility for social change within the moral integrity of the individual rather than in social structures or institutions.

This kind of interpretation is often supported by reference to a much-quoted exchange of letters between Mrs Gaskell and her publishers, Chapman & Hall, which reveals that Edward Chapman persuaded a reluctant Mrs Gaskell to change the title from *John Barton* to *Mary Barton*, and thus to emphasise the book's identity as domestic romance rather than as social polemic. Uglow surmises that Chapman 'may have been reluctant to shock the public by having the name of a murderer, John Barton, as the title'.[22] The comment is significant for it echoes an assumption which has persisted in any number of accounts of *Mary Barton*, that the use of melodrama and romance was made principally for political or ideological reasons. So, for example, in John Lucas's view the melodramatic murder plot was necessary to '*simplify* a complexity which [had] become too terrific for her to accept consciously';[23] and for Raymond Williams, it betrayed Gaskell's 'real' politics – an underlying middle-class fear of working-class violence. John Barton, according to Williams, was 'a dramatisation of the *fear of violence* which was widespread among the upper and middle classes at the time and which penetrated, as an arresting and controlling factor, even into the deep imaginative sympathy of a Mrs Gaskell'.[24] In accounts such as these the alleged tension between descriptive radicalism and narrative conservatism – between identifying the problem and finding a solution – is resolved ideologically: in them Gaskell (unlike, say, Dickens) is seen to have imaginatively glimpsed the truth but to have drawn back from it, fearful of her readers' sensibilities, or (depending upon the prejudices of the particular critic in question) jealous of her reputation. The obvious difficulty with this kind of interpretation (which I have already outlined in an earlier chapter) is that such a basic contradiction between description and narrative form appears to be more a product of the particular values of the modern critic than of the confused intentions of Mrs Gaskell. It depends upon a prior assumption that a certain (sociological) way of understanding social problems was available in the mid-nineteenth century, but was for some personal reason refused or relinquished by Gaskell.[25]

In the Preface to *Mary Barton*, written at the prompting of her publisher Edward Chapman,[26] Gaskell makes two large and related claims: the first is a claim for the authenticity of her novel – its 'truthfulness' – which in turn derives its force from her second claim, a self-confessed naïvety – that she is ignorant of 'large' political and economic issues: 'I know nothing of Political Economy; or the theories of trade. I have tried to write truthfully; and if my accounts agree or clash with any system, the agreement or disagreement is unintentional.' Surprisingly, perhaps, this confession of ignorance has often been taken at face value, and the dichotomy which it seems to imply between systematic argument on the one hand and 'truth' (or moral insight) on the other has been taken as a paradigm for reading the novel. It is exactly this opposition which underlies the conflict between description and narrative, where the moral plotting of melodrama and romance is cited as evidence of Gaskell's inability (or unwillingness) to address political and economic issues. However, Jenny Uglow's gloss on Gaskell's Preface points to a rather different explanation: she argues that Gaskell's disclaimer was 'deliberately' designed to distance herself 'from Harriet Martineau and other professed experts' on political economy.[27] This suggests a careful strategy underlying an apparently naïve confession of ignorance. Indeed Uglow notes elsewhere that Gaskell's confessions of intellectual modesty – her claims 'not to have read economics, not to understand science, not to like sermons, not to be "metaphysical"' – are generally to be distrusted. As a child Gaskell had been warned against the impropriety of 'displayed learning' and in adult life had learnt to 'hide her cleverness', becoming what Uglow terms a 'closet scholar'.[28] In this particular instance Gaskell's concern was to distinguish herself from a certain way of thinking about economics, rather than from economic thinking in itself. This may seem a fine distinction but it is an important one, for it opens up the possibility that Gaskell's emphasis on morality, far from being a way of avoiding economic theorising, was in fact a way of engaging with it. As the previous chapter has demonstrated, the opposition of the economic to the moral was not arbitrary; it was a consequence of the conceptually limited ways in which dissenting individuals were able to contest the tenets of political economy. In such a context, Gaskell's disclaimer is all the more understandable: it seems likely that her real worry was a fear of being mistaken for someone (like Harriet Martineau) who *supported* political economy. The absence in the mid-nineteenth century of an alternative economic theory made it difficult for those unhappy with economic orthodoxy to present what their present-day counterparts would call 'clear water' between themselves and their opponents. Of course there were radical alternatives to political economy, such as that embodied in Owenite collectivism; but these sorts of answers, as I have suggested in the previous chapter, were not endorsed by coherent *economic* argument, and were generally ridiculed by economic orthodoxy. The most important consequence of all this was that serious economic debate tended to take place within the conceptual paradigms already established by political economy. Hence the difficulty for Gaskell was not the impossibility of articulating an alternative economic theory (although it is worth reiterating that the intellectual tools for such a critique were not available until the 1870s and the 'marginal' revolution of Jevons, Menger and Walras), but the more pressing problem of how to make the arguments which she could marshal seem sufficiently distinctive and sufficiently critical.

Paradoxically, then, I would suggest that Gaskell's confession of ignorance in her Preface disguises the opposite state of affairs: that in practice she was all too knowledgeable of political economy – not, perhaps, of the precise details of its complex body of theory, but certainly (like Dickens) aware of the hegemony of its doctrines, and of the intellectual difficulties involved in combating them. As I shall argue below, Gaskell's background and upbringing make it simply unbelievable that she 'knew nothing' of such matters. This interpretation of Gaskell's comments in turn suggests a new way of reading *Mary Barton*: that, far from being a work which assiduously avoids discussing economics or 'theories of trade', *Mary Barton* is absorbed by the topic, almost to the point of obsession. Evidence for this interest derives from several sources: most obviously, it appears in the novel's compulsive detailing of financial transactions. There are few nineteenth-century novels which are so concerned with documenting – almost invoicing, we might call it – the exact cost of living, with setting a precise price for moral integrity. In *Mary Barton* the economic and the moral, far from being alternatives (as they are in *Hard Times*), are inextricably intertwined, and a central theme of the novel is the attempt to define how each can be placed in a proper relationship to the other. Gaskell takes as her explicit subject-matter what Dickens merely alludes to: the problematic role of morality in the contemporary market-place. In simple terms, the conundrum which *Mary Barton* poses is as follows: can a moral life determine economic conduct, or does economics determine the conditions for living a moral life? Despite the 'anxieties' which Dickens betrays, the argument of *Hard Times* ostensibly supported the first position. As I suggested earlier, that novel, in keeping with much of Dickens's *oeuvre*, insists that commerce is always a source of moral corruption. So for Dickens, the economic and the moral must be rigidly marked off from each other – an opposition which in turn explains Dickens's frequently fastidious treatment of the theme of money. Although several of his novels are obsessed with the corrupting effects of greed and materialism, unlike Gaskell, he has little or no interest in the precise details of financial transactions. In Dickens's world the sources of money are often mysterious – from convicts, inheritances, benefactors, but never from market transactions (except with dire consequences). For the novels to document such information would of course be to taint the narrative consciousness with precisely the kind of knowledge which the novels themselves satirise as corrupt. At the same time, though, the reward for moral probity paradoxically often turns out to be financial: so the career of many of Dickens's early heroes – from Martin Chuzzlewit and Oliver Twist to Pip Pirrip – is to be pauperised in order to learn to be moral. The reward for that lesson is financial independence, often derived (as I have hinted) from an inheritance or from marriage. Dickens's separation of the economic and the moral forces him to view money in 'fairy-tale' terms – to divest it, that is, from any kind of economic reality or market significance. By contrast, part of the 'realism' of *Mary Barton* derives precisely from Gaskell's willingness to be 'tainted' – to examine money in terms of cost as well as value.

More obviously, *Mary Barton* is also marked by unusually detailed set-piece discussions of economy theory by both characters and by the author herself (in the form of a long digression in which she attempts to 'state the case' for the reader). In some of these set-piece discussions the economic polemic comes close to the orthodoxies of political economy: so, for example, Job Legh, an articulate, educated working-class character rather surprisingly turns out to be a well-informed advocate of free trade. A superficial reading of these passages might seem to endorse Gaskell's alleged political conservatism (Legh, after all, is also anti-Union and anti-Owenism). However, a fuller appreciation of the significance of these passages requires them to be read in relation to Gaskell's detailing of financial transactions which I alluded to earlier. These two ways of discussing economic issues amount to a distinction between micro- and macro-economic analyses, and it is in the relationship between these sorts of analyses – between the rather stilted set-piece discussions of economic theory, and the careful attention to the precise details of an individual's economic circumstances – that we can glimpse Gaskell trying to work out a coherent economic thesis. As I shall argue, one advantage of focusing on what might be termed the novel's 'embedded' economic critique is that it resolves several of the contradictions which earlier critics have perceived in *Mary Barton*; specifically, it removes the alleged discrepancy between descriptive detail and narrative form. Such a reading does not, however, deny that tensions exist in the novel; but it does suggest that they chiefly concern the problematic relationship between morality and economics, and are in turn a result of the conceptually limited way in which Gaskell was able to address and understand economic issues. Importantly, these tensions are not simply due to personal confusion, emotional withdrawal, or the limitations of certain fictional forms. On the contrary, I want to suggest that when *Mary Barton* is viewed in its *own* terms it turns out to be a novel consistently thoughtful in its attempt to formulate a solution to contemporary social problems (although not necessarily in a way which conforms to the political prejudices acceptable to a modern reader).

One of the many merits of Jenny Uglow's meticulous biography of Gaskell is the way in which it documents the intellectual richness of her domestic environment. Gaskell may have been a 'housewife' who saw as her first responsibility her husband and children, but she nevertheless enjoyed a hectic social life, entertaining and being entertained by a host of intellectual luminaries. The Gaskells were extremely well-connected, related to both the Wedgwood and Darwin families, a connection which in turn permitted introductions to figures such as the Carlyles. William Gaskell, Elizabeth's husband, was a prominent Unitarian minister, and his involvement with the central Unitarian establishment in Manchester, Cross Street Chapel, introduced Elizabeth to many of the leading radicals both within and related to that movement, including such distinguished social campaigners as Edwin Chadwick and Thomas Southwood Smith. It is simply inconceivable that, in such an environment, Gaskell did not know about or did not discuss economics; she was after all surrounded by people who were deeply involved in urgent contemporary questions of social reform. As a group, Unitarians were particularly active in early nineteenth-century Manchester, and played a formative role in establishing any number of public institutions including the Literary and Philosophical Society, the Natural History Society, the Royal Manchester Institution, the Mechanical Institute, the Royal Medical College and the *Manchester Guardian*. In addition to charitable and philanthropic work, Unitarians were also prominent in Manchester manufacturing as factory-owners, engineers and bankers. The Manchester Unitarian MPs Mark Philips and John Potter made important contributions to contentious Commons debates about factory legislation, and in 1838 Cross Street Chapel became the meeting-place for the Manchester Anti-Corn Law Association.[29] This last event is particularly significant, for it illustrates an important characteristic of Unitarian radicalism, its ability to accommodate what seems to modern eyes to be the apparently conservative tenets of political economy. As Uglow argues, 'Radicals they might be, but these Manchester Unitarians [i.e. the factory owners and bankers] held to an ideal of individualism rather than one of equality, to the ethic of the market as much as to that of the Gospels'.[30] In fact the relationship between Unitarian beliefs and contemporary economic orthodoxies was more complex than this, and there were those within the movement who were less happy with the idea of free trade and of minimising state intervention. The merits of the market and of *laissez-faire* were, in Uglow's terms, 'hotly debated' in Cross Street Chapel throughout the late 1830s and 1840s.[31]

In teasing out the relationship between political economy and Unitarian doctrines, it is not the differences or ambiguities in the various Unitarian responses to contemporary economic orthodoxies which strike the modern reader, but rather the apparent inability of those who disagreed with free trade or *laissez-faire* to elaborate an alternative economic doctrine. Why was this? Why did those Unitarians (like Gaskell) who were deeply involved in social reform, and who were acutely aware of the appalling conditions of the urban working classes, *not* develop a theory of poverty which linked it to social structures? Why, in other words, was Unitarian theology (of whatever character) unable to overcome the limitations of contemporary economic debate? As I have suggested in the previous chapter, part of the answer lies in certain fundamental continuities between Unitarianism and political economy, particularly the concern with the individual. Just as political economy took the individual as the basic unit of analysis in explaining society, so too Unitarian belief (whether of the necessitarian or free-will variety) emphasised the importance of individual responsibility and personal action. Indeed it was precisely this 'individualism' which formed the basis of Unitarianism's ethical commitment to equality (before God) and moral justice, and hence became the motor for its radicalism. The reforming zeal of Unitarianism proceeded directly from an emphasis on the individual's responsibility for rational enquiry into the world about him (or her – unusually for Victorian Britain equality was extended to women). Unitarian radicalism is thus an important reminder of the close relationship in early and mid-Victorian Britain between dissent, social reform and individualism: it was precisely this individualist paradigm, rather than any large-scale structural changes implied by socialist thought, which dominated responses to social disorder.[32] It should therefore come as no surprise that for Mrs Gaskell, as for many of her fellow Unitarians, unease with current economic orthodoxies itself came to be articulated in terms of the very concepts underlying those orthodoxies – individual agency and responsibility. Indeed this was precisely why Unitarian beliefs could be marshalled in support of both advocates *and* critics of *laissez-faire* free trade. Nowhere is this more true than in the work of Gaskell's own father, William Stevenson.

Between 1824 and 1825 Blackwoods published a series of essays by Stevenson entitled 'The Political Economist'. Gaskell was only fourteen when they appeared, and there is no direct evidence that she read them. However, we do know that Stevenson took a very keen interest in his daughter's education, encouraging her to read much more widely than was then usual for a girl; moreover, when initially considering whether to publish *Mary Barton* under a male pseudonym, Gaskell offered Chapman the name 'Stephen Berwick', a composite reference, as Uglow notes, to Gaskell's father and to his birthplace. From the death of Gaskell's mother, and her father's remarriage, the relationship between father and daughter was difficult, and in trying to account for the unexpected tribute, Uglow wonders whether Gaskell was 'perhaps remembering Stevenson's *Blackwood* articles'.[33] The hint is useful, for a close examination of Stevenson's work reveals some surprising similarities between his argument and the kind of approach to economics which we find in Gaskell's novel.

Stevenson's aim in his essays was to rescue the science of political economy from two mutually opposed (and in his view equally damaging) kinds of criticism: the polemic associated with those he termed the 'perfectionists', those who admitted of no error or improvement in the doctrines of political economy; and the arguments of critics who simply dismissed out of hand everything which political economy had to say, denying that it could have any relevance to human affairs.[34] Significantly, the potential which Stevenson sees in political economy, and which makes it worthy of defence in the first instance, concerns its close attention to the individual, and to the way in which individual interests relate to those of the community:

> There is no branch of human inquiry or science which we apprehend is so singularly situated; certainly none which draws, as Political Economy does, or ought to do, all its facts or principles from circumstances and events constantly occurring; and, we may add, from the observation and experience of every individual. For though it respects ... whatever relates to the real nature of national wealth, to the means by which it may be acquired, secured, and increased ... yet, as nations are composed of individuals; as the mode in which an individual conducts his business, redoubles in its effect the effects of the Political Economy of the government under which he lives, and as the influence of his wise or injudicious conduct of his affairs extends beyond himself into the community of which he forms a part, – from all these causes, individual as well as national experience offers ample and various illustration of the principles of Political Economy, to those who will attentively examine and study it.[35]

In keeping with the demands of *Blackwoods Magazine*'s varied readership Stevenson avoided discussing complex theoretical issues, focusing instead on the simpler (and rhetorically more effective) task of demonstrating the confusions and contradictions which in his view obtained among contemporary political economists. 'Wealth', 'value', 'price', 'wages', 'capital' – all these terms, according to Stevenson, were contested; moreover, there was equal confusion about what he termed 'practical questions', such as what constituted 'money', what kind of 'trade' ('domestic' or 'foreign') was most beneficial to a nation, how useful were the 'Corn Laws' and 'navigation laws', and so on.[36] The overriding problem in all these cases is a lack of attention to what Stevenson terms the 'facts'. Indeed Stevenson's overall argument is that political economy *can* be a science (and a useful one), but that it is as yet 'imperfect', for it was founded on insecure and inadequate evidence. Such a criticism of political economy, as I indicated in the previous chapter, was fairly commonplace at the time. Stevenson is more interesting in his insistence on the need to discriminate between relevant and irrelevant facts – to decide upon the *status* of factual evidence. Scathingly dismissive of 'practical or matter-of fact men' – the 'statistical collectors' – Stevenson notes that the facts offered by such individuals were too often partial and biased:

> What are called facts are not always such; that they are often mixed up with theory and prejudices; and that even when political arithmeticians [statisticians] or practical men state what is really the case, they do not state the whole case; that when they assert that a certain measure is beneficial or injurious, they most frequently have viewed it only as regards their own interest, or particular line of inquiry or business, or in its immediate and temporary results, and *not as it effects the interest of the community at large, and displays itself in its remote and permanent consequences.*[37]

In Stevenson's view, what is needed to improve political economy, to make it more 'scientific', is a more certain method of adducing correct or relevant facts, where the criterion of correctness is a certainty about having seen the whole picture – that is, *all* the circumstances and consequences which attend particular facts. In the final essay, Stevenson suggests how such an objective might be achieved. He argues that all knowledge (that is, all questions about evidence and its status) rests upon two fundamental precepts: on the 'permanence or stability of the appearances and operations of nature', and on 'that fundamental law of human mind, on which rests the association of our ideas'.[38] Truth – correct or relevant facts – emerges from the interplay of these two factors, from the constant testing of associations through observation and experiment against the permanence of nature. When it is applied to political economy, such an argument suggests that the relevant facts can only be determined by testing them against the permanent 'order of nature' as it is exhibited in the human race. In simple terms, facts are relevant if they accord to the known universals of human nature; the difficulty, of course, as Stevenson readily admits, is in defining precisely what is permanent and universal in humankind:

> The order of nature is as stable and permanent in what relates to man in all his relations and actions, as it is in what relates to matter; but it is much more difficult to trace this order, and to separate what is universally true from what is only generally so, and what is more generally true from what is so in various diminishing degrees. Till this be done, our associations must be erroneous; in our belief and expectation, things will be united as cause and effect, which are not united in nature; hence our belief will be erroneous – our expectations disappointed – our predictions will prove false, and our conduct will be at variance with our substantial good.[39]

To the modern reader, Stevenson's argument may not amount to much: his insight that the 'facts' adduced to support the arguments of political economy are often biased is not adequately answered by an appeal to human nature (a concept which modern readers will perhaps see as equally unstable and contested). Yet, as will become clear, it is exactly this kind of argument which seems to inform *Mary Barton*. In the first place, the novel engages with the 'laws' of political economy through an obsession with factual detail, particularly with those 'awkward' facts which do not fit easily into current 'theories of trade'. Indeed the source of the 'muddle' which characters such as John Barton so frequently refer to is the mismatch between theory (the tenets of political economy) and evidence (the 'facts' of working-class poverty). As her father recommended, Gaskell seems concerned to look at precisely those 'consequences' and 'circumstances' ignored by the experts; she focuses, that is, on the consequences of economic doctrines for 'the interest of the community at large', where community includes workers, employers and consumers. Furthermore, Gaskell constantly tests the 'truth' of her evidence – of the 'facts' she enumerates – against a knowledge of human nature. So a central theme of the novel is to show that reactions to extreme poverty, even violent ones, are in some sense 'natural'. In so doing, Gaskell successfully exposes the arbitrary injustices of current market conditions, injustices which the supposedly immutable 'laws' of political economy effectively concealed. Where Gaskell is less effective, however, is in formulating or outlining a new economic orthodoxy to explain or counter those uncomfortable facts. But perhaps we should remember that this was a task which her father (and most of her contemporaries) had also failed to address.

This very brief account of some of the circumstances of Gaskell's upbringing shows, I hope, how we should be careful not to pre-judge her novel; Gaskell's concern with individual conduct, far from being the mark of a naïve conservatism (as the modern critic has too often assumed), is rather the foundation – and perhaps the only possible *coherent* foundation – of her radicalism. However, an appreciation of that radicalism, as I indicated earlier, does require careful reading – an understanding of the various elements of Gaskell's analysis of the economics of her society, and of the ways in which they interrelate with one another. A good place to begin is with the problematic plotting of *Mary Barton*.

The novel's main plot seems to imply that conflicts between masters and men can be resolved on an individual level through Christian understanding and proper education. Such an argument explains the emblematic reconciliation between Barton and Carson near the end of the novel, which seems to read as a simple assertion of Christian optimism, of the power of moral benevolence – of 'deep and genuine feeling' – to overcome social discord. The meeting between master and man symbolically bridges the gap in understanding which Barton believed to be the root cause of class conflict. As Job Legh later explains at some length to Carson:

> John Barton was no fool. No need to tell him that were all men equal to-night, some would get the start by rising an hour earlier to-morrow. Nor yet did he care for goods, nor wealth; no man less, so that he could get daily bread for him and his; but what hurt him sore, and rankled in him as long as I knew him ... was that those who wore finer clothes, and eat better food, and had more money in their pockets, kept him at arm's length, and cared not whether his heart was sorry or glad ... It seemed hard to him that a heap of gold should part him and his brother so far asunder. For he was a loving man before he grew mad with seeing such as he was slighted, as if Christ himself had not been poor.[40]

The reasoning here is exactly that of the parable of Dives and Lazarus cited by Barton much earlier in the novel, and often noted by modern critics. For the modern reader it seems that complex political and economic issues – questions about power and the distribution of wealth – are being collapsed into simple moral platitudes. As Carson muses to himself, social conflict might disappear if only 'a perfect understanding, and complete confidence and love, might exist between masters and men'. He goes on to wish that:

> the truth might be recognized that the interests of one were the interests of all; and as such, required the consideration and deliberation of all; that hence it was most desirable to have educated workers, capable of judging, not mere machines of ignorant men; and to have them bound to their employers by the ties of respect and affection, not by mere money bargains alone; in short, to acknowledge the Spirit of Christ as the regulating law between both parties.[41]

The language here is a curious mixture of the moral and economic; indeed the whole of the conversation between Carson and Job Legh which leads up to this insight centres on an attempt to define the right relationship between morality and the market. At one point Carson, for example, claims that the operations of the market are simply given: 'how in the world can we help it', he appeals to Legh, '[w]e cannot regulate the demand for labour. No man or set of men can do it. It depends on events which God alone can control.' Legh's response is more supportive than we might have expected, for not being what he terms 'given to Political Economy' he too is unable to understand the market. At the same time, though, Legh (like Carson) recognises a divine presence in the very technological developments which defined the contemporary market, and which had helped to put so many of his colleagues out of work:

> It's true it was a sore time for the hand-loom weavers when power-looms came in: them new-fangled things make a man's life like a lottery; and yet I'll never misdoubt that power-looms, and railways, and all such-like inventions, are the gifts of God.[42]

The dilemma which confronts both Carson and Legh is the mysteriousness of the operations of the market: while both recognise the harsh consequences of the organisation of labour, and the gross inequalities of wealth which it produces, neither can envisage any economic alternative. The laws of the market are simply 'given';

that the consequences of their operation should be so unfair is 'the mysterious problem of life'. Such language is appropriately religious in tone, suggesting that such vexed problems are simply beyond the scope (therefore also the responsibility) of humanity. Ironically, perhaps, it is precisely their shared ignorance of this matter which permits master and men to converse so freely – to interact for the first time as near equals, although at an intellectual rather than political level. Ignorance over an alternative economic structure is the one issue over which all points of view in the novel (authorial and those of the various characters) converge; conversations about 'political economy' and 'theories of trade' tend to arrive at the same impasse or mystery. As Legh is finally forced to acknowledge, on the one hand there are simply 'facts' (the givenness of market conditions – of trade cycles, 'commercial depressions', and so on), on the other hand there are 'feelings'. All that can be done is to hope that 'feeling' might make those 'facts' more palatable.

If this was all *Mary Barton* had to say about economics, readers might indeed be justified in seeing in this apparent 'ignorance' of the market little more than a justification for preserving the political status quo. By itself, the main plot might seem to provide evidence of a profound conservatism. For two quite distinct reasons, though, such a reading would be misleading. In the first place, it ignores the fact that Gaskell (like Dickens) simply did not have an alternative economic argument to hand: in this respect, she was as 'honestly' ignorant of an alternative set of economic laws as any of her characters are. Second, and much more important, allegations that *Mary Barton* is at heart a conservative work ignore the novel's *self-consciousness* about that ignorance. *Mary Barton* is a novel remarkable for articulating a scepticism about the very solution to social problems which it appears to offer: although it suggests that moral benevolence may act as some kind of buffer between the individual and the harshness of economic laws, the novel simultaneously presents morality as almost impossible to sustain within a modern market economy. This 'counter-critique' (for that is what it amounts to) is to be found in the novel's descriptive detail – in the 'facts' about individuals' circumstances which Gaskell so painstakingly describes. Importantly, these facts, far from being 'contained' or 'explained away' by the plot, provide the all-important context (in William Stevenson's terms, the 'true' evidence) by which the narrative's significance can finally be grasped.

The suggestion in the main plot that social conflict might be over-come by benevolence presupposes a certain view of human nature, that all individuals, however selfish, mean-minded or misdirected, nevertheless possess an inner moral core, for brotherhood can only possibly 'work' as a solution to social problems if individuals are in the first place capable of moral redemption. Gaskell, however, does not take such moral integrity for granted, and much of *Mary Barton* is concerned with examining whether it is indeed possible for a basic humanity to transcend the harshness of contemporary social conditions, and thereby to bring about a more equitable form of social life. To this end, and like Dickens in *Hard Times*, Gaskell uses plot situations taken from melodrama and romance to test her Christian humanism by examining the resilience of moral integrity in extreme situations. Of course it is precisely here that we meet the common objection that melodrama and romance are unrealistic forms. Concerned with ideals rather than ideology, they are judged to be inappropriate to Gaskell's politically charged subject-matter. But at this point we need to remember that Gaskell chose to express her views via the novel and (unlike her father) not via a treatise or periodical essay, and we should therefore not be surprised when (like Dickens) she uses fictional devices which had already proved popular with her intended audience. More importantly, though, while murders and deaths certainly do not occur with such regular-ity in life as they do in *Mary Burton*, the presentation of such events in the novel in fact bypasses the limitations of the fictional genres which are their source. Underlying the sensationalism of the plot devices there is a counter-insistence on a mundane economic reality. This emphasis, wholly in keeping with the novel's praised descriptive power, serves as an ironic but deeply serious commen-tary on the otherwise naïve optimism of reconciliation which Christian brotherhood makes possible. Like *Hard Times*, but in a much more thoroughgoing way, it implicates a scepticism in the faith that human nature alone (suitably redescribed) could indeed form the basis of a new kind of social life.

A detailed attention to what I earlier termed the 'micro-economic analysis' of *Mary Barton* reveals that actions in the novel are nearly always motivated by financial expediency: this is obvious in the first half of the novel where the disintegration of working-class family life and of individual morality (particularly in John Barton and Esther) is traced directly to the pressures of poverty. Indeed it is precisely this gesture towards a social explanation of working-class violence and moral degradation which many critics have commended in the novel. By contrast, little attention has been given to the fact that money is just as central to the more melodramatic events in the second half of the novel. For example, the suspense surrounding the arrest of Jem, the search for Jem's alibi and the ensuing trial scenes all depend crucially upon financial transactions which are documented with Gaskell's customary precision. Initially it is Carson's great wealth which permits him to put up a reward that leads to Jem's sudden arrest; the amount of money, described as 'a temptation' for the police, is set at a 'thousand pounds' rather than the superintendent's suggestion of the 'munificent' sum of 'three, or five hundred pounds'. Carson believes that he can buy justice; he can afford the 'attorneys skilled in criminal practice' and the 'barristers coming from the Northern Circuit' who, he believes, will ensure a 'speedy conviction, a speedy execution'. By contrast, the case for the defence is constantly threatened by the absence of money: poverty nearly prevents Mary from travelling to Liverpool (she has to rely on a sovereign lent to her by Margaret); and when she does arrive, lack of money again nearly thwarts her attempt to contact Will (she is unable to pay the full fare for the boat trip). Once the court proceedings are under way, money continues to be central in the creation of dramatic tension. The effort expended on contacting Will and his dramatic entrance into the courtroom seem doomed when the prosecution casts doubt on his evidence by suggesting that he had been paid for his story by 'good coin of her majesty's realm'. Will's indignant reply echoes a theme central to the first half of the book: that the possession of money corrupts the wealthy far more than its absence corrupts the poor.

> Will you tell the judge and jury how much money you've been paid for your impudence towards one, who has told God's blessed truth, and who would scorn to tell a lie, or blackguard any one, for the biggest fee as ever a lawyer got for doing dirty work. Will you tell, sir? – But I'm ready, my lord judge, to take my oath as many times as your lordship or the jury would like, to testify to things having happened just as I said.[43]

It is fitting that the evidence in question concerns Will's inability to afford a 'three-and-sixpence' train-fare to Liverpool. Possessing only a 'jingling ... few coppers', he had been forced to walk, and Jem's agreement to accompany him as far as Parkside provides the all-important alibi. On this evidence the jury eventually acquits Jem, but there is little sense of victory. On the contrary, the verdict is described as 'unsatisfactory', the jurors 'neither being convinced of his innocence, nor yet quite willing to believe him guilty'. The resulting ambiguity taints Jem's reputation and eventually forces him to leave England. At this point the story is far from endorsing the values of melodrama and romance; there is no simple triumph of right over wrong, of Christian virtue over financial expediency. Rather the opposite: the attention given to the economics of every situation is a forcible reminder of how vulnerable morality is to money. One incident in particular provides a poignant illustration of the inevitable interconnection between morality and the market. When Mary returns home after the trial she is shocked to encounter her father 'still and motionless' beside the cold fire-grate in their former home. Mary's earlier revulsion at his crime is immediately overcome by compassion for his 'smitten helplessness'. The strength of blood-ties – 'He was her father! her own dear father!' – is a typical melodramatic trope, and Mary's emotional response to her father's plight is entirely appropriate to the genre: 'Tenderly did she treat him, and fondly did she serve him in every way that heart could devise or hand execute.' However, this generalised expression of compassion immediately finds its expression in economic terms: 'comfort' for John Barton turns out to be material as well as spiritual. It involves some 'purchases', those necessary to furnish a house which 'was bare as when Mary had left it, of coal, or of candle, of food, or of blessing in any shape'. Ironically, Mary is only able to afford these commodities because 'she had some money about her, the price of her strange services as a witness'. Here, as everywhere in *Mary Barton*, conventional expressions of piety (a daughter's dutiful love for her father) are registered in terms of their economic cost.

The most sustained example of this interpenetration of the moral and the economic is provided in the early chapters of the novel, in the detailed descriptions of working-class culture. The main way in which we are introduced to that culture is through witnessing working-class meals, either within families or, more often, by small celebrations which accompany meetings between families. The purchase, preparation and consumption of food are not just to sustain life; they are also important social rituals. And it is through these rituals that the working classes enact their sense of community: compassion and benevolence are typically demonstrated through giving and receiving food. Our very first introduction to urban working-class culture is via the preparation of a meal by the Bartons for their friends the Wilsons. A succession of meals at various homes – at Alice's cellar, at the Leghs', at the Davenports' – follows, and in each case the nature of the specific meals is an index both of the moral character of the giver and of the strength of community between giver and receiver. In this respect the failure of the Carsons even to think of offering George Wilson any sustenance when he visits them is indicative not only of the absence of community between the two classes, but also of the Carsons' own moral inadequacies. They feel no sense of unease in consuming an elaborate breakfast while Wilson stands in front of them faint with hunger. Eventually it is the cook, a servant in fact, who 'thinks' to offer Wilson some 'meat and bread' just as he is leaving. The stark contrast between the selfishness of the rich and the generosity of the poor (the scene at the Carson home is immediately followed by a visit to the Davenports) is biblical in tone; it enacts the distinction between 'Dives and Lazarus' alluded to earlier. It is significant, though, that the biblical reference comes from Barton, not from the narrator; Gaskell's understanding of the relationship between money and morality is, as I have suggested, more subtle than the simple opposition to which Barton refers.

The first working-class meal which we witness is prefaced by 'a long whispering, and chinking of money' as the Bartons consult to see if they can afford to be hospitable. Similarly their guests, although 'too polite to attend' to this consultation, are themselves only too aware that accepting the meal will incur costs when the favour has to be returned. The reader is then given a shopping list which details the cost of the bread, eggs, ham, milk, tea and rum needed to turn alimentation into a communal event. Later in the novel, when the money for provisions runs out, the sense of community becomes fragile and threatened. In homes where there is no work and no wages there are 'desperate fathers ... bitter-tongued mothers ... reckless children'; in 'trial and distress', the narrative continues, 'the very closest bonds of nature were snapped'. In the very same passage the reader is also reminded (in biblical terms) that the same circumstances produced 'Faith such as the rich can never imagine on earth; there was "Love strong as death"; and self-denial, among rude, coarse men'. Certainly these qualities are exhibited by working-class characters in the novel, but significantly they are most consistent in those who are *not* subject to 'trial and distress' – that is, those who are not totally impoverished. Margaret Legh, for example, the moral paragon of the novel, never falls into absolute penury; her blindness, although preventing her from earning a living by sewing, allows her a more profitable career in singing. Moreover she and her father have substantial savings – a 'mint ... laid by in an old teapot'. Described as a 'hoard', this 'mint' contains enough money to pay the fees for Jem Wilson's lawyer.

Jem, another moral paragon, is also financially secure. He works in a foundry and not in a mill, and as a result is protected from the cyclical poverty experienced by Barton. Moreover, the success of his 'invention' provides an income of 'twenty pound a year' for his mother and aunt, enough money for 'the best o'schooling, and ... bellyfulls o' food'. Even when Jem is eventually forced out of his job, a good reference from his previous employer ensures he finds profitable work in Canada. In contrast to all this are the finances of the Barton household. Extreme poverty leads both father and daughter to exhibit some of that 'desperation, recklessness and bitter-tongued speech' associated with times of 'trial and distress'. Barton becomes violent, first towards his daughter and later (and more dramatically) towards Carson; in response Mary is sullen and resentful, emotions which in turn contribute to her incautious flirtation with Harry Carson. Parent and child also become estranged from each other and the family breaks down. Mary is forced to seek friendship and moral guidance from outside her own home. Importantly she turns to Margaret and Job Legh; neither are directly involved in the strike, and consequently their home is one of the few still able to *afford* hospitality and community. We are forcefully reminded that sustaining Christian virtues of morality, community and benevolence, whether in a Manchester cellar or in a Liverpool courtroom, requires money. Put crudely, Christian brotherhood appears to have a price; morality paradoxically turns out to be vulnerable to exactly the realm of action – that of the economic – which it is supposed to transcend. In formal terms, it is in the carefully contrived *interaction* between the novel's realism and its melodrama – between matters of 'fact' and a concern with 'human nature' – that we glimpse Gaskell's self-consciousness about the weakness of moral critiques of political economy.

There are two related suggestions which Gaskell puts forward to suggest how economic conditions might be improved sufficiently to permit morality (and therefore charity to others) to flourish. Very early in the novel the narrator comments that one of the problems for the working classes was the huge discrepancy between 'the amount of the earnings ... and the price of their food'; all too often the gap was unbridgeable and resulted in 'disease and death'. Much of the first half of the novel is devoted to demonstrating the truth of this insight. The cost of living, as I have already noted, is an obsessive preoccupation with Gaskell and it leads to a compulsive description of financial transactions in which the precise cost of the goods is detailed with laborious care. Why do we need this information, and why do we need it in such abundance? One obvious reason is related to Gaskell's interest in the relationship between price and value.

About a third of the way through the novel there is a long story-within-a-story. Job Legh relates the poignantly comic tale of his attempt with his daughter's father-in-law, Jennings, to convey their orphan grand-daughter back to Manchester. The tale makes much of the traditional literary oppositions between town and country, London and the provinces, rich and poor, inn and home; it is also full of examples of native wit and warmth, and seems intended to illustrate the strength of community among the Manchester working classes. There are two related moments in the tale when all these values crystallise; the first occurs when Legh and Jennings come to pay for their meal at an inn in 'Brummagen' (as we might expect, mealtimes, for the men and the baby, are a focal point of the tale). The shocking price is 'half-a-crown apiece' (for food which they had hardly tasted) together with 'a shilling for th'bread and milk as were possetted all over the baby's clothes'. Legh and Jennings vainly protest against this injustice: 'We spoke up again it; but every body said it were the rule, so what could two poor oud chaps like us do again it?' Next morning they leave Brummagem (as 'black a place as Manchester, without looking so much like home') in disgust, and penury forces them to walk all day and through the night before early the following morning, and close to Manchester, they finally stop for refreshment at a cottage. They are invited in to a 'cheery, clean' room, and given a hearty breakfast while the baby is looked after by a womanly hand. When it comes to paying for these generous services, Legh is momentarily embarrassed:

'So giving Jennings a sharp nudge ... I says, "Missis, what's to pay?" pulling out my money wi' a jingle that she might na guess we were all bare o'cash. So she looks at her husband, who said

ne'er a word, but were listening wi'all his ears nevertheless; and
when she saw he would na say, she said, hesitating, as if pulled
two ways, by her fear o'him, "Should you think sixpence over
much?" It were so different to public-house reckoning'.[44]

The price is low because the wife had recently lost her own baby
and enjoyed the company, particularly that of the child. At the inn
the price of food had been determined wholly by profit, and was
rigidly fixed – it was 'the rule' to pay 'half-a-crown'. In the cottage,
however, price is negotiable, and is defined in part by moral
feeling. A similar contrast between what might be called a 'moral'
value and a purely 'economic' price occurs during the haggling
over the cost of the boat-trip to contact Will. Initially, the boatmen
demand 'thirty shillings' for the fare, but this is subsequently
reduced to 'a sovereign', then 'fourteen shillings and ninepence
plus a shawl', until finally the fare accepted is the plain 'fourteen
and ninepence'. They arrive back at the quayside and as Mary
alights one of the boatmen apologises for the rough way in which
she had initially been treated, commenting that the haggling over
money 'were only for to try you, – some folks say they've no more
blunt, when all the while they've getten a mint'. In these incidents
Gaskell seems to suggest that financial transactions should be
infused with moral value: that there is both an honest price and a
dishonest or exploitative price. The second kind of price is one
determined solely by market values: it is, in the language of
economics, the highest price which the market will bear. The
former, by contrast, results from the divorce of value from market
conditions; it is a negotiation between individuals based on what a
particular individual can reasonably *afford* to pay. Like Dickens,
Gaskell is attempting to replace the selfish, profit-seeking model of
humanity (derived from the market and assumed by political
economy) with the notion that individuals should be motivated by
moral feeling and community spirit. Where Gaskell differs from
Dickens, though, is in her insistence that such moral individuals
can still be *economic* agents. Indeed it is a moral model of humanity
which in her view defines the proper or 'ideal' economic agent –
someone whose decisions about cost, value and price are made not
on the basis of private interest, but rather in terms of how individual financial needs relate to those of the community. Such ideas are
very similar to John Ruskin's strident attack on political economy
in *Unto this Last* (1860). On publication, Ruskin's arguments were

ridiculed, not least because in the eyes of 'professional' economists the notion of an 'honest' price wholly failed to recognise the complexity of the relationship between cost and value. Indeed it is perhaps not an accident that the most sustained argument in the nineteenth century for 'honest' pricing is to found in another work of fiction – William Morris's Utopian novel, *News from Nowhere* (1890).

Gaskell's second suggestion concerns the idea of a subsistence wage. In *Mary Barton* it is significant that we know much more about the price of a loaf of bread and a couple of eggs than we do about the price of cold partridge and broiled steaks. The difference in treatment is partly explained by the emotive contrast between wealth and poverty; for the working class, partridges will always be beyond their means, so for them their actual cost is wholly irrelevant. When the price of upper-middle-class living is occasionally mentioned, such as Harry Carson's 'half-a-crown' for a bunch of lilies of the valley, it is only as an index of the huge disparity between rich and poor: the same amount of money would buy many meals for the starving Barton. But as I suggested earlier, Gaskell does not confine her energy simply to exhibiting the vulgar contrast between middle-class wealth and working-class poverty. On the contrary, one consequence of her energetic detailing of working-class lives is to focus attention on the more subtle topic of the relative nature of poverty *within* a class. What we see in Gaskell's detailed portrait of an urban working-class community is a hierarchy of working-class incomes which in turn permit the possibility of morality and benevolence. Rather than address the vexed question of the distribution of wealth, Gaskell opts for the safer topic of defining a 'subsistence' wage. Here we can see the thematic importance of the apparently causal reference to the 'twenty pound' a year which Jem judges to be sufficient to provide for his mother and aunt. It is the amount of money below which it is unreasonable to expect an individual to live and to remain fully human – to act, that is, as a moral agent.

To the modern reader this strategy will of course seem like an evasion of political responsibility. But we need to recognise that Gaskell did not have a real alternative in the sense that there was no coherent economic theory which she could draw upon to theorise a new concept of wealth distribution. Socialist explanations of value were simply not available to her (nor perhaps would they have been of much practical help on the issue). By contrast, though, the whole issue of subsistence would have been a familiar one. Since Ricardo's formulation of the notorious 'iron law of wages', subsistence, or minimal income, had become central to political economy's understanding of wealth distribution. The law, which drew upon Malthus's views about population, stated that labour had a natural price, one which permitted the worker to survive, but which at the same time, through the threat of starvation, prevented the working population as a whole from increasing or decreasing. In practice the law could be used to justify poverty as an unfortunate but necessary consequence of a market economy; certainly it denied the need for government intervention to control wages. In focusing on subsistence rather than on the equality of wealth, Gaskell is clearly only working within the conceptual paradigms established by political economy. Where she was challenging, however, was in her expanded definition of what subsistence involved. In *Mary Barton* subsistence means not simply staying alive (feeding oneself and one's family) but being part of a human community. In other words, the notion of subsistence ceases to be solely an economic issue (as political economists had assumed), and becomes instead a moral and political one.

In economic terms, Gaskell's attention to 'honest' pricing and subsistence wages seems naïve in the extreme. Certainly such proposals could not in any way resolve the fundamental macro-economic problem of the gap between wages and prices. The failure, though, is understandable given a mid-nineteenth-century frame of reference. What is commendable is Gaskell's willingness in *Mary Barton* to address such problems in the first place – her willingness, that is, to use the resources of fiction (the interplay of realism and melodrama) to see them *as problems*. Certainly Gaskell does not engage directly with the 'theory' or laws of political economy. Instead she follows her father's example and focuses on details – on discovering those awkward facts and *all* their circumstances. That evidence is then used to expose the complacency of political economy. Like Dickens, Gaskell suggests that the heart of the problem is the model of humanity with which political economists work; unlike Dickens, though, she goes on to argue that morality and economics (moral agency and economic agency), far from being mutually opposed, *must* be reconciled, for the first requires the second. In the end, Gaskell is of course unable to fix the right relationship between the moral and the economic. But such failure is a measure not of confusion or timidity, but rather of courage. In *Mary Barton*, Gaskell refuses to opt for the simple answer, for those Christian platitudes of which modern critics have too glibly accused her.

III

A fuller knowledge of their intellectual context points us towards new ways of understanding the limitations of *Hard Times* and *Mary Barton*. The framework sketched in Chapter 2 is equally fruitful when applied to the other social-problem novels. The following account of *North and South*, *Sybil* and *Alton Locke* aims, however, to be suggestive rather than comprehensive for, as I suggested earlier, I am not concerned with a detailed treatment of all the works in the sub-genre.

Critics of the social-problem novel have paid rather less attention to *North and South* than to *Mary Barton*. This situation is perhaps in part due to the heterogeneity of its themes which, as Martin Dodsworth has argued, are less easily identified with those generally associated with the sub-genre.[45] Most importantly, the centre of the novel's narrative interest is the relationship between two middle-class characters, Margaret Hale and John Thornton, and the conflicts between masters and men which the novel describes (that is, the strike and the violent mob reaction which accompanies it) are worked out through an account of a traditionally troped romance between two superficially dissimilar individuals. At one level the novel's narrative of the attraction of opposites is one familiar in nineteenth-century romantic fiction, from *Pride and Prejudice* to *Jane Eyre*, *Wuthering Heights* and *Middlemarch*. In contrast to *Mary Barton*, then, the social-problem element of *North and South* can seem little more than a topical but relatively un-important framing device for a traditional love story.[46] At the same time, though, the final reconciliation between the two lovers depends upon their overcoming certain prejudices about how con-temporary problems of social disorder (particularly those asso-ciated with industrial labour relations) are to be understood. In this respect, the novel seems to indicate that the new understanding demanded of both Margaret and Thornton can be a prototype of a new solution to contemporary social problems. In so doing it appears to locate responsibility for social order firmly within the hands of the middle classes, and in this sense it is tempting to see

North and South beginning at the point where *Mary Barton* leaves off; that is, *North and South* is concerned with describing the *nature* of the moral re-education which is necessary if reactionary masters like Henry Carson are to learn to live amicably with figures like John Barton, Job Legh or indeed Nicholas Higgins, who, taken together, represent working-class honesty and decency. More specifically *North and South* may also be an attempt to use the resources of fiction to educate a middle-class novel readership (which we know was composed mostly of young women) into the values of the public world of which they (like the protagonist Margaret Hale) would have been largely ignorant – the world of trade and commerce, of factories and strikes.

Such a reading of *North and South*, where romance is understood as troping a debate about social reform, presents two critical problems. The first, once again, is a question of plot – that is, whether the romantic narrative (Margaret and Thornton's 'star-crossed' relationship) connects coherently with the political narrative (the conflicts between mill-owners and workers). The second is one of judgement – whether this particular way of connecting the private with the public (or, more exactly, the personal with the political) is in itself valuable. Generally speaking, these two questions have tended to be run together, for the inconsistencies of plot have typically been explained by reference to the limitations inherent in Gaskell's social criticism. A good example of this concerns the way in which Gaskell treats the central theme of personal integrity or moral probity, for (as in *Mary Barton*) certain details of the plot seem to intimate that private morality is vulnerable to the values of a public world.

The most obvious instance of this equivocation occurs in the scene where Margaret lies in order to protect her brother Frederick from the prospect of being arrested by the police. Margaret is tortured by guilt about her action; she sees it as a kind of 'degradation', a personal falling-off from the high moral standards which she had tried to represent. Initially the focus of her anxiety is her shame at having compromised herself in the eyes of Thornton, who had previously viewed her emphasis on religion and moral probity with scepticism: 'She was a liar. But she had no thought of penitence before God; nothing but chaos and night surrounded the one lurid fact that, in Mr Thornton's eyes, she was degraded.' Later Margaret discusses the matter with Mr Bell (a kind of father-figure), who tries to persuade her that 'under the circumstances ... [the lie]

was necessary', and that it was quite excusable for Margaret to have forgotten herself 'in thought for another'. Dissatisfied with Mr Bell's reply (which she interprets as an attempt to be kind), Margaret realises that the true nature of her sin was lack of trust in God, an 'instinctive want of faith' – 'trusting to herself, she had fallen'. She thus prays that 'she might have the strength to speak and act the truth for evermore'. It has been noted that the problem at this point in the novel is that the reason for Margaret's lie was her concern with the inability of the public institutions of law and order to protect Frederick's innocence. However, there is no suggestion in the novel about how prayer might rectify such a situation; indeed Margaret's lie proves to have been unnecessary, not because of the fairness of legal institutions or the foresight of the Almighty, but because Frederick had already evaded detection. In other words, such an incident (so important to the romantic plot) appears to undermine the novel's political argument, for it seems to concede that moral probity, however desirable it might be for its own sake, has little real power to effect social justice. As Catherine Gallagher has pertinently commented, in incidents such as this the novel appears to 'cast doubt' on its central thesis that 'social reform depends on private ethics'.[47]

A similar equivocation is evident in Gaskell's treatment of philanthropy. In Chapter 15 Margaret and Thornton have a heated conversation about 'masters and men'. Margaret's parting words are an ironic allusion to Corinthians: 'When I see men violent and obstinate in pursuit of their rights, I may safely infer that the master is the same; that he is a little ignorant of that spirit which suffereth long, and is kind, and seeketh not her own.' The submerged reference is to St Paul's comments on charity: 'Charity suffereth long, and is kind; charity envieth not; charity vaunteth not itself, is not puffed up, doth not behave itself unseemly, seeketh not her own, is not easily provoked, thinketh no evil.' It was precisely this view of charity which informed nineteenth-century philanthropic work, and in mid-Victorian Britain philanthropy was one of the main avenues through which Christian benevolence was expressed. Moreover, as I suggested in the previous chapter, philanthropy also formed the basis of a strong opposition to the hegemony of political economy. It is entirely appropriate, then, that Margaret's attempt to put into practice her own views about resolving class conflicts should take the form of a philanthropic visit to the poor. This activity, however, is explicitly associated with her former life in

Helstone in the New Forest, and therefore with her 'ignorance' of
urban industrial life.

We are told that the 'people' who lived on Helstone's commons –
'wild, free, living creatures' – were 'her people':

> She made hearty friends with them; learned and delighted in
> using their peculiar words; took up freedom amongst them;
> nursed their babies; talked or read with slow distinctness to their
> old people; carried dainty messes to their sick; resolved before
> long to teach at the school, where her father went every day.[48]

Significantly, we also learn that this charitable work was in part
undertaken by Margaret as compensation for the boredom, the 'discontent' and 'monotony' of her 'in-doors life' in a small village. The
same mixed motives underlie Margaret's charitable visit to the
Higgins household in Milton. Margaret is relieved and delighted to
have finally found some 'human interest' in the dismal northern
town. Ironically, however, she finds that her benevolence is not
wholly welcomed; Higgins is initially suspicious of her questions
and correctly recognises that Margaret's interest in his family is
partly selfish, born of a mixture of curiosity and conscience rather
than real sympathy. 'Whatten yo'asking for?' he says, rather
bluntly, when she asks for his address and his name. Margaret is in
turn surprised at Higgins's rebuff: 'at Helstone it would have been
an understood thing, after the enquiries she had made, that she
intended to come and call upon any poor neighbour whose name
and habitation she had asked for'. Like Thornton's arrogance in his
dealings with the working classes, Margaret too has been guilty of
presuming too much, for she too has taken it for granted that the
'justness' of her actions will be immediately recognised by those to
whom they are directed. Here Gaskell seems to be hinting that
philanthropy has a politics, and that it is merely patronising to the
poor. In explaining herself to Higgins, Margaret realises her former
presumption:

> 'I thought – I meant to come and see you.' She suddenly felt
> rather shy of offering the visit, without having any reason to give
> for her wish to make it, beyond a kindly interest in a stranger. It
> seemed all at once to take the shape of an impertinence on her
> part; she read this meaning too in the man's eyes.[49]

Nevertheless Margaret is still 'half-nettled' to find that in Milton she needs 'permission' to be charitable.

More importantly we also see that Margaret's charity is both limited in conception and ineffective in practice. So on that first visit Margaret rejects Bessy's request for real (that is, economic) help – her request that Margaret should offer Bessy's 'slatternly' sister Mary a position as a servant:

> 'She could not do' – Margaret glanced unconsciously at the uncleaned corners of the room – 'She could hardly undertake a servant's place, could she ...? But even though she may not be exactly fitted to come and live with us as a servant – and I don't know about that – I will always try and be a friend to her for your sake, Bessy'.[50]

As Margaret comes to know the Higgins and Boucher families better, and as she gains a fuller knowledge of the special circumstances which attend urban working-class poverty, she realises that friendship must mean more than moral guidance; it is money – economic support – which the family really needs. Hence when she later witnesses Boucher's distress at the prospect of his 'little ones clemming' she reacts by immediately taking out her purse:

> Margaret sat utterly silent. How was she ever to go away into comfort and forget that man's voice, with the tone of unutterable agony, telling more by far than his words of what he had to suffer? She took out her purse; she had not much in it of what she could call her own, but what she had she put into Bessy's hands without speaking.[51]

Of course this is still quintessentially Victorian philanthropy, for it is an individual act of benevolence which does not resolve the underlying cause of Boucher's distress (his unemployment), although it makes Margaret feel less uncomfortable. Bessy thanks Margaret for the gift, but points out that Boucher will be looked after in any case: 'father won't let 'em want, now he knows ... Yo're not to think we'd ha'letten 'em clem, for all we're a bit pressed oursel'; if neighbours doesn't see after neighbours, I dunno who will'. The sentiment is expressive of exactly the kind of community feeling among the working class which Gaskell had described in

Mary Barton, and which is part of her attempt to show the decency of the poor. But here it also acts to undermine the worth of Margaret's philanthropy for once again she is reminded of the limitations of her actions. Her desire to help the Boucher family might have its origins in the purest of motives, from Christian feeling for the suffering of a fellow human, but nevertheless it is still inadequate: moral concern is of limited help when it is not linked to financial resources. The concession is an important one, and it is reminiscent of the dialectic between the moral and the economic in *Mary Barton*. Margaret's timely inheritance at the end of the novel demonstrates that philanthropy only becomes effective when moral sympathy is combined with both economic good sense and real money. In the novel, then, the domain of private morality, far from revaluing the public world of commerce, remains indebted to it for, as with *Mary Barton*, conscience is only of value when it is empowered by money. Indeed Margaret turns out to be obligated to the worldly business skills of Captain Lennox; it is his good management of her investments which realises the money which she eventually uses to finance Thornton's experiment in labour relations. At the end of the novel, then, the traditional opposition between private ethics (associated with female expertise) and public success (associated with male competence) is still firmly in place.

As I suggested above, the equivocation in *North and South* over the power of morality to affect the economic world – the marketplace – has been noted. However it has proved much more difficult to explain that equivocation than to register it. My suggestion is that the inconsistencies in Gaskell's novel exist as an inevitable consequence of the limitations inherent in the mid-Victorians' conceptual set; that is, the underlying problem in *North and South* is exactly that glimpsed in *Mary Barton*. Gaskell's evident dismay at certain aspects of contemporary social life – the conflicts produced by industrial labour relations – is compromised by her inability to contest the economic 'realities' which she acknowledges determine those relationships.

Gaskell admitted to being unhappy with the ending of *North and South*, and complained to a friend that her 'poor story' was 'like a pantomime figure with a great large head and a very small trunk'.[52] She placed the blame squarely on the demands of serialisation, and in the Preface to the book version of the novel she apologised for having been 'compelled to hurry on events with an improbable rapidity towards the close'. She then drew her readers' attention to the addition of 'various short passages' and 'several new chapters' intended to 'remedy this obvious defect'.[53] Despite Gaskell's additions, the defects have remained, and the connection between the romantic and political plots – or, more exactly, the translation of individual understanding into social reform – still seems to be the novel's weakness. This suggests that the cause of our (and her) dissatisfaction with the novel has little to do with the pressure under which it was composed. A more likely reason is a profound paradox which lies at its very heart, one which she could hardly have avoided. As I have indicated, the plotting of *North and South* explicitly identifies social change (a resolution of the conflict between masters and men) with changes which take place within individuals' moral understanding (Margaret's gradual appreciation of the values of commerce and manufacturing, and Thornton's gradual appreciation of the importance of feeling and emotion in business relationships). It also implies that the *kind* of social change needed is one where the public world of commerce (specifically, industrial production) is infused with the moral values associated with the private or domestic realm. For this argument to be coherent we have to be convinced that the world of commerce, of economic activity, is amenable to modification by the actions of such morally empowered individuals. However, it was exactly this assumption which the orthodoxies of contemporary economic thought denied; as I have already indicated, the central tenet of political economy was that the market – trade cycles, the relationship between prices and wages, and so on – was immune to individual action. Moreover, it is exactly this assumption which *North and South* (and *Mary Barton*) is unable to contest.

Throughout the discussions of the strike the central issue is the vexed relationship between 'wages' and 'the state of trade'. Broadly speaking, employees such as Higgins believe that the rate of wages is determined by individual decisions, and that the impoverishment of the workers is a direct result of the personal selfishness and greed of the masters:

> State o' trade! That's just a piece o' masters' humbug. It's rate o' wages I was talking of. Th' masters keep th' state o' trade in their own hands; and just walk it forward like a black bug-a-boo, to frighten naughty children with into being good. I'll tell yo' it's their part ... to beat us down, to swell their fortunes; and it's ours to stand up and fight hard'.[54]

By contrast, for employers such as Thornton the opposite relationship holds; in his view, it is the economics of the market – trade
cycles and so on – which sets the level of wages. Hence the poverty
of the working classes cannot be held to be the responsibility of any
individual or group of individuals:

> Mr Hale brought all his budget of grievances, and laid it before
> Mr Thornton, for him, with his experience as a master, to arrange
> them, and explain their origin; which he always did, on sound
> economical principles; showing that, as trade was conducted,
> there must always be a waxing and waning of commercial
> prosperity; and that in the waning a certain number of masters,
> as well as of men, must go down in the ruin, and be no more seen
> among the ranks of the prosperous.[55]

This argument is also held (in a slightly different form) by both
Margaret and by Mr Hale – by, that is, those very characters who
are associated with moral probity, and whose moral constitution
holds out the possibility of a remedy to the inequalities which so
perplex Higgins. Indeed it is particularly significant that Margaret,
who admits to knowing 'so little about strikes, and the rate of
wages, and capital, and labour', nevertheless knows enough to
suggest to Higgins that 'the state of trade may be such as not to
enable them [the masters] to give you [the men] the same remuneration'. The argument about the 'state of trade' is also one associated
with 'books', and therefore with authority, a point which Mr Hale
puts to Higgins, although rather more elaborately: 'granting to the
full the offensiveness, the folly, the unchristianness of Mr Hamper's
way of speaking to you in recommending his friend's book, yet if it
told you what he said it did, that wages find their own level, and
that the most successful strike can only force them up for a
moment, to sink in far greater proportion afterwards, in consequence of that very strike, the book would have told you the truth'.
Higgins virtually concedes Hale's point, suggesting that his real
dissatisfaction is not with the terms of the argument, but with the
fact that it is never properly explained to the workers (who of
course are unable to read books of the kind lent to Higgins):

> 'Well, sir,' said Higgins, rather doggedly; 'it might, or it might
> not. There's two opinions go to settling that point. But suppose it
> was truth double strong, it were no truth to me if I couldna take

it in. I dare say there's truth in yon Latin books on your shelves; but it's gibberish and not truth to me, unless I know the meaning o'the words. If yo', sir, or any other knowledgeable, patient man come to me, and says he'll larn me what the words mean, and not blow me up if I'm a bit stupid, or forget how one thing hangs on another – why, in time I may get to see the truth of it; or I may not.'[56]

This exchange strikes a discordant note partly because it reproduces exactly that patronising attitude towards the poor which characters such as Margaret have learned to be wary of. More importantly, though, the line of argument which Mr Hale articulates is exactly one which we would associate with a nineteenth-century political economist. Paradoxically, however, it is precisely the science of political economy (and its assumptions about human agency) which has been the object of Gaskell's censure for most of the novel. Our dissatisfaction with the plot's resolution, then, has nothing to do with Gaskell's complaint about the pressures or speed of composition, but much more to do with what is a fundamental thematic inconsistency in the novel.

The Thornton whom we (and Margaret) see in the early part of the novel – the arrogant, stubborn mill-owner who has not yet learned the importance of feeling and emotion – is presented as a parody of a political economist. He represents exactly that type of unbending dogmatism satirised as the 'perfectionist' by Gaskell's father in his *Blackwoods* essays. So, for example, very early in the story we learn that Thornton is an enthusiastic supporter of *laissez-faire* policies; he is vehemently opposed to any form of government intervention in the workings of the market, particularly those attempts to formalise relations between masters and men through legislation. In Thornton's view employers and employees should fight their own battles. As he explains to Margaret: 'We will hardly submit to the decision of an umpire, much less to the interference of a meddler with only a smattering of the knowledge of the real facts of the case, even though that meddler be called the High Court of Parliament.' This reference to 'the real facts' is yet another clue to Thornton's identity as an 'unreformed' political economist. Like Dickens's Gradgrind (surely very fresh in the minds of Gaskell's readers – *North and South* had begun serialisation in *Household Words* less than a month after *Hard Times* finished), Thornton's 'usual mode of talk' is 'about facts, not opinions, far less feelings'.

Indeed for Thornton, truth is always 'plain matter-of-fact'. 'I only state the fact', he says at one point, thinking that it will somehow be the last word on the matter. As with Dickens's Mr McChoakumchild it is as if, in the face of the facts, there is simply nothing more to be said, nothing more to argue about. Thornton's language throughout the early part of the book is saturated with the jargon of the political economist: so he talks not only of 'facts' but also of 'laws', 'interests' and 'systems'. He has no time for what he terms 'humbug or philanthropic feeling', relying instead on his own 'best discretion ... to make wise laws and come to just decisions'. This linking of justice to law has a Benthamite ring to it, and it is one reinforced by Thornton's aloof disregard for his men's personal feelings. In Thornton's view, because the law is self-evidently right, any explanation of trade cycles, of their effects on employment and wages, and so on, is simply unnecessary: 'I will neither be forced to give my reasons, nor flinch from what I have once declared to be my resolution. Let them turn out! I shall suffer as well as they: but in the end they will find I have not bated nor altered one jot.' There is more than personal stubbornness in his attitude: Thornton's arrogance is born of his faith in the system, and of his knowledge of the inability of the individual to change its workings. Indeed this is precisely why Thornton, following one of the central ambitions of political economy, tends always to collapse political questions (about power and responsibility) into economic ones: for him justice and right – social harmony – are completely identified with the natural order of the market:

> It is one of the great beauties of our system, that a working-man may raise himself into the power and position of a master by his own exertions and behaviour; that, in fact, every one who rules himself to decency and sobriety of conduct, and attention to his duties, comes over to our ranks; it may not always be as a master, but as an overlooker, a cashier, a book-keeper, a clerk, one on the side of authority and order.[57]

All this should by now sound very familiar, for like the good political economist that he is, Thornton assumes that human nature is fundamentally selfish, and that every man (employer and employee) is motivated by the desire to 'get on' at the expense of others. He also holds to the political economist's belief that the 'true' interests between master and 'work-people' are always 'identical', and that those individuals who do not recognise where their true interests lie are simply 'self-indulgent', 'dishonest' or of 'poor character'. It is just this reasoned dismissal of the individuality of his workers which permits Thornton to argue that his real duty lies not with people at all; rather, in his view, employers 'have a wide commercial character to maintain', and it is the value of commerce as an end in itself, divorced from the specificity of individual wants, which makes manufacturers like Thornton, 'the great pioneers of civilisation'. To use the terms proposed in *Mary Barton*, we can see here how completely the economic has replaced the moral in Thornton's outlook.

It is precisely the substitution of economic dogma for moral value which Thornton must learn to undo, primarily through his relationship with Margaret and then through his relationship with Higgins and the rest of his employees. The education of the hero (and heroine) into new and more socially responsible values had of course been a traditional theme in prose fiction since novels of the 1750s; in *North and South*, though, those values are given a specific economic colouring. Just as Margaret understands that she must engage with the values of the business world if her philanthropy is to be effective, so Thornton comes to understand the limitations of the 'cash-nexus' and the importance of infusing industrial relations with what he calls 'personal intercourse'. The difficulty here is that this new understanding (symbolised through Margaret and Thornton's marriage) in no way impinges upon the status or authority of those very economic axioms (about trade cycles and so on) which Thornton had earlier so trenchantly articulated. Another way of describing this paradox is to say that the arrogance of political economists (as represented by the Thornton of the early part of the novel) is held up for the reader's censure, but those very economic doctrines which permitted that arrogance in the first place are not. Moral feeling unfortunately cannot change the 'axioms of trade', and it cannot change the nature of economic activity. Morality (as the exchange between Higgins and Mr Hale demonstrates) can only serve to make those axioms more comprehensible to those who did not at first fully understand them, a group which includes young, middle-class women as well as working-class men. Thornton acknowledges as much when he admits to Margaret the limitations of his proposed 'experiment' in labour relations:

My utmost expectation only goes as far as this – that they may render strikes not the bitter, venomous sources of hatred they have hitherto been. A more hopeful man might imagine that a closer and more genial intercourse between classes might do away with strikes. But I am not a hopeful man.[58]

Thornton's plan will not prevent future strikes (and the poverty and hardships which they cause) because it will always be at the mercy of economic 'laws' – the fluctuations in trade cycles – which produce the conflicts between masters and men in the first instance. Thornton (like Carson, like Job Legh, and like Gaskell herself) is simply unable to envisage a different kind of market, one where prices and wages might exist in a different sort of relationship. Although he has learned the need to 'humanise' political economy, he simultaneously recognises the power of the market to resist such a moralising or humanising process. The paradox of the novel, then, is that on the one hand the impetus of the 'romantic' plot seems to argue that private ethics (that is, the moral integrity associated with Margaret) should in some way inform the public world of commerce (as represented by Thornton); but on the other hand the 'political' plot (the account of strikes, their origins, and their consequences) shows quite clearly that the market is impervious to all such moralising.

It is for precisely this reason that the connection between the romantic and the political plots inevitably fails to convince: matters could not be otherwise, for the change which takes place within the individual characters (the moral development of Margaret and Thornton) *cannot* result in parallel changes in the operation of the economy. Perhaps the most dramatic example of the imperviousness of the economy to individual intervention (moral or otherwise) occurs near the end of the novel – the 'daring speculation' which Thornton refuses to gamble on, but which earns his brother-in-law an 'enormous fortune'. As the narrative voice wryly comments, his brother-in-law's 'success brought with it its worldly consequence of extreme admiration. No one was considered so wise and far-seeing as Mr Watson'. Here we see quite clearly the arbitrariness of the market; it rewards the selfish gambler and punishes the moral, selfless individual who put the needs of the community before his own. We are reminded once more of the tenuous nature of the relationship between personal morality and social justice, and, more importantly, between individual agency and social (here, that is, economic) change.

IV

In distinction to *Hard Times*, *Mary Barton* and *North and South*, the intellectual debts of Charles Kingsley's *Alton Locke* are registered in a much more self-conscious way: in it normalised concepts of the social are given an explicitly national colour. The last chapter of the novel is subtitled 'Freedom, Equality, and Brotherhood', a reference, of course, to the rallying call of the French Revolution, 'liberté, égalité, fraternité'. Kingley's use of an English translation is pointed, for one of the main themes of the novel (and certainly of Alton's education) is to suggest how these terms need to be re-interpreted in order to make them relevant to the social discontents of mid-nineteenth-century Britain. The discontents themselves are familiar enough, although they are seen as far wider-ranging than in some of the other social-problem novels (for example, the novel's scope extends from the sweat-shops of Bermondsey to the 'thatched hovels' of agricultural labourers). Kingsley's concern is with the frustration of the increasingly impoverished working classes (both urban and rural), and the apparent obliviousness of the middle classes – especially 'government and parliament' – to their plight. Those discontents in turn are focused by the activities of the Chartist movement and the threat to social order which it appears to pose.

In fact Kingsley's portrayal of Chartism is not unsympathetic. Some of its members are caricatured (for example, the unprincipled proprietor of the *Weekly Warwhoop*, O'Flynn, is modelled on the Chartist leader Feargus O'Connor), but other participants (particularly Alton's friend Crossthwaite) are shown to be intelligent, articulate and well-meaning. Moreover in a chapter subtitled 'How folks turn Chartist' the reader is invited to understand that 'political discontent' had its roots 'not merely in fanciful ambition, but in misery and slavery most real and agonizing' and in 'terrible physical realities – of hunger, degradation, and despair'. Indeed some of the most memorable passages in the book are Kingsley's vivid descriptions of these 'physical realities' – the tailors' workroom, the sweaters' den, and the rat-invested slum which is the home of the

Downes family. Nevertheless, Kingsley's overarching aim is to show that Chartism is wrong-headed, and that the desire for political representation through working-class 'combination' represents a French (and therefore wholly inappropriate) understanding of what is meant by 'freedom, equality, and brotherhood'. Indeed throughout the novel the limitations (and dangers) of Chartism are explicitly troped by reference to the French Revolution. So, for example, the news of the fall of Louis-Philippe – the 'French incubus' – is cited as inspiration for the presentation of the Charter; and Crossthwaite's political rhetoric always takes its cue from France. For him, political action is the 'ordre du jour' and it has to involve a 'coup de main' – as Alton drily comments, 'poor Crossthwaite was always quoting French in those days'. There are also the familiar references to mob violence, particularly the 'pandemonium', 'reckless fury' and 'madness' which accompany the burning of Hall Farm, and during Alton's appearance in court the prosecuting counsel 'imputes' to him 'every seditious atrocity which had been committed in England or France since 1793'.[59]

In contrast to all of this is an English interpretation of 'freedom, equality, and brotherhood'. As Eleanor, the novel's saintly heroine and Alton Locke's spiritual saviour, explains:

> Freedom, Equality, and Brotherhood are here. Realize them in thine own self, and so alone thou helpest to make them realities for all. Not from without, from Charters and Republics, but from within, from the Spirit working in each; not by wrath and haste, but by patience made perfect through suffering, canst thou proclaim their good news to the groaning masses, and deliver them, as thy Master did before thee, by the cross, and not the sword.[60]

Eleanor's revaluation of French Revolutionary rhetoric is obviously indebted to the work of Thomas Carlyle; it locates true (that is, permanent or authentic) change as taking place within individuals, within the spirit or conscience. Moreover, it is through realising this spirituality that individuals assert their true humanity. In *Alton Locke*, as in other social-problem novels, we once again find that the possibility of equality and brotherhood is grounded in the assertion of a universal human nature which in turn is defined in terms of individuals' identity as 'children of God'.[61] The main consequence of Eleanor's translation of French terms is therefore to shift the meaning of revolution from the realm of politics to morality, and from an emphasis on collective action to a valorisation of the actions of the individual. Social change, in Eleanor's view, will arise naturally from spiritually transformed individuals. Or, to be more precise, it is only spiritually transformed individuals who will be in a position to benefit from the kinds of social transformations which will be the reward for 'giving up their will to God's will'.[62] In her argument the nature of those social changes remains unspecific, as do the precise mechanisms which will bring them about. Indeed to try to anticipate these changes, as Alton learns to his cost, is not only futile (Chartism fails and Alton's personal involvement in the movement lands him in prison for three years), but it is also to commit the sin of pride – to trust in what Margaret Hale called the agency of the 'self', in man-made 'systems', rather than in divine providence. As Eleanor once again explains:

> before you attempt to obtain them [social reforms], make your-
> self worthy of them – perhaps by that process you will find some
> of them have become less needful. At all events, do not ask, do
> not hope, that He will give them to you, before you are able to
> profit by them. Believe that He has kept them from you hitherto,
> because they would have been curses, and not blessings ... [L]et
> them [the working classes] show that they are willing to give up
> their will to God's will; to compass those social reforms by the
> means which God puts in their way, and wait for His own good
> time to give them, or not to give them, those means which they in
> their own minds prefer.[63]

Given Eleanor's injunction to realise 'freedom, equality, and brotherhood' in 'thine own self', it is appropriate that *Alton Locke* is written as a spiritual autobiography. The form itself dramatises the novel's central thesis: that before social justice can even be contemplated, all individuals (particularly those involved in reform movements such as Chartism) must follow Alton's personal journey towards moral enlightenment. Alton's life history thus becomes both the pattern and the mechanism for social reform. It follows from this that the novel's success – the plausibility of its thesis – will depend crucially on the way in which Alton's character is realised and, more particularly, on the nature of the transition from his false understanding of social reform (his involvement in Chartism) to the true understanding described by Eleanor. At this point, though, critics have pointed to some intractable difficulties in the novel. First, there is Alton himself: he seems wholly unrepresentative of the working classes – in speech, education and experience. He is clearly intended to be a figure who can mediate the differences between classes because he appeals to elements in them both. As well as feeling solidarity with his fellow tailors, his 'natural' intelligence also permits him to make friends with the Dean and to find a niche at Cambridge proof-reading for Lord Lynedale. One consequence of these protean abilities, as Catherine Gallagher notes, is that Alton's identity is curiously ill-defined, and many of his attainments are simply unexplained.[64] Much more problematic is the fact that Alton's final enlightenment does not follow logically from lessons learned through experience (the traditional pattern of the *Bildüngsroman*); rather they result from the strange dream sequence described in Chapter 36.

The final failure of the Charter leaves Alton exhausted, depressed and bereft of ideas, a state aggravated by the 'poisonous fever gases' he inhales when visiting Downes's cellar. He returns to his lodgings and collapses, slipping into the semi-delirious state described as 'dream-land'. In the dream sequence which follows we are offered a quasi-mythical interpretation of the disparate elements of Alton's previous life. All his personal struggles and discontents together with the social conflicts between classes are symbolically mapped on to a much larger evolutionary scheme which culminates in the prophesy of man's spiritual and moral perfection. Alton wakes from his 'fevers' with a mind newly receptive to the sermon which Eleanor is waiting to preach: he becomes converted to true knowledge – that is, to an English understanding of 'freedom, equality, and brotherhood'. In providing a final interpretation of Alton's life, the dream sequence invokes a wholly new, non-rational, order of explanation; moreover, the fact that the explanation occurs when Alton is hallucinating makes its status doubly difficult to ascertain. One reason for its inclusion clearly relates to Kingsley's emphasis on social reform through spiritual transformation; indeed the experimental style of the dream sequence, which jars so oddly with the verisimilitude of other parts of the novel, may be an attempt to find a form appropriate to describing the complex workings of the psyche. A further and more interesting reason concerns Kingsley's simple inability to provide a rational or realistic account of the kind of society which would result from morally transformed individuals such as Alton.

To be convincing, Eleanor's suggestion that the solution to social discontent lies in individual moral redemption must be seen to be superior to the alternative solutions to social discontent which the novel earlier characterises as false or mistaken. The most important of these, as I suggested above, is the Chartist demand for social reform by political representation. This argument is dismissed by Kingsley on the grounds that the demand for political equality does not attend to the important question of human morality or goodness – it is an argument which is '*about* man, and not *in* him'. It cannot resolve inequality because it does not guarantee the one attribute – a common humanity realised in individuals' moral nature – which in Kingsley's view makes a more equitable form of social life possible. Of course in *Alton Locke*, the Chartists do not understand equality in moral terms; for them it is primarily an economic and a political question, and their discontents arise directly from poverty and the resulting 'hunger, degradation, and despair'. Unsurprisingly, then, the main target of the Chartists' criticism is the complacency of Parliament and the political economists who dictate government policy. As Crossthwaite explains to his colleagues:

But you can recollect as well as I can, when a deputation of us went up to a member of parliament ... and set before him the ever-increasing penury and misery of our trade and of those connected with it; you recollect the answer – that, however glad he would be to help us, it was impossible – he could not alter the laws of nature – that wages were regulated by the amount of competition among men themselves, and that it was no business of government, or any one else, to interfere in contracts between the employer and employed, that those things regulated themselves by the laws of political economy, which it was madness and suicide to oppose. He may have been a wise man. I only know that he was a rich one. Everyone speaks well of the bridge which carries him over. Every one fancies the laws which fill his pockets to be God's laws.[65]

Properly speaking, it is this economic case (rather than the political demand for representation) which Eleanor's notion of individual moral redemption must answer. To put this point in terms comparable to the dilemma articulated by the other novelists I have discussed, Kingsley must show how moral equality will bring about economic equality. He must identify the precise sort of economic activity which is genuinely 'natural' and which does indeed follow from 'God's laws'.

The sorts of difficulties involved in such a task are glimpsed in the conversations between the farm labourers which take place in Chapter 28. The conundrum which faces them is why some labourers are starving while others get 'ten shillings a-week all the year round, and harvesting, and a pig, and a 'lotment'. Significantly none of them is able to formulate a coherent answer, and in their frustration they resort to crime, to looting and burning the nearby farm. By contrast, Eleanor, the moral paragon of the novel, *is* able to propose a solution. She describes to Alton how in thinking about 'the problems of society' she first resorted to philanthropy, to 'giving largely to every charitable institution I could hear of'. However, like Margaret Hale in *North and South*, she realises that this attempt to ameliorate economic conditions is inadequate, partly because it derives from selfish motives and partly because it did not affect in any way the workings of a market economy: 'One by one, every institution disappointed me; they seemed, after all, only means for keeping the poor in their degradation, by making it just not intolerable for them – means for enabling Mammon to draw fresh victims into his den, by taking off his hands those whom he had already worn into uselessness.'[66] Eleanor then tries 'association among my own sex', by placing working women 'in a position in which they might work for each other, and not for a single tyrant; in which that tyrant's profits might be divided among the slaves themselves.' The idea that poverty (low wages) results solely from the personal greed of individual manufacturers is an argument rehearsed much earlier in the novel by Alton, when he muses that the labourer's wages 'are used up every Saturday night', but when 'he [the labourer] stops working [the employers] have in [their] pockets the whole real profits of his nearly fifty years' labour'. It also appears in a different form in the parable of the Mountain in the 'dream-land' sequence. Eleanor goes on to describe how 'experienced men' warned her 'that such a plan would be destroyed by the innate selfishness and rivalry of human nature; that it demanded what was impossible to find, good faith, fraternal love, overruling moral influence'. She continues:

> I answered, that I knew that already; that nothing but Christianity could supply that want, but that it could and should

apply it; that I would teach them to live as sisters, by living among them as their sister myself ... And I have succeeded – as others will succeed, long after my name, my small endeavours, are forgotten amid the great new world – new Church I should have said – of enfranchised and fraternal labour.[67]

Here the political economist's concept of humanity – man considered principally as a selfish, profit-seeking agent – has been replaced by a Christian concept of humanity – man as moral being. Moreover it is assumed that a new social and economic order will simply arise naturally from the activities of these individual moral agents.

To return briefly to Alton's own experiences as a tailor: the immediate reason for his unemployment and impoverishment is his new employer's decision to make more money by contracting 'sweaters' to work in their own homes. The decision is presented as a purely personal one, motivated by greed, by what Alton refers to as 'the present code of commercial morality'. In other words, in distinction to the arguments of political economists, Kingsley seems to suggest that economic activity – the market – *is* capable of being modified by individual actions. However, the problem which Kingsley's argument presents for the modern reader is that he gives no account of the precise nature of the economic activities and institutions which will result from individuals acting as moral agents, and which (more importantly) will in turn produce enough money to alleviate poverty and despair. Another way of putting this is to say that Kingsley (unlike, for example, Gaskell) does address the issue of the distribution of wealth, but in a way which divorces it from the equally important question of wealth creation. In this respect Kingley's solutions are not really economic ones at all, and therefore they do not answer the political economist's case. The lacuna at the heart of Kingsley's account is, once more, one of economic knowledge. A model for a more equal society is not fully realised by Kingsley (and is therefore not available to persuade Alton) because it simply could not be; the intellectual resources – the appropriate economic arguments which could be mapped on to the 'individualism' of Kingsley's Christian socialism – were not available to him. So Kingsley invokes the authority of divine providence (which of course cannot be anticipated or legislated for); and he includes the dream sequence as the only possible (because non-logical) evidence for the existence of that providential plan. The resort to religious authority can of course be partly explained by the details of Kingsley's biography: he became rector of Eversley in Hampshire in 1844 and retained the living there until his death in 1875. But the dilemma which religious faith has to resolve is not one unique to Kingsley; as I have shown, it is a dilemma which confronts all the social-problem novelists because it is one produced by the limitations of a mid-nineteenth-century conceptual set. In this respect it is interesting that Kingsley should have defended the dream sequence on the grounds that he wanted to take 'the story off the ground of the actual into the deeper and wider one of the ideal'.[68] In such an ambition we see very clearly the distinction between his work and that of Gaskell and Dickens. All three writers work with exactly the same intellectual resources – an emphasis on individual agency, the location of brotherhood in the constancies of human nature and the opposition between the moral and the economic. With Dickens and (especially) with Gaskell, attention to the 'actual' serves to expose the limitation of those resources; in Kingsley, however, those limitations are consciously brushed aside by the use of a form of explanation for which 'the actual' can have no possible relevance, a reworking of the medieval device of the dream – as vision.

V

Benjamin Disraeli's *Sybil*, one of the first of the social-problem novels to be published, may seem to define the terms of the sub-genre: so in this novel we find an identification of 'two nations' – of a society divided by an apparently unbridgeable gap between what Disraeli terms 'the rich and the poor'. We also find what amounts to a synopsis of the sub-genre's main themes: corruption among the ruling classes, degradation of the working classes (both urban and rural), their resort to 'combination' or collective action, the organisation of a strike, the mob violence which results from it, and so forth. At the same time, however, there are also some significant differences between *Sybil* and the other novels I have discussed, and they centre on Disraeli's understanding of what is meant by a 'social' problem. Most obviously, *Sybil* is a party-political tract. It forms the second novel in what is known as the 'Young England' trilogy which included *Coningsby* (1844) and *Tancred* (1847). In these works Disraeli attempted to make a case for the political relevance of the Tory party (or rather, for his particular understanding of Toryism). In his view, the effective exclusion of the Tories from power for the past two hundred years or so was the direct result of the corruption he saw endemic in the Whig oligarchy. Hence the contemporary divide between rich and poor, and the social discontents and unrest which resulted from it, were of interest to Disraeli in so far as they provided evidence for political mismanagement, for what he termed in *Sybil* the 'political infidelity[,]... mean passions and petty thoughts' of the ruling Whigs. For Disraeli, then, the central critical problem was not defining the nature or grounds for a more cohesive society, but legitimating the power structures (the Tory aristocracy) which in his view were best fitted to secure such a goal. In *Sybil*, in contrast to the other novels I have discussed, social problems are understood first and foremost as political problems, and they raise questions about the legitimacy of political life, rather than the nature of the social.

In an early scene in the novel Egremont, the aristocratic hero, is contemplating the ruins of Marney Abbey. He begins musing about the relationship between past and present as follows:

> Why was England not the same land as in the days of his light-hearted youth? Why were these hard times for the poor? He stood among the ruins that, as the farmer had well observed, has seen many changes: changes of creeds, of dynasties, of laws, of manners. New orders of men had arisen in the country, new sources of wealth had opened, new dispositions of power to which that wealth had necessarily led ... And the People – the millions of Toil, on whose unconscious energies during these changeful centuries all rested – what changes had these centuries brought to them? Had their advance in the national scale borne a due relation to that progress of their rulers which had accu-mulated in the treasuries of a limited class the riches of the world ...? Were there any rick burners in the times of the lord abbots? And if not, why not? And why should the stacks of the Earls of Marney be destroyed, and those of the Abbots spared?[69]

Egremont's perspective on contemporary social problems is defined by a nostalgia for the past, for a time when there was 'com-munity' rather than 'aggregation', and 'unity' rather than 'dissoci-ation'. The ruined abbey stands as testimony both to the destruction of this ideal, but also to the possibility for its recovery. This location of authority in the past – in historical precedent – is exactly what we might expect from Disraeli's conservative politics, and it produces a novel with very different kinds of emphasis from the other works I have discussed. Most obviously, many of the specificities of mid-nineteenth-century social life which so obsessed writers such as Gaskell and Dickens – that is, the machinery of industrial production, the workings of a market economy and so forth, as well as the doctrines employed to explain these activities and processes – for Disraeli, this sort of detail is of relatively minor concern. It provides useful local colour; indeed *Sybil* is a novel which abounds in topical reference, much of it plundered from Victorian Blue Books. At the same time, though, such detail does not contribute significantly towards the proposed solution to social discontent. To put matters in the terms I have used before, factual detail in *Sybil* is often simply accumulated; it is not interpreted, or rather its interpretation is not registered as problematic or contradictory, in the way that it is in, say, *Mary Barton*.

For example, the character of Lord Marney – 'cynical, devoid of sentiment, arrogant, literal, hard' – is troped, as we might expect, in terms of Marney's 'acquaintance with the doctrines of the economists' and support for the Benthamite new Poor Law. The 'manufacturing' town of Mowbray is described by Lady Marney as a place where 'you never have a clear sky' and 'your toilette table is covered with blacks'. This kind of evaluation is similar to that which we find in *Hard Times*; also familiar is Disraeli's use of caricature in figures such as 'Devilsdust'. More interestingly at times Disraeli seems to hint at a connection between character and environment. So, for example, Devilsdust is described as being formed by his abandonment as a baby by his mother (who had to return to work in 'her factory'), and by his subsequent employment since the age of five in the 'Wadding Hole', 'a place for the manufacture of waste and damaged cotton'. By seventeen, Devilsdust is a 'first-rate workman' who receives 'high wages'; but the harsh upbringing has bred a youth who is 'dark and melancholy ... ambitious and discontented', and who 'read and pondered on the rights of labour, and sighed to vindicate his order'. This association between industrial manufacturing processes and the breakdown of family life (and therefore of morality and social order) is repeated in the circumstances of the Warner family. The father, a hand-loom weaver, has been squeezed out of the market by mechanisation. His loom is not even worth the price of 'old firewood', and he finds himself living in penury in a squalid cellar, unable to feed himself, his wife and his children. To make matters worse his eldest daughter, who is employed at Webster's factory, has left home, selfishly preferring to keep her wages for herself. She is described by the mother as the 'infamous Harriet' and a 'shameless hussy'. In a similar way, the working conditions and labour practices at the mines are cited as being responsible for the 'hideous coarseness' of the miners' language and the 'savage rudeness of their lives'. Together with the 'tommy-shop' system of payment, they contribute towards the miners' 'insurrection', in turn described as particularly 'violent' and difficult to control. In all of this Disraeli appears to make a connection between the specificity of contemporary labour relations (those arising from an industrial economy) and particular forms of contemporary social unrest (the organisation of a national strike, and the violence which accompanies it). Indeed in one passage he even explains those labour relations (and the poverty and discontent which result from them) in terms of the operations of the market:

The rate of wages which for several years in this district had undergone a continuous depression, had just received another downward impulse and was threatened with still further reduction, for the price of iron became every day lower in the market, and the article itself so little in demand that few but the great capitalists who could afford to accumulate their produce were able to maintain the furnaces in action. The little men who still continued their speculations could only do so partially, by diminishing the days of service and increasing their stints or toil and by decreasing the rate of wages as well as paying them entirely in goods.[70]

Most information in *Sybil* about wages and the relationship between 'capital' and 'labour' is derived from conversations between characters, particularly between Lord Marney and his supporters, and between Dandy Mick and Devilsdust. Its status is therefore unreliable; indeed explanations of social unrest by reference to the market more often than not indicate the ignorance or naïvety of the speaker in question.

Taken together these kinds of detail might seem to point towards an understanding of contemporary social divisions in terms of the specificities of mid-nineteenth-century society – that is, the particular circumstances which attend industrial labour relations and a modern market economy. It might even seem to suggest a social or environmental (as opposed to individual) understanding of the causes of contemporary unrest. However, such hints are never followed through in the novel. By contrast the proposals which Disraeli offers, as R. A. Butler has commented, fall far short indeed from providing any 'proper long-term solution to the strife and violence portrayed in *Sybil*'. The idea of a strong church, a strong monarchy, and the restoration to power of a Tory aristocracy is too vague, too generic, to answer the specificity of the problems which the novel highlights. As Butler pithily suggests, there is 'no prescription in the novel to equal the *de*scription'.[71] Such a disjunction, however, should not be surprising, for it is an inevitable consequence of the historicising perspective outlined at the very beginning of *Sybil*. Despite the contemporary detail he marshals, Disraeli's concern is with social division *per se*, rather than with the particular form of contemporary social divisions. For it is only social division understood in the most general way (rather than in terms of, say, the particular kinds of antagonisms produced by industrial labour relations) which will correlate with two hundred years of Whig rule, and therefore with Disraeli's political polemic. Indeed this is why Disraeli's 'two nations' are identified in the first place archetypally as 'the rich and the poor', rather than the more specifically contemporary 'masters' and 'men'.[72] The consequence, though, is that the kinds of problems which so taxed Dickens, Gaskell and Kingsley – that, for example, the main determinant of contemporary social divisions (the market economy) seemed impervious to individual intervention – this kind of conundrum is never registered by Disraeli, despite the fact that some of the descriptive detail in his novel appears to point directly to it.

Even if we take *Sybil* on its own terms and ignore the tensions between the topical and the historical and the general and the particular, there are still some profound difficulties with Disraeli's thesis, and they mainly concern his use of history. If history is the source of authority, then a central issue will be how to discriminate between false history and true history. In *Sybil*, the former is associated with Whig corruption, and with the attempt by the Whigs to maintain power by creating false historical precedents to authorise themselves and their activities. This politicisation of history is epitomised by Baptiste Hatton, a specialist in 'heraldic antiquity' who earns his money 'by claiming the ancient baronies ... for obscure pretenders' in order to enable them to take up 'seats in parliament'. True history, by contrast, is represented by the dispossessed Gerard family who (like Disraeli's genuine Tory aristocracy) have been excluded from their rightful title and therefore from power. The agent in that exclusion (aided by Hatton) is the corrupt Whig landowner, Lord Mowbray; his suppression of the documents which prove the Gerard lineage thus enacts at individual level the pattern of corruption which Disraeli sees in the past two hundred years of history. Similarly the successful recovery of these documents at the end of the novel is meant to symbolise both the restoration of the 'true' Tory aristocracy and the triumph of 'true' history. The romantic plotting of *Sybil* thus resolves social discontent by restoring the rightful rulers to power and confirming their right to rule. As I have indicated, though, there is a profound difficulty with this scheme. The reading of history which authorises Disraeli's Tory politics (described at tedious length in Book One) is eccentric; in places it is wholly inaccurate, even for the Victorian reader. A modern reader will almost certainly object to its illiberalism and the apparent rejection of a whole tradition of democratic reform. As Thom Braun has wryly commented, Disraeli's 'idiosyncratic historical perspective was only one facet of a mind which was often alarming in its individuality'.[73] In other words, *Sybil* will fail to convince because the basis of its authority, the relationship which it posits between true history and false history, appears to be compromised: that is, Disraeli's 'true' reading of history (which authorises the 'apostolic' succession of Tory aristocrats) will seem no less politically 'interested' than the 'false' reading of history which legitimates the Whigs.

By the time Dickens, Gaskell and Kingsley came to write their novels, the existence of the 'two nations' was fairly widely acknowledged. For them, however, this 'historic' divide took on an entirely new dimension. Unlike Disraeli, they located the source of social divisions and discontents within contemporary circumstances – within the economic and cultural changes associated with industrialisation. In so doing they raised an entirely new set of problems, the most fundamental of which concerned the relationship between *theories* of sociability and *actual* social conditions. The paradox of their work is that their recognition that the basis of social life had to be 'rethought' simultaneously led them to divorce the results of that 'rethinking' from the very circumstances which had motivated it. In short, the models of social life which these novelists offer do not adequately answer to those circumstances which precipitated a demand for them in the first place. I have argued that the principal reason for this paradox lies not in an ambivalence about those circumstances – about, say, a sympathy with working-class poverty combined with a desire to preserve class distinctions. It is rather to be glimpsed in the limited ways in which the social could be theorised. The twin emphases on individual agency and the constancies of human nature demanded that the basis of social life was to be redefined in a way which logically *had* to exclude circumstances. Human nature, that is, was conceived as an essentialist category. As we have seen, some authors, most notably Gaskell, were aware of this paradox, but they could not resolve it. So Gaskell's attempt to suggest how moral agency might influence the market merely testified to the ineffectiveness of morality. One novelist who had a particularly acute awareness of this cul-de-sac was George Eliot. As the final chapter will demonstrate, Eliot's sense of the vulnerability of the moral agency which the social-problem novelists champion is so pressing that it comes close to undermining the whole argument for that agency.

5

The Individual versus the Community

The starting point for explaining Eliot's views on civil society is often taken to be her 1856 essay in the *Westminster Review* on the German social scientist, Wilhelm von Riehl.[1] The date, less than two years after the publication of *North and South*, is significant, for it locates the development of Eliot's understanding of the social within broadly the same period as that of the other social-problem novels – a circumstance which partly reduces the chronological gulf which might otherwise appear to separate *Felix Holt* from the other works in the sub-genre.

Entitled 'The Natural History of German Life', Eliot's essay took the form of a review of the first two parts of Riehl's *Naturgeschichte des Volkes: Die Bürgerliche Gesellschaft* (1855) and *Land und Leute* (1856). Eliot admired Riehl's attention to what she termed a 'natural history' of 'social classes' – that is, his attention to describing their particularity. She contrasted what she understood as Riehl's 'inductive process' (his attempt to attend to the 'concrete', to 'specific facts', freed from 'aforegone conclusion' or 'a professional point of view') with contemporary tendencies towards deductive abstractions, exemplified in the use of terms such as '"the people," "the masses," "the proletariat," "the peasantry"'. For Eliot, the 'images called up' by such terms were devoid of 'concrete knowledge'; they were 'as far from completely representing the complex facts summed up in the collective term, as the railway images of [a] non-locomotive gentleman'.[2] The principal origin of this bent towards abstraction is made clear a little later in the essay, when Eliot refers to 'the tendency created by the splendid conquests of modern generalization, to believe that all social science questions are merged in economical science, and that the relations of men to their neighbours may be settled by algebraic equations'.[3] It will be recalled that it was exactly this sort of alignment of interests between professional bodies, Utilitarians and political economists

187

which underlay the polemic of Dickens and Gaskell. For Gaskell, in particular, the hostility towards abstractions such as 'economic man' were to be countered by an attention to what her father had referred to as 'the facts' – to, that is, exactly the 'specific details' of working-class lives which Eliot claims have been ignored. Indeed it is notable that Eliot too comments on 'how little the real characterization of the working-classes are known to those who are outside them'; and how little abstractions have to say about their 'psychological character – their conceptions of life, and their emotions'.[4] Eliot also points (once again like Gaskell) to the importance of infusing facts with what she terms 'moral sentiment'; and it is this task, she suggests, which is particularly suited to the artist. 'Appeals' founded on 'statistics' alone are of little value because they take for granted an interpretation of raw facts which only art can provide; they have to assume in the reader a 'sympathy ready-made, a moral sentiment already in activity'.[5] At the same time, though, there is also a significant but subtle difference between Eliot's and Gaskell's moralising attention to facts.

In Gaskell's work we saw how difficult it was for the nineteenth-century author to formulate a coherent narrative from accumulated facts, and how the 'difference' they articulated was ultimately contained by an assertion, made via the simplifying moral scaffolding of melodrama and romance, of a universal human nature. For Eliot, by contrast, the variety or difference exhibited by an attention to concrete detail serves to undermine the possibility of *any* kind of generalisation or universalism. It is for this reason that she rejects solutions offered for social disorder from both party-political positions. So the socialist ideal that 'the working-classes are in a condition to enter at once into a millenial state of *altruism*' and the 'aristocratic dilettantism which attempts to restore the "good old times" by a sort of idyllic masquerade' are both vitiated by their simplistic assumptions about human nature, by their lack of any 'real knowledge of the People'.[6] Later in the essay she comments on some studies which have paid attention to the working classes, to the 'Parisian proletariat' or to 'factory-operatives', but which are nevertheless of limited value precisely because they try to generalise from the narrow base of their evidence; they use as 'the basis of a theory' only 'a single fragment of society'. Eliot concludes (in paraphrase of Riehl) that 'the more deeply we penetrate into the knowledge of society in its details, the more thoroughly we shall be convinced that *a universal social policy has no validity except on paper, and can never be carried into successful practice*'.[7] Eliot's premise about the importance of attending to specificities, together with her hostility towards all forms of generalisation and abstraction, not only works against generic policy decisions, but, as Peter Coveney has suggested, it also appears to deny the possibility of 'social theory, *qua* theory'.[8] Actually it would be more accurate to say that it is not that Eliot's view of the social is atheoretical (as Coveney implies), but rather that it is theorised differently from, say, modern social science. Eliot, like the other social-problem novelists I have discussed, sees the form of social life determined by the behaviour and dispositions of individuals, and not the other way round. In her understanding of a 'natural history' of 'social bodies' or 'social classes' the proper object of study is the individual in all his or her particularity. Exactly this conclusion is indicated in a comparison Eliot makes with an attempt to create a universal language. She suggests that the resulting rationalisation 'may be a perfect medium of expression to science, but will never express *life*'; any attempt to purge or smooth out the 'anomalies and inconvenience of historical language' will result in a loss of 'its music and its passion ... its vital qualities as an expression of individual character'.[9] However, Eliot's attention to an individual's uniqueness (for which her favourite term is their 'private life') brings its own problems. If the result of Eliot's 'observation' is a perception of the variety (rather than sameness) among humanity, then where exactly does she locate the source of social cohesion? How exactly can 'moral sentiment' succeed in 'extending our contact with our fellow-men beyond the bounds of our personal lot'? More precisely, what kind of interpretation does moral sympathy give to factual detail?

Like Gaskell, Eliot hints that it can help to 'link the higher classes with lower' thus 'obliterating' what she terms 'the vulgarity of exclusiveness'. Later this notion of exclusiveness is taken up again in her portrait of the quintessentially 'anti-social' human being whom she labels (after Riehl) the *Philister* or Philistine. According to Eliot, Riehl defines the *Philister* as:

one who is indifferent to all social interests, all public life, as distinguished from selfish and private interests; he has no sympathy with political and social events except as they affect his own comfort and prosperity, as they offer him material for amusement or opportunity for gratifying his vanity. He has no social or political creed, but is always of the opinion which is most convenient to him for the moment.[10]

She goes on to amplify this definition, suggesting that 'the epithet *Philister* has usually a wider meaning than this'; it is 'the personification of the spirit which judges everything from a lower point of view than the subject demands – which judges the affairs of the parish from the egotistical or purely personal point of view – which judges the affairs of the nation from the parochial point of view, and does not hesitate to measure the merits of the universe from the human point of view'.[11] The kind of egotism described here is exactly that which we find in a Bounderby, or in Eliot's Mr Chubb whose 'political idée' was that 'society existed for the sake of the individual, and that the name of the individual was Chubb'. In some respects the *Philister* is simply an elaboration of the selfish, profit-seeking agent posited by political economy. Interestingly a link between anti-social behaviour and what Carlyle termed the 'cash-nexus' is hinted at earlier in the essay in Eliot's discussion of what she refers to as the 'degeneration' of the peasant character by a dependence on 'ready money'. In her view the replacement of a barter system of payment by straightforward cash payments leaves the peasant vulnerable to 'the chances of the market', and therefore at the mercy of the corrupt 'money lenders': 'social policy', she comments, 'clashes with a purely economical policy'.[12] This sort of evaluation is very similar to that found in Dickens and Gaskell; it should therefore come as no surprise to learn that for Eliot the more socially-minded individual is once again defined by selflessness. 'Co-operation', she argues, requires 'a provincial subordination of egotism'; it requires a disposition characterised by 'comprehensiveness' and 'sympathy' – exactly those moral qualities Eliot had attributed to the artist.

The oppositions we see here, between the economic and the moral, and between the selfish and the selfless, are precisely those which permitted the redefinition of social life found in the work of the other social-problem novelists. The distinctiveness of Eliot, however, lies in her location of selflessness in an ethic of renunciation. More importantly, this ethic, instead of being a given of (or a possibility derived from) a universal human nature, has to be acquired or learned by individuals for themselves. It is only with the gradual accumulation of such willed individual transformations that society may eventually evolve to a better state; as the narrator in *Felix Holt* comments:

> we see human heroism broken into units and say, this unit did little – might as well not have been. But in this way we might break up a great army into units; in this way we might break the sunlight into fragments, and think that this and the other might be cheaply parted with. Let us rather raise a monument to the soldiers whose brave hearts only kept the ranks unbroken, and met death – a monument to the faithful who were not famous, and who are precious as the continuity of the sunbeams is precious, though some of them fall unseen and on barrenness.[13]

Eliot's metaphor of the soldier is revealing. The identity of the soldier stems from his membership of an army – from, that is, a collective body: soldiers, by definition, cannot be 'different'. More precisely, in joining the army a soldier is compelled to relinquish his difference. In the army, then, community is unproblematic precisely because individuality is not at issue. As an analogy for social life in general, Eliot's metaphor suggests that there must be an element of coercion if the 'difference' of individuals (as acknowledged by her 'natural history') is to be reconciled with community. At the same time, though, Eliot simultaneously evades that dilemma by locating the responsibility for communal life within the individual – specifically, within *private* efforts of will. As a result, the sociability she articulates seems curiously fragile and negative: individuals must renounce their self-interest for a greater social good, but the nature of that good – the nature of the values or principles (economic, political or whatever) which will form the basis of communal life – is never specified.

For Eliot, the great merit of Riehl was his recognition that 'the external conditions which society has inherited from the past' – conditions which might have been mistaken for what the French sociologist, Emile Durkheim, would later call 'social facts' – were 'but the manifestation of inherited internal conditions in the human beings who compose it'.[14] Theoretical blueprints for new forms of social life, and the mechanisms for social change which they proposed, were worthless in so far as their model of the social was abstracted from life, from the particular behaviours of individuals objectified by the historical process. In reversing this procedure, by theorising about the social from the behaviour of the individual,

Eliot unsurprisingly reveals herself to be an inhabitant of exactly the intellectual world occupied by Dickens, Kingsley or Gaskell and which Chapter 3 has described. At the same time, though, her insistence on the difference of individuals, on the variety of social life revealed by acute 'observation', marks an important point of departure. As I have hinted, deprived of Kingsley's, Gaskell's, or even Dickens's faith in a universal – in a fundamentally moral – human nature, Eliot is left with the problem of having to account for the ethical basis of sociability (as well, we might add, as the social basis of ethics). In fact there are two elements to this problem. The first is practical: if individuals are not 'naturally' good, then how are they to be persuaded into selfless behaviour? Second, and perhaps more important, if goodness is not a given (of, say, human nature), then from where is it derived? From what kinds of values?

In *Felix Holt* the first of these questions is focused by Esther's choice of husband, and as a consequence by her choice of lifestyle and value-system; and the second is to be found in the character-isation of Felix, who stands as both the possibility for and the em-bodiment of moral goodness. Ironically, it is exactly these aspects of the novel which have caused difficulties for modern critics; so criticism has typically been directed towards the credibility of Felix's character and the plausibility of the complexities of the legal plot which provide the mechanism for Esther's moral dilemma. We should notice in this kind of account a very familiar pattern, for once again attention is being drawn to the relationship between the moral solution offered by a social-problem novelist and the fictional devices through which it is articulated. The difference is that in the work of Dickens, Gaskell or Kingsley, dissatisfaction with their alleged moral platitudes was connected to their use of melodrama and romance; by contrast in Eliot it relates to what appears to be the opposite, her realism.[15] The reason, though, should be obvious: Eliot's commitment to the 'facts', and so to the variety and com-plexity of human experience, combined with a hostility to gen-eralisation and universalism, would have made the moral simplifications of melodrama and romance (so appropriate for exhibiting the constancies of human nature) of little practical use to her.

The much praised Introduction of *Felix Holt* covers a familiar nineteenth-century terrain. Using the device of a coach-journey across the Midlands, Eliot describes those changes in demography, landscape and sensibility associated with the accelerating industrialisation of the British economy. As we pass 'from one phase of English life to another' we are given a series of striking juxtapositions which are testimony to the impressiveness of recent developments in England's history. We see the 'village dingy with coal-dust, noisy with the shaking looms' and 'a parish all of fields, high hedges, and deep-rutted lanes'; the 'pavement of a manufacturing town, the scenes of riots and trades-union meetings' and 'a rural region, where the neighbourhood of the town was only felt in the advantages of a near market for corn, cheese and hay'; the 'busy scenes of the shuttle and the wheel, of the roaring furnace of the shaft and the pulley' and the 'large-spaced, slow-moving life of homesteads and far-away cottages and oak-sheltered parks'; miners 'walking queerly with knees bent outward' and a 'basket-maker peeling his willow wands in the sunshine'. In all of it we seem to have the pattern setting of a social-problem novel; familiar, too, are the oppositions between town and country, natural fecundity and urban stuntedness, rural labour and industrial mechanisation. However, in the novel itself many of the sub-genre's familiar tropes are surprisingly absent; or, in the case of, say, the figuring of social disorder through a riot, they are subtly but significantly altered.

Most obviously Eliot does not pursue in detail the hint in the Introduction that contemporary social ills were directly connected with the specificities of industrial production and labour relations – the idea, that is, that it was the 'breath of the manufacturing town ... diffused ... over all the surrounding country' which was 'filling the air with eager unrest'. The theme is briefly reasserted in Chapter 3 in the description of Treby Magna where Eliot again seems to suggest a causal link between the town's transformation to 'the more complex life brought by mines and manufactures' and changes in its inhabitants' political awareness – in Treby Magna's readiness 'when political agitation swept in a great current through the country' to 'vibrate'. However, the falling 'prices', rises in 'poor-rates' and inflexibility of 'rent and tithe' which Eliot associates with a modern market economy, and which form the basis for discussion by the various electoral candidates and their supporters, in practice turn out to be of minimal importance in the political drama which follows. So the riot (the familiar trope of social disorder) which takes place in Treby Magna, unlike those we witness in *Alton Locke* or *North and South*, has no recognisable cause or principle behind it. 'There was', the narrator comments, 'no evidence of any distinctly mischievous design. There was only evidence that the majority of the crowd were excited with drink.' The same view is repeated by Felix, who comments that it was a 'sort of mob, which was animated by no real political passion or fury against social distinction'; and a little later he muses on the 'multitudinous small wickedness of small selfish ends, really undirected towards any larger result, [which] had issued in widely-shared mischief that might yet be hideous'. This 'depoliticisation' of the mob is very different from the justifiably angry workers whom we see confronting John Thornton; and different again from the noisy crowd incited by local and national grievances which descends on Hall Farm in *Alton Locke*. Eliot's account voids the mob of any sort of class or group interest, and in so doing she dissociates its violence from the specificities of contemporary social conditions, from those falling prices and the rise in poor-rates to which the novel had alluded earlier. In *Felix Holt*, Eliot's *perception* of social disorder or fragmentation may be familiar from the social-problem novel sub-genre, but (as with Disraeli's *Sybil*) her diagnosis of its cause is much less easily accommodated to that tradition. The main reason concerns the connection between what we might usefully call Eliot's 'historical sense' – her Burkean desire to maintain a formative but fluid connection between past and present – and the distinctiveness of the novel's contemporary agenda, that is, its relation to the events of the mid-*1860s*, rather than the late 1840s or 1850s.

Although *Felix Holt* is set in the early 1830s, and although it contains many 'Condition-of-England' references, its politics in fact relate to much more recent events – to debates in the 1860s about franchise reform, and the controversies which had been fuelled by writers such as Matthew Arnold in his *Cornhill* essays, later to be collected in his anti-democratic tract, *Culture and Anarchy* (1869). The riot which accompanies the 1832 elections in Treby Magna stands as a warning to those in 1865 who were contemplating enfranchising the members of that mob. In such a scheme, Eliot clearly *has* to decouple the rioters' violent 'unreasonableness' from the kinds of topical circumstances – the trade cycles and economic slumps – cited by Gaskell or Kingsley; if (as in so much Victorian historiography) the significance of the past was to point lessons for the future, then to some extent historical specificity had to be obscured. So although the riot originates in contemporary events, in the unscrupulous activities of electoral agents (which Eliot had read about in an 1835 Parliamentary Select Committee Report on

'Bribery at Elections'),[16] nevertheless the root cause of the violent behaviour which leads to Tommy Trounsem's death is the un-civilised desire of the ill-educated working classes for alcohol. It is this weakness of individual character, as prevalent, Eliot suggests, in the 1860s as it was in the 1830s, which permits the working classes to be exploited by an agent like Johnson in the first instance. It is also, for Eliot, a powerful reason for being cautious before offering the franchise to the working classes. In this respect the polemic of *Felix Holt* was both straightforward and, for the group of readers imagined by Arnold, comfortingly familiar: that the working classes lacked the education necessary for political responsibility. As Felix explains to the assembled crowd in the High Street:

> I want the working men to have power ... But there are two sorts of power. There's a power to do mischief – to undo what has been done with great expense and labour, to waste and destroy, to be cruel to the weak, to lie and quarrel, and to talk poisonous nonsense. That's the sort of power that ignorant numbers have. It never made a joint stool or planted a potato. Do you think it is likely to do much towards governing a great country, and making wise laws, and giving shelter, food, and clothes to millions of men? Ignorant power comes in the end to the same thing as wicked power; it makes misery.[17]

The same argument was aired more thoroughly in Eliot's 'Address to Working Men, by Felix Holt', written in November 1867 at Blackwoods' prompting, and published in 1868 in the January edition of the *Magazine*:

> No political institution will alter the nature of Ignorance, or hinder it from producing vice and misery. Let Ignorance start how it will, it must run the same round of low appetites, poverty, slavery, and superstition ... To get the chief power into the hands of the wisest, which means to get our life regulated according to the truest principles mankind is in possession of, is a problem as old as the very notion of wisdom.[18]

Eliot's diagnosis of the 'Condition-of-England' thus involves not so much the perception of a new set of social problems thrown up by new circumstances; rather, she isolates a generic problem (moral and intellectual ignorance) which happens for topical reasons (agitation for the reform of the franchise) to have reasserted itself in a new and particularly urgent way. Superficially, such an analysis seems to have much in common with Disraeli's use of history in *Sybil*, a novel which was equally concerned with the corrupt nature of contemporary political life. In both works history testifies that the origins of contemporary problems of social division and disorder are independent of local circumstances; more particularly, they reside in British political institutions, rather than the vicissitudes of the market. For Eliot, though, and in contrast to Disraeli, this line of reasoning does not entail a return to the past in order to reform social life – a complacent attempt to re-establish some lost golden age of politics. On the contrary, she remains alive to the difficulties of social improvement, largely because (like the other social-problem novelists) she recognises the vulnerability and impotence of the moral probity which she identifies as the prerequisite for political engagement. Importantly, and as I hinted earlier, the source of that fragility (as well, paradoxically, as its alleged strength) derives from the fact that moral acts have to be willed, by each individual and *against* the contingencies of local circumstances. As Esther comments, the 'best life' is 'where one bears and does everything because of some great and strong feeling – so that this and that in one's circumstances don't signify'. As I argued in the previous chapter, Disraeli's historicising perspective produces a gross complacency about the relationship between ideals and circumstances; by contrast, Eliot's 'historical sense' testifies to an inevitable tension between them, one which her fiction attempts to resolve, although with little success.

In *Felix Holt* that tension is exhibited most dramatically in the problems which accompany the characterisation of Felix. Although he is ostensibly the hero of the novel, Felix is in fact absent for large sections of its narrative. Moreover, even when he does appear, he remains, like so many of Eliot's idealised male characters, curiously insubstantial, despite the fact that she takes great pains to establish him as a robust physical presence. On first meeting Felix we are told that he was a 'shaggy-headed, large-eyed, strong-limbed person'; when he is in the dock, the narrator comments that Felix 'might have come from the hands of a sculptor in the later Roman period, when the plastic impulse was stirred by the grandeur of barbaric forms'. The reference to sculpture echoes an earlier and equally striking portrait in which Felix is favourably compared to a 'trades-union man':

The effect of his figure in relief against the stone background was unlike that of the previous speaker. He was considerably taller, his head and neck were more massive, and the expression of his mouth and eyes was something very different from the mere acuteness and rather hard-lipped antagonism of the trades-union man. Felix Holt's face had the look of the habitual meditative abstraction from objects of mere personal vanity or desire, which is the peculiar stamp of culture, and makes a very roughly-cut face worthy to be called 'the human face divine'.[19]

It is the 'grandeur of his full yet firm mouth, and the calm grey clearness of his eyes' which impress the crowd, gaining Felix their attention. The use of bodily health, and particularly candour of expression, as an index of moral probity was a familiar Victorian device, one which would later be ruthlessly satirised by Oscar Wilde. Reading such passages one is reminded of Basil Hallward's ironically inapposite comment to Dorian Gray in Wilde's novel: 'sin is a thing that writes itself across a man's face ... But you, Dorian, with your pure, bright, innocent face ... I can't believe anything against you.' For Eliot, though, the trope is serious, and it is used consistently, whether to index the selfish 'calculation' of the 'thin and sallow' Chubb, the 'clouded visage' of Jermyn, or the more suave form of egotism in Felix's rival, Harold Transome.

Significantly, when Transome is first introduced to the reader he is displaying his 'plump hands' and wondering about his 'trick of getting fat'. Overweight is a sign not only of Transome's wealth, but also of his self-indulgence – moral as well as sensual; Transome is Riehl's *Philister* writ large:

He naturally supposed that he might take the abjuration to be entirely in his own favour. And his face did look very pleasant; she could not help liking him, although he was certainly too particular about sauces, gravies, and wines, and had a way of virtually measuring the value of everything by the contribution it made to his own pleasure. His very good-nature was unsympathetic ... an arrangement of his for the happiness of others, which, if they were sensible, ought to succeed ... [A]n inevitable comparison ... showed her the same quality in his political views: the utmost enjoyment of his own advantages was the solvent that blended pride in his family and position, with the adhesion to changes that were to obliterate tradition and melt down enchased gold heirlooms into the plating for the egg-spoons of 'the people'.[20]

Felix stands as the antithesis to all this; his physical robustness signifying a kind of selfless asceticism, where Transome's fleshiness signs a pleasure-seeking egotism. The schematic nature of these oppositions is partly offset by some subtleties of characterisation, particularly in Harold, who must appear attractive enough to make Esther's choice a real one. After all, her probity would be compromised if (like Louisa Gradgrind) she were seen to be too strongly attracted to a corrupt figure. Nevertheless, the basic formulas at work here, those oppositions between the economic and the moral (or 'circumstance' and 'great feeling') and between the selfish and the selfless, are all too familiar. They explain why Felix is given the occupation of watch-making, for it is an activity (like circus acts) which is largely removed from the modern market-place and therefore from the moral contamination which, Eliot seems to suggest, commerce entails. (Interestingly we actually see very little of Felix at work; the same is true of Eliot's other heroes, such as Will Ladislaw or Adam Bede.) Watch-making is also an essentially individual trade, a circumstance which focuses the limitations of Felix's character. For a figure who must embody the principle of sociability, he is oddly isolated: his very 'difference' – the moral integrity, or the realisation of an Arnoldian 'best self' which, Eliot suggests, will form the basis of a better social life – seems in practice to be asocial, or even anti-social. (Significantly, Felix is generally seen in the novel as a figure set apart: for example, on the edge of the crowd, looking on, or trying to be its leader. Both roles mark out his distinctiveness – that is, his difference and separation from ordinary men.) With the exception of Esther, Felix is remarkably unsuccessful in persuading other individuals (particularly the members of the 'mob') to undergo a similar 'conversion' or 'renunciation' to his own. Dissatisfaction with Felix's character, the sense that he is insubstantial or ineffective, thus largely derives from this apparent discrepancy between the principle he represents and the social role he occupies in the narrative: his ideals are never realised in practice, nor is the precise form of social life to which they point ever specified. The problem for Eliot (as for Dickens, Gaskell and Kingsley) is once again describing how 'great feeling' will answer to circumstance – how, more precisely, it will transform an economic system which empowers Harold Transome and disables Felix

Holt. The problem is exhibited in a particularly acute way in Eliot's attempt to define for the reader the *value* of Felix's (appropriately named) 'vision'.

As we have seen in Eliot's methods of characterisation, Felix (and the goodness he represents) are troped as 'other'. So Felix and his vision represent what Transome, Jermyn, Chubb and the trades-union man are not. We know that Felix is good, and his vision worthwhile, in proportion to our sense that other figures are corrupt. In Eliot's scheme of values, the anti-social egotism of the *Philister* is defined by worldliness and materialism, by possessions and by the desire to possess. The *Philister*'s measure of value, like that of 'economic man', is always a rational 'calculation' whose axis, as political economy had suggested, was the selfish needs of the individual. Importantly, this kind of immorality is easy to represent precisely because it finds its embodiment (indeed its whole rationale) in 'things', in those objects-in-the-world, the 'concrete details', which Eliot's form of realism was so alert to and so adept at enumerating. Just as Gaskell tropes the selfishness of the Carsons or the arrogance of the Thorntons via their possessions (their lace curtains, polished tables, expensive button-holes, and so forth), so too we get the measure of Harold Transome by witnessing the expense he lavishes on fitting out not only Transome Court (with 'noiseless carpets', 'fine-matting' and chairs and curtains of 'rose-coloured satin'), but also his own mother. Seen against this 'fresh background with a gown of rich new stuff', she is just one more object, one more possession to signify Transome's value of himself. Moreover, it is exactly this kind of value-system which Esther too is initially in thrall to; like Transome, she too judges others (and herself) in terms of objects, spending her earnings on 'finest cambric handkerchiefs and freshest gloves'.

By contrast, Felix's moral goodness is a negation of such mater-ialism: it is other-wordly, anti-economic and incapable of rational calculation. As such it is, as Catherine Gallagher has suggested, 'pure value'.[21] The difficulty, however, is that pure value (unlike the moral human nature suggested by Gaskell and Dickens) has by definition no point of reference in the material world of the novel; and it is precisely because it corresponds to nothing in the world, because it is, as Esther comments, independent not only of circum-stance but also of people, that we can only know it in terms of *what it is not*. Moral probity *has* to be suggested negatively because it cannot be represented (at least through the devices of realism).[22]

The problem, though, with negative definitions is that they are not very persuasive; they require an act of faith by the reader. And it is exactly Felix's *faith* in his ideal, the tenacity with which he holds to it in the face of temptation, failure and personal hardship, which is his character's most positive recommendation, and which elicits admiration (and even awe) in Esther. As I argued earlier, moral probity, for Eliot, is defined by an act of renunciation; and we can now see why this is so. Acts and objects, unlike pure value, *can* be represented; hence in *Felix Holt* it is the act of renunciation (significantly another form of negation), rather than the specific ideal that motivates it, which the novel dramatises, largely through Esther's choice of husband (Felix's conversion has taken place prior to the events recounted in the novel). It is Esther's decision to renounce her life at Transome Hall which figures the value of Felix's morality. Interestingly, Eliot took great care to make the basis of Esther's choice as realistic as possible, consulting legal experts, such as Frederick Harrison, in order to ensure the plausibility of the complex law of entailment.[23] However, the irony noted by so many contemporary and modern readers is that the resulting accuracy seems to work *against* the novel's purpose in that it produces a plot of such unwieldy complexity – Fred C. Thompson memorably describes it as 'labyrinthine, artistically unmalleable'[24] – that the reader is either bored or confused (or both).

Part of the frustration we may feel in reading *Felix Holt* derives from the suspicion that this attention to detail is directed at the wrong subject; that it makes the absence of 'concrete' detail on Felix's morality (and on how it will transform society) all the more conspicuous. There are difficulties too with the character of Esther who seems (like Felix) too insubstantial to carry the weight of Eliot's argument. Peter Coveney suggests that the problem is the narrow timescale which 'precludes [Eliot] from conveying a sense of moral development in her characters'. He goes on: 'Esther Lyon is the moral heart of the novel ... The speed however with which the process of her moralizing revolution must be effected precludes a sense of the kind of moral development in Esther which we associate with *Middlemarch*.'[25] This may be the case, but the modern reader is much more likely to be dismayed by the utterly conventional way in which Eliot (like Dickens) defines moral probity in terms of sexual continence. It is important to remember that Esther refuses Harold not in the certainty of marrying Felix (whose 'presence and love' were then 'only a quivering hope'), but simply to give her life up to his higher ideal. Marriage is her reward only *after* she has learned (unlike Mrs Transome, Jermyn, and indeed Harold in his first inauspicious marriage) that sexual desire is inherently selfish and therefore socially destructive: 'supreme love', Esther recognises 'is not to be had where and how she wills'.

It emerges from all this that Eliot is at one with Dickens, Gaskell and Kingsley in suggesting that social life may only be transformed by changes within the behaviours of individuals – that sociability depends upon individuals becoming more moral (that is, less selfish and less materialistic). She is also at one with them in defining that moral agency in opposition to economic activity. Where Eliot differs from her predecessors, though, is in her location of this moral principle – not in a universal human nature, but in an ideal, one which is only to be glimpsed through individual acts of renunciation. As we see in *Felix Holt*, however, the effect of this shift of focus is to expose dramatically the limitations of the individualist paradigm, for by divorcing moral principle from *any* basis in the world, she demonstrates how fragile – and, paradoxically, how *asocial* – such a concept of sociability could be. The suggestion that, as human beings, we simply *are* altruistic (or, in Eliot's case, have to be willing to become so) implies that sociability is in some sense a 'natural' state, and therefore independent of local circumstances (such as, for example, the conditions of a market economy). This proposition in turn permitted the social-problem novelists to avoid many of the questions which immediately strike the modern reader – questions such as: what exactly *is* a community? Is it based on an identity of political or economic interests? Are those interests in turn compatible with each other? Is communal life *always* coercive? And so forth. The paradox of the social-problem novelists is that their individualist concept of social life turns out to have nothing to say about the very issue which makes sociability so problematic – that is, the nature of group interests. The aim of this book has simply been to show *how* that paradox arose, and *why* it was not as obvious to the mid-nineteenth-century mind as it is to the modern reader.

Ending my discussion with Eliot's exposure of the limitations of the individualist paradigm suggests that it marks some kind of watershed between mid- and late nineteenth-century responses to social problems. Clearly it cannot be the subject of this book to describe in any detail those later developments. Nevertheless it is interesting to glimpse the way in which later Victorian critiques of social life tend to retain, but simultaneously invert, the premises of Eliot's argument. A dissatisfaction with contemporary social life continues to be figured via an attention to the individual, but the relationship between the individual and the social is understood in very different ways. Two (admittedly brief) examples will demonstrate the nature of that difference. In the work of late nineteenth-century writers such as Oscar Wilde and Walter Pater, the asocial dimension of individuality becomes a source for celebration rather than containment. Wilde, for example, suggests that the route to a better social life is to politicise difference: in Wilde's ideal society, politics (or the state), far from requiring as a prerequisite the 'sameness' of our 'best selves', will in fact function to enfranchise us all to be 'other'. It is for this reason that the purpose of Socialism, in Wilde's view, is to empower Individualism. In Pater's work, social life is renounced altogether in favour (once again) of enfranchising individual difference. The fiction of Thomas Hardy and George Gissing, two of the late nineteenth century's most vehement critics of contemporary society, also testifies to the importance of *protecting* individual difference rather than assimilating it. Once again both see in the conformity or 'sameness' demanded by 'the social' a debilitating and destructive principle. What marks off the fictional worlds of Hardy or Gissing from those of Wilde is that individuality becomes impossible to sustain, and the pressures of conformity – the pressures, we might say, of *being social* – are subsequently registered as psychological, rather than political. We should notice, though, that in each of these examples the possibility of communal life has been abandoned: so Wilde's individual is typically defined by transgression, by being 'other'; Pater's is locked in a kind of solipsism – 'each mind as a solitary prisoner, its own dream of a world'; while for Hardy and Gissing, to be oneself is to be inevitably alienated from others.

Of course there are also other late nineteenth-century writers – William Morris or George Bernard Shaw are the examples which spring to mind – who depart completely from the individualist paradigm, and who seek a new principle of sociability by arguing for changes in social structures. Such developments are to be expected given the sustained and serious interest in Britain in socialism and French social thought in the last quarter of the century. However, the existence of such a tradition of social critique makes it all the more striking to see just how much late nineteenth-century fiction continues to register dissatisfaction with contemporary social life by reference to the individual. Why, we might ask, did the individualist paradigm, albeit in its inverted 'Wildean' or 'Paterian' form, continue to exercise such a fascination for dissident writers, not only those of the late nineteenth century, but also many of those we associate with modernism? A possible way of explaining such a situation is to look at other areas of political thought, for the most striking difference between, say, Wilde and Eliot is not the valorisation of difference over sameness, but rather the explicit *politicisation* of that difference. We need to understand why and how in the late nineteenth century the individualist paradigm becomes a means of addressing the political, instead of (as in the work of Eliot, or indeed Gaskell, Kingsley and Dickens) avoiding it. But we equally need to understand why so many late nineteenth-century writers registered their dissatisfaction with their society by renouncing the possibility of communal life altogether.

Notes

Notes to Chapter 1

1. See, e.g., Kathleen Tillotson, *Novels of the Eighteen-Forties* (Oxford, 1954); Arnold Kettle, 'The Early Victorian Social Problem Novel' in Boris Ford (ed.), *Dickens to Hardy: The Pelican Guide to English Literature*, Vol. 6 (Harmondsworth, 1958) pp. 169–87; Raymond Williams, *Culture and Society 1780–1950* (London, 1958). As I point out in the following chapter, the very first identification of the sub-genre was in fact in 1903 by the French scholar, Louis Cazamian. However, Cazamian's work was not widely available in Britain until the 1970s, and systematic study of the sub-genre did not begin until the 1950s.
2. The exception is of course *Felix Holt*, published in 1866. This novel is generally included within the sub-genre because it is seen to address similar sorts of issues. However the fact that it was written over a decade after the other works raises some problems about the concept of periodicity. In particular, we might ask what role do historical circumstances play in defining the specific and local features of the sub-genre if the historical period in question stretches over thirty years.
3. For a more detailed discussion of the significance of the debate between Leavis and Bateson, see Josephine M. Guy and Ian Small, *Politics and Value in English Studies* (Cambridge, 1993) pp. 73–6.
4. See Charles Dickens, *Hard Times*, ed. David Craig (Harmondsworth, 1969); Elizabeth Gaskell, *Mary Barton*, ed. Stephen Gill (Harmondsworth, 1970); Michael Wheeler, *English Fiction of the Victorian Period 1830–1890* (London, 1985) pp. 34-6.
5. See Stephen Greenblatt, *Shakespearean Negotiations* (Oxford, 1988) pp. 1–20. A useful description of the principles underlying new historicism can be found in Stephen Greenblatt, 'Resonance and Wonder', in Peter Collier and Helga Geyer-Ryan (eds), *Literary Theory Today* (Oxford, 1990) pp. 74–90; see also Marjorie Levinson, 'The New Historicism: Back to the Future', in Marjorie Levinson, Marilyn Butler, Jerome McGann and Paul Hamilton, *Rethinking Historicism* (Oxford, 1989) pp. 18–63.
6. Thomas Carlyle, *Chartism*, in *Thomas Carlyle: Selected Writings*, ed. Alan Shelston (Harmondsworth, 1971, 1986) p. 151.

Notes to Chapter 2

1. F. R. Leavis, *The Great Tradition* (London, 1948, 1973) pp. 227 and 234.
2. Ibid., p. 227.
3. Ibid., p. 236.

4. Ibid., p. 233; Leavis is quoting Dickens – see Charles Dickens, *Hard Times*, ed. David Craig (Harmondsworth, 1969, 1986) p. 77.
5. Leavis, pp. 233–4.
6. Ibid., p. 234.
7. Ibid., p. 236.
8. David Lodge, *Language of Fiction* (London, 1966, 1979).
9. See Jonathan Culler, *Structuralist Poetics* (London, 1975) pp. 32–109.
10. Ibid., p. 12.
11. David Lodge (ed.), *Modern Criticism and Theory: A Reader* (London, 1988) p. 31.
12. Roman Jakobson, 'Closing Statement', in ibid., p. 33.
13. Lodge, *Language of Fiction*, p. 6.
14. Ibid., pp. 38 and 46.
15. Ibid., p. 65.
16. Ibid., pp. 68–9.
17. Ibid., p. 78.
18. Ibid., p. 79.
19. Ibid., pp. 149 and 150.
20. Ibid., p. 151.
21. Ibid., p. 153.
22. Ibid., p. 162.
23. For an early example of this kind of literary history, see L. C. Knights, *Drama and Society in the Age of Jonson* (London, 1937). It is worth emphasising at this point that there is an important distinction between the kind of Marxist historiography represented by Knights or by Williams or Kettle, and more recent varieties of Marxism, such as 'cultural materialism'. The first group, although they see the politics of a particular work as ideologically determined, nevertheless tend to view its aesthetic or literary elements – sometimes referred to as its 'imaginative qualities' – as relatively autonomous; the latter kinds of Marxism sees *all* aspects of literary production as determined.
24. Raymond Williams, *Culture and Society* (London, 1958; Harmondsworth, 1963) p. 13.
25. Ibid., p. 119.
26. Ibid., p. 99.
27. For a detailed but lucid discussion of these issues, see Marinus C. Doeser, 'Can the Dichotomy of Fact and Value be Maintained?', in M. C. Doeser and J. N. Kraay (eds), *Facts and Values* (Dordrecht, 1986) pp. 1–20.
28. Arnold Kettle, 'The Early Victorian Social Problem Novel', in Boris Ford (ed.), *Dickens to Hardy: The Pelican Guide to English Literature*, Vol. 6 (Harmondsworth, 1958, 1976) pp. 169–87.
29. See Louis Cazamian, *The Social Novel in England 1830–1850*, trans. Martin Fido (London, 1973); and Kathleen Tillotson, *Novels of the Eighteen-Forties* (Oxford, 1954, 1985). All subsequent references to Tillotson and Cazamian are to these editions.
30. Kettle, 'The Early Victorian Social Problem Novel', p. 170.
31. Ibid., p. 172.
32. Ibid., p. 173.

33. Ibid., p. 178.
34. John Lucas, 'Mrs Gaskell and Brotherhood', in David Howard, John Lucas and John Goode (eds), *Tradition and Tolerance in Nineteenth-Century Fiction* (London, 1966) p. 143.
35. Ibid.
36. Ibid., p. 141.
37. Ibid., p. 147.
38. Ibid., p. 146.
39. These debates were given a new impetus in the late 1960s and early 1970s through the introduction into Britain of the work of the French philosopher, Louis Althusser. Althusser's attempt to resolve some of these complex questions resulted in a radical retheorising of the Marxist concept of ideology. See Louis Althusser, *For Marx*, trans. Ben Brewster (London, 1969) and *Politics and History*, trans. Ben Brewster (London, 1974). For a discussion of Althusser's influence in Britain see Susan James, 'Althusserian Materialism in England', in Ceri Crossley and Ian Small (eds), *Studies in Anglo-French Cultural Relations* (London, 1988) pp. 187–219.
40. Lucas, 'Mrs Gaskell and Brotherhood', pp. 141–2.
41. Regenia Gagnier, *Subjectivities* (Oxford, 1991) p. 113.
42. Cazamian, *The Social Novel in England*, p. 3.
43. See Kathleen Tillotson, *Novels of the Eighteen-Forties*, p. 123; and Sheila Smith, *The Other Nation: The Poor in English Novels of the 1840s and 1850s* (Oxford, 1980) p. 266.
44. See Cazamian, *The Social Novel in England*, pp. 14–16.
45. See, for example, Dorothy Thompson, *The Chartists: Popular Politics in the Industrial Revolution* (Hounslow, 1984).
46. See note 29.
47. Cazamian, *The Social Novel in England*, pp. ix–xii.
48. Ibid., p. ix.
49. Ibid., p. 4.
50. Ibid., p. 8.
51. Ibid., p. 81.
52. Ibid., p. 90.
53. Ibid., p. 9.
54. Ibid., p. 6; my emphasis.
55. Ibid., p. 9; my emphasis.
56. Ibid., pp. 9–10.
57. Ibid., p. 12.
58. Tillotson, *Novels of the Eighteen-Forties*, p. 123.
59. Ibid., p. 89.
60. Ibid., pp. 123–4.
61. Ibid., pp. 212–13.
62. At one point, for example, Tillotson comments that 'the moral content of *Mary Barton*, as distinct from all its accretion of specific, documentary detail, is also that of *Dombey and Son* and of *Past and Present*' (p. 212).
63. Ibid., p. 202.
64. Smith, *The Other Nation*, p. 2.

65. Ibid., p. 3.
66. Ibid., p. 254.
67. Ibid.
68. John Holloway, 'Hard Times: A History and a Criticism', in John Gross and Gabriel Pearson (eds), *Dickens and the Twentieth Century* (London, 1962, 1966) pp. 159–74.
69. Ibid., p. 159.
70. Ibid., pp. 159–60.
71. Ibid., p. 161.
72. Ibid., p. 166.
73. Ibid., p. 160. In *Alton Locke* Kingsley also refers to McCulloch's work as authoritative reading; so when Lord Lynedale becomes interested in economics it is 'McCulloch on taxation' which lies open on his desk. See Charles Kingsley, *Alton Locke*, ed. Elizabeth Cripps (Oxford, 1983) p. 146.
74. Catherine Gallagher, *The Industrial Reformation of English Fiction* (London, 1985) p. xiv.
75. Ibid., pp. xi–xii.
76. Ibid., pp. xiii–iv.
77. Ibid., p. xii.
78. It is perhaps worth noting that Gallagher's use of these terms is specific to her argument and differs from their general usage in philosophy to which I have referred in note 27.
79. At one point Gallagher rather gnomically comments that 'readers will probably detect in the three major subdivisions of the book (free will versus determinism, private versus public, fact versus value) resemblances to Georg Lukács's "antinomies of bourgeois thought"'. She goes on to criticise Lukács on the grounds that his use of the term 'bourgeois' is 'limiting and insufficiently specific', and comments that nineteenth-century discussion of these 'antinomies' was not in fact defined by class interests. Interestingly, Gallagher does not see that the identification of the 'antinomies' themselves, and their relevance to problems in society, might also be the product of a particular, historically contingent frame of reference. See Gallagher, *The Industrial Reformation of English Fiction*, p. xiv.
80. Ibid., p. 187.
81. Ibid., p. xv.

Notes to Chapter 3

1. For a more detailed account of these aspects of nineteenth-century intellectual life, see Ian Small, *Conditions for Criticism: Authority, Knowledge, and Literature in the Late Nineteenth Century* (Oxford, 1991).
2. See the early work of Michel Foucault, in particular *The Order of Things* (London, 1970) and *The Archaeology of Knowledge* (London, 1972). It is perhaps worth noting the distinction between the notion of the episteme and Foucault's later, and more popular, idea of

discourse, in which, as I suggested in relation to the work of Catherine Gallagher, there is no concept of boundary, so discourse can never be known in its totality. Hence ideas of status or authority cannot be broached.

3. See Stefan Collini, *Liberalism and Sociology: L. T. Hobhouse and Political Argument in England 1880–1914* (Cambridge, 1979) p. 9. Collini describes himself as 'heavily indebted' to the work of Quentin Skinner, and although largely ignored by literary critics and literary historians, Skinner's essay, 'Meaning and understanding in the history of ideas', *History and Theory*, 8 (1969) pp. 3–53, remains one of the most intelligent accounts of how to 'do' intellectual history. The reader may also find useful Collini's pragmatic dismissal of the currently fashionable view that history is nothing more than our modern views imposed upon the past. While recognising that there is a 'tension' between 'on the one hand, attempting to recover the past in its own terms, and, on the other, recognizing that selection on the basis of our criteria is inherent in the enterprise', Collini nevertheless argues that this tension 'need not, if properly handled, necessarily prove to be damaging in practice'. He goes on: 'while we constantly need to be reminded that the past is another country where they speak what in many respects is a foreign language, the impassability of the divide can be exaggerated. To declare that the historian is inescapably the child of his time is only to announce a rather obvious truth, not to "unmask" some sinister distorting influence. Foreign languages are among the things that historians, like other children, can learn; even our preconceptions are corrigible, and historical scholarship is in fact one of the means by which we correct them' (p. 7). A more detailed philosophical discussion of the issue of relativism in historical knowledge can be found in Arthur C. Danto, *Narration and Knowledge* (New York, 1985); an account of its relationship to literary history can be found in Josephine M. Guy and Ian Small, *Politics and Value in English Studies* (Cambridge, 1993) pp. 119–29.

4. Henry Plotkin, for example, has recently pointed out that there are now no 'substantive alternative ways' (with the exception of a 'small minority of creationists') of understanding evolution. See Henry Plotkin, *The Nature of Knowledge* (London, 1994) p. xiv.

5. Ian Small, *Conditions for Criticism*, p. 48.

6. For a useful account of the individualist emphasis of psychology and aesthetics see Small, ibid., pp. 64–88. The role of human agency in Victorian histories (and the exceptional nature of Buckle's work) is also discussed by Small, pp. 45–53. It is worth noting here that the first volume of Buckle's *History of Civilization in England* was not in fact published until 1857 (that is, *after* most of the social-problem novels had been written); moreover, even then, it remained highly controversial and was roundly rejected by the academic establishment.

7. Some economic historians have suggested that classical political economy was in fact the origin of the individualist conceptual set which I am discussing. Prior to Smith's publication of *The Wealth of*

Nations, economic thought had been piecemeal and unsystematic, arising largely from reactions by individuals to contemporary events. Historians generally divide pre-classical economic thought into three groups: scholasticism (that is, the body of work developed by the scholastics, particularly Thomas Aquinas, who wrote from the thirteenth to the sixteenth century), mercantilism (the name given to the economic literature written between 1500 and 1750) and physiocracy (a short-lived 'movement', from about 1750 to 1780, exclusive to France). In this history, the most important distinction to bear in mind is that between mercantilism and classical political economy. The basic tenet of mercantilism was that the total wealth in the world was a fixed quantity, hence when trade took place, gain for one party necessarily involved a loss for another. Moreover, this argument was seen to hold true for both individual transactions and for those which took place between nations. In this respect, the overall wealth of the nation was considered to depend upon the balance of trade between nations in the sense that an actual gain for one country inevitably resulted in an actual loss for another. In the words of Harry Landreth and David C. Colander, for the mercantilists 'the wealth of the nation was not defined in terms of the sum of individual wealth ... [Rather] they advocated increasing the nation's wealth by simultaneously encouraging production, increasing exports, and holding down domestic consumption. Thus the wealth of the nation was based on the poverty of the many' (Harry Landreth and David C. Colander, *History of Economic Thought*, 2nd edn (Boston, Mass., 1980) p. 30). In this respect, mercantilism posited a conflict-model of economic activity whereby there were inevitable disharmonies both between trading states and between one state and its individual citizens, for the impoverishment of individuals was seen to be necessary if the domestic economy was to compete successfully in national trade. In such a view individual or private self-interest was inevitably in conflict with public interest, hence the need for the state or the statesman to intervene in order to regulate economic life. The main focus of attention for the mercantilist was therefore, *not* on the individual, but rather on understanding the basic laws or rules by which the economy operated so that effective legislation could be enacted to control the course of economic events. In practice, such interventionist legislation involved controls on individuals via matters such as price control, regulation of labour, monopolies and special privileges, and attempts to control the productivity of other states through navigation acts, colonisation, import duties, bounties and so forth. (See Robert Lekachman, *A History of Economic Ideas* (New York, 1959) pp. 44–9.) For the purpose of my argument, however, the main point of interest in all of this is that mercantilist thought, unlike political economy, did *not* theorise from the needs of individuals. It is true that late mercantile thought gives some attention to the notion of 'economic man' as a selfish agent motived by profit; however, the emphasis is still on discovering a set of abstract laws or institutions which can channel such egoistic drives in order to increase the prosperity of the nation (see Landreth and Colander, *History of Economic Thought*, p. 34). Finally, political economy may have been the origin of an individualist understanding of the social; however, it is equally plausible that it was the increasing dominance of the individual in many other areas of thought which was partly responsible for the initial 'acceptance' of political economy.

8. For example, one kind of history describes the period of classical political economy beginning in 1776 with Smith's *An Enquiry into the Nature and Causes of the Wealth of Nations* and ending in 1848 with John Stuart Mill's *Principles of Political Economy*, while another sees it beginning in the middle of the eighteenth century with the work of the 'Physiocrats' and ending in the mid-1880s with the death of Karl Marx.

9. For an accessible introduction to what is meant by the terms 'political economy' and 'classical political economy', see James A. Caporaso and David P. Levine, *Theories of Political Economy* (Cambridge, 1992).

10. Caporaso and Levine, *Theories of Political Economy*, p. 34.

11. Ibid.

12. Ibid., p. 36.

13. The precise details of how the market or civil society operates is not of importance to my argument, although it is worth pointing out that writers within the tradition of classical political economy differed substantially on these issues. For example, David Ricardo's explanation of how the market works was quite different from that proposed by Adam Smith; indeed Ricardo's work marked a theoretical shift away from Smith's concentration on what determines the wealth of the nation, and towards the rather different topic of the distribution of wealth. This in turn led Ricardo to formulate distinct theories about labour, value, wages and economic growth. There is also an important methodological debate within classical political economy about the relative merits of induction (that is, the practice of deriving theoretical inferences from attention to the 'facts' of experience) and deduction (that is, the abstract formulation of laws from *a priori* axioms which are then used to explain the 'facts' of experience).

14. Caporaso and Levine, *Theories of Political Economy*, p. 43. It is worth noting here that the public good is defined in political economy in a very narrow way. So for Adam Smith, for example, it is synonymous with the wealth of the nation or the increase in society's stock of capital.

15. Again, it is worth noting that in Smith's view the state becomes an administrative rather than a political body; so, as Caporaso and Levine argue, Smith's state 'would not deliberate on the appropriate ways of life in a well-ordered society; it would not concern itself with collective judgements on the nature of the public good; it would not take responsibility for the welfare of those whose private activities fail adequately to sustain them' (see Caporaso and Levine, *Theories of Political Economy*, p. 45).

16. In fact the extent and nature of early and mid-nineteenth-century social legislation has led some historians to argue that the origins of the modern welfare state can be located in a pattern of legislation

which began in the early nineteenth century and grew steadily
through the following decades. See, for example, David Roberts,
Victorian Origins of the British Welfare State (New Haven, Conn., 1960).

17. Collini, *Liberalism and Sociology*, p. 14.
18. Philip Abrams, *The Origins of British Sociology 1834–1914* (Chicago, Ill.,
     1968, 1972) p. 9.
19. Ibid., p. 10.
20. Caporaso and Levine, *Theories of Political Economy*, p. 39.
21. Ibid., p. 44.
22. John Stuart Mill, 'On the Definition of Political Economy; and on the
     Method of Investigation Proper to it', in J. M. Robson (ed.), *Collected
     Works of John Stuart Mill*. Vol. IV: *Essays on Economics and Society*
     (Toronto, 1967) p. 318.
23. Mill, 'On the Definition of Political Economy', ibid., p. 321. See also
     Samuel Hollander, *The Economics of John Stuart Mill*. Vol. I: *Theory and
     Method* (Basil Blackwell, 1985) p. 107.
24. Mill, 'On the Definition of Political Economy', p. 336.
25. Mill, *A System of Logic: Ratiocinative and Inductive. Collected Works*,
     Vol. VIII, p. 901. It is worth noting that Mill was aware of some of the
     difficulties posed by such a methodology. In the first place, he
     realised the possible dangers of specialist study, and insisted that the
     conclusions from accounts of different social phenomena should
     always be 'afterwards corrected for practice by the modifications
     supplied by the others' (*A System of Logic*, p. 906). And he even went
     so far as to admit that in instances where behaviour was not homoge-
     nous but (in his words) 'mixed up', specialist study would be impos-
     sible. Mill was also aware that the foundational axioms of political
     economy (that individuals are motivated in their behaviour by 'a
     desire of wealth' and by a 'preference for a greater proportion of
     wealth to a smaller') might be true only for Britain and America.
     Because axioms about individual behaviour were deduced from
     contemporary empirical observation, they always ran the risk of
     being relative to time and place. The result was that the arguments of
     political economy could only be assumed to hold true for a particular
     environment; political economy could therefore neither be predictive
     nor universal. This caveat aside, Mill nevertheless believed that
     behavioural axioms could be deduced from observations about indi-
     viduals, and that such axioms (whether or not provisional) were the
     proper starting-point of a scientific study of society. Indeed he argued
     for a separate science of what he called 'human character formation'
     or 'ethology' in which such generalisations about human behaviour
     'should be connected deductively with the laws of nature from which
     they result'. 'The science of Human Nature may be said to exist,' Mill
     argued, 'in proportion as the approximate truths, which compose a
     practical knowledge of mankind, can be exhibited as corollaries from
     the universal laws of human nature on which they rest' (ibid., p. 848).
     In the absence of such a science, however, political economists had
     simply to be cautious about the universality of their foundational
     axioms. For a detailed discussion of Mill's methodology see Samuel

Hollander, *The Economics of John Stuart Mill*, pp. 66–159. I have drawn substantially on Hollander's lucid exposition.

26. This way of thinking about the relationship between the individual and the social had been developed earlier in the century, chiefly in the work of Robert Owen and his followers. However, Owenism remained marginal to British intellectual culture until the revival of socialist thought in the 1880s. Owen's reputation and the impact of his ideas is discussed in a later section of this chapter.

27. As I argue later, it is not until the very late 1850s that sustained attention was given to the specificity or difference of individuals. This change of emphasis is marked by the publication of John Stuart Mill's *On Liberty* (1859); it also underwrites developments in several other areas of late nineteenth-century thought, particularly in psychology, and the development of marginal utility theory in economics. See Ian Small, *Conditions for Criticism*, and Regenia Gagnier, 'On the Insatiability of Human Wants: Economic and Aesthetic Man', *Victorian Studies*, 36, 2 (1993) pp. 125–53. Both critics have drawn attention to the significance of these developments for understanding late nineteenth-century literary movements such as Aestheticism.

28. A further distinction to bear in mind is that between 'individualist' and 'Individualism'. Classical political economy was a theory based on individual behaviour; this, however, does not mean that it is concerned with the ideology associated with Individualism. The term 'individualist' was used to describe what Stefan Collini (quoting from the *Oxford English Dictionary*) has termed a 'general sense common throughout the nineteenth century, of "self-centred feeling or conduct as a principle; a mode of life in which the individual pursues his own ends or follows out his own ideas; free and independent individual action or thought; egoism"'. By contrast 'Individualism' refers to '"the social theory which advocates the free and independent action of the individual as opposed to communistic methods of organization and state interference; opposed to Collectivism and Socialism"' (Collini, *Liberalism and Sociology*, p. 16). Individualism thus implies a *politics*, and in a general sense this politics is what distinguishes it from what is meant by individualist. Importantly, Individualism understood in this political sense does not become current until the 1880s. In other words, in the early and mid-nineteenth century, references to individual behaviour do not entail an interest in subjectivity, nor do they imply an individual's political right to self-expression. Finally, the distinction made between 'individualist' and 'Individualist' with a capital 'I' is also significant. I use the term 'individualist' (lower-case 'i') descriptively to refer to an atomistic conception of society where the unit of understanding is individual behaviour. This usage should not be confused with the specialist late nineteenth-century term 'Individualist' (with a capital 'I') which was used by advocates of a political doctrine of Individualism to identify themselves. When the term 'individualism' (with a lower-case 'i') is used before the 1880s it refers pejoratively to those modes of thought which I describe as individualistic. For the purposes of this book, the

Notes 213

reader need simply note that Individualism and 'Individualist' (with a capital 'I') denote a specialised, historically-specific understanding of these terms which belongs to late nineteenth-century thought; and 'individualism' or 'individualist' (with a lower-case 'i') are simply descriptive terms. A useful discussion of these complexities of definition may be found in the following works: Steven Lukes, *Individualism* (Oxford, 1973); Stefan Collini, *Liberalism and Sociology*; and (perhaps most helpfully) M. W. Taylor, *Men Versus the State: Herbert Spencer and Late Victorian Individualism* (Oxford, 1992).

29. See John Plamenatz, *The English Utilitarians* (Oxford 1958, 1966) p. 59. My account of Bentham generally follows what P. J. Kelly has called the 'received interpretation' of his work. In *Utilitarianism and Distributive Justice* (Oxford, 1990), Kelly draws extensively on Bentham's unpublished material – the Civil and Distributive Law manuscripts – in order to overturn this interpretation. His argument is that Bentham's political morality was 'more complex' than is usually acknowledged. More specifically he claims that Bentham's Utilitarianism was more accommodating to 'the liberal values of liberty, equality and personal inviolability' than critics (such as John Rawls) have been prepared to admit. Indeed Kelly goes as far as to suggest that while Bentham shares much with 'classical laissez-faire theory', he also 'can consistently adopt positions that are described as 'collectivist' (*Utilitarianism and Distributive Justice*, p. 10). Discussion of Kelly's complex and detailed argument is clearly beyond the scope of the present book. The case he argues might indeed be correct, in the sense that Bentham might have been developing lines of philosophical argument different from those in his published work. However, I am concerned with the public dimension of Bentham's work and consequently I have felt justified in reproducing the 'received interpretation', which is derived largely from Bentham's most popular work, *An Introduction to the Principles of Morals and Legislation*, on the grounds that this was the interpretation of Utilitarianism most widely available to (and therefore most influential for) Bentham's Victorian audience. Indeed it is significant, as M. W. Taylor has more recently argued, that the 'Individualists', a late nineteenth-century group of thinkers who advocated extreme anti-interventionist policies, could claim themselves to be 'the only legitimate heirs of the Benthamite heritage'. As Taylor acknowledges, such an argument necessarily involved a certain kind of interpretation of Bentham, one which privileged the economic elements of Utilitarianism over its politics. Nevertheless, the significant point is that this interpretation at the time was seen to be coherent and legitimate. As Taylor argues, 'Leslie Stephen's characterization of Bentham as "in the main an adherent of what he calls the laissez-nous faire principle" ... [i]n the context of the late nineteenth century ... was not a particularly contentious interpretation ... [I]t is only much more recently that scholarship has established Bentham's own views with regard to the legitimate province of the State were complex, and often allowed for a considerable degree of governmental action.' See

Taylor, *Men Versus the State*, pp. 37 and 39. This popular association of Bentham (and Utilitarianism) with *laissez-faire* policies (in spite of the many legislative reforms enacted under the auspices of Utilitarian theory) is in keeping with my general argument that the nexus of ideas underlying political economy and Utilitarianism were antithetical to a sociological understanding of society.

30. H. L. A. Hart, 'Introduction', in Jeremy Bentham, *An Introduction to the Principles of Morals and Legislation*, eds J. H. Burns and H. L. A. Hart (London, 1970, 1982) p. xxxiv.

31. Bentham, *An Introduction to the Principles of Morals and Legislation*, p. 11. As I have suggested, the Victorian reader was most likely to have known Bentham through Dumont's French 'redactions', or, later in the century, through Bowring's edition. Both these works are now no longer easily available, and for ease of reference I have therefore cited all quotations from Burns's and Hart's modern edition which prints (to use their words) 'essentially' the 1823 text (that is, the second edition of *An Introduction to the Principles of Morals and Legislation*) as 'approved by Bentham' (see Burns and Hart, p. xliii). It is worth stressing that the kinds of general points which I wish to make about Bentham's way of thinking are not fundamentally influenced by the textual variants which I have mentioned.

32. Bentham, *Principles of Morals and Legislation*, p. 12.

33. Ibid., pp. 12–13.

34. Hart, 'Introduction', p. xxxviii.

35. Bentham, *Principles of Morals and Legislation*, p. 51.

36. This brief summary draws upon Hart's 'Introduction'; a more detailed introductory account (with different points of emphasis) is given in Plamenatz, *The English Utilitarians*, pp. 70–82.

37. Plamenatz, ibid., p. 71.

38. Ibid., p. 72.

39. Hart, 'Introduction', p. xliii.

40. Bentham, quoted by Hart, ibid., pp. xlvi–xlvii. Hart in turn cites Bowring as his source; see John Bowring (ed.), *The Works of Jeremy Bentham*, Vol. III (Edinburgh, 1843), p. 459.

41. Hart, 'Introduction', p. xlvii.

42. For a list of such interpretations and for his own 'contribution' see Hart, ibid., pp. xlvii–xlix.

43. T. R. Malthus, *An Essay on the Principle of Population*, ed. Donald Winch (Cambridge, 1992) p. xiii. The standard modern edition of Malthus's *Essay* is the variorum edition produced by Patricia James (Cambridge, 1987) which documents textual changes made between 1803 and 1826, as well as identifying Malthus's sources. A more accessible text for the non-specialist is Donald Winch's selected extracts from the *Essay* (cited here) which is based on James's text. All references to the *Essay* are from Winch's edition.

44. The most obvious point of departure between Malthus's arguments and political economy concerns his support for the Corn Laws and therefore his defence of a form of protectionism as an 'exception' to *laissez-faire* principles of free trade. For a brief discussion of this issue

(and other distinctions between Malthus and political economy) see Donald Winch, *Malthus* (Oxford, 1987) pp. 54–93.

45. Malthus, *Essay*, p. 214.
46. Ibid., p. 213. The immediate source of Malthus's Utilitarian framework was the 'theological Utilitarianism' of William Paley in his *Principles of Moral and Political Philosophy* (London, 1785).
47. Malthus, *Essay*, p. 213.
48. Ibid., p. 208.
49. Ibid., pp. 223–4.
50. Ibid., p. 226.
51. Ibid., p. 325.
52. Ibid., p. 327.
53. See Robert Lekachman, *A History of Economic Ideas*, p. 133.
54. It is worth noting in passing that M. W. Taylor has recently drawn attention to an apparent incompatibility between Utilitarianism and political economy. In discussing what he terms the 'Benthamite heritage', he has noted 'a potential conflict between Benthamism as a creed of the rational reform of political institutions – which were consequently regarded as artificial structures subject to human design – and as an economic creed which preached legislative impotence by treating the system of production and distribution as a "natural" organization, governed by laws analogous to those of the physical science' (Taylor, *Men Versus the State*, p. 37). It is Taylor's argument that interpreters of Benthamism in the second half of the century tended to focus on one or other of these strands. So by emphasising *either* the political or the economic, Benthamism could be used to endorse both interventionist and anti-interventionist thought. Hence Benthamism was historically invoked as a precursor of both liberalism and Individualism. Importantly, however, in the early decades of the nineteenth century this contradiction was not readily apparent, mainly because the kind of legal reforms which Bentham suggested, and the kind of legislation which (as I suggested) classical political economists advocated, were not necessarily interpreted as interventionist. Importantly, such legislation did not implicate fundamental changes in social structures, and was not justified by any appeal to the necessity for social change. In this sense the partial application of *laissez-faire* doctrines did not necessarily undermine the classical political economists' position; nor was the radicalism of Bentham's legal reforms necessarily incompatible with a theoretical stand-point which assumed that individuals could not intervene to change the underlying laws of social life. The basic point to remember is that legislation – government action – did not imply an attempt to mould the *social* order. Rather the opposite: legislation (intervention) tended to be justified on the grounds that it would 'enable or force men [individuals] to square their lives with the natural laws of society where these were known but not working freely'.
55. Economic historians refer to that alternative economic theory as marginal utility theory, and the process by which it replaced political economy is known as the marginal revolution. The nature of that

revolution is complex, and attempts to understand it have generated a large body of critical work. For a brief account of some of the areas of controversy see Ian Small, *Conditions for Criticism*, pp. 62–3; and for a useful general account of the marginal revolution see T. W. Hutchinson, *Review of Economic Doctrines 1870–1929* (Westport, Conn., 1975) and *On Revolutions and Progress in Economic Knowledge* (Cambridge, 1978). There was also in the late decades of the nineteenth century a sustained (though still marginal) attempt to articulate a socialist theory of economic activity – that is, a socialist critique of free-market economics. See, for example, the popular adaptation of some aspects of Marxist theory by H. M. Hyndman in *England for All: The Text Book of Democracy* (London, 1881); see especially Chapters II and III entitled 'Labour' and 'Capital' respectively.

56. By the term 'ideology', Althusser refers to the totalising control exercised by a system of ideas which is analogous to a belief-system (see Chapter 1, note 39). For useful general accounts of the concept of ideology, see Raymond Guess, *The Idea of a Critical Theory* (Cambridge, 1981); and David McLellan, *Ideology* (Milton Keynes, 1986).

57. Nassau William Senior, *An Outline of the Science of Political Economy* (London, 1836) p. 1.

58. Landreth and Colander, *History of Economic Thought*, p. 134.

59. Mark Blaug, *Ricardian Economics: A Historical Study* (New Haven, Conn., 1958) p. 187; quoted in Landreth and Colander, *History of Economic Thought* p. 135.

60. Landreth and Colander, *History of Economic Thought*, p. 138.

61. Ibid., p. 144.

62. John Stuart Mill, *Principles of Political Economy. Collected Works*, Vol. II, p. 199.

63. Mill, *Principles of Political Economy. Collected Works*, Vol. III, p. 794; the quotation is from the third edition of the *Principles* published in 1852. In that third edition (and in the previous second edition of 1849), Mill had expanded his discussion of socialism (in Part IV, Chapter vii, 'On the Probable Futurity of the Labouring Classes') in a way which was, broadly speaking, more favourable than the first edition of 1848. Importantly, though, despite an increasing sympathy for some socialist ideas he still maintained his critical distance. This is also true of his most mature statement on socialism in the unfinished *Chapters on Socialism* edited and published posthumously by Helen Taylor in 1879, six years after Mill's death.

64. Mill, *Principles of Political Economy. Collected Works*, Vol. II, p. 208.

65. Lekachman, *A History of Economic Ideas*, p. 195. Interestingly, Melvin Richter has noted that in the nineteenth century, 'intellectuals who share the dominant assumptions and values of their society, but who deplore the extent to which the practices and institutions of that society failed to embody them, will characteristically formulate their criticisms in moral terms'; see Richter, 'Intellectual and class alienation: Oxford Idealist diagnoses and prescription', *Archives européennes de sociologie*, VII (1966) pp. 1–26. As I argue, this concentration on the moral behaviour of individuals, rather than on social

institutions, is a characteristic of the social-problem novelists. In their case I suggest that it results from the way they share the same conceptual framework as that which underwrites the doctrines which they attempt to criticise.

66. Lekachman, *A History of Economic Ideas*, pp. 195–6.
67. Mill's continuing engagement with classical political economy, particularly through changes made in the subsequent editions of the *Principles*, led him in 1869 to repudiate one of its major tenets, the Wages Fund theory. The recantation appeared in a review of a book by William Thornton. Interestingly, however, in the seventh edition of the *Principles*, published in 1871, no revisions were made to accommodate this change in position. Landreth and Colander comment that Mill had 'held that these new developments [were] "not yet ripe for incorporation in a general treatise on Political Economy"', despite the fact that the fifth edition of the *Principles* (1862) had already anticipated some of Thornton's arguments. They conclude that the 'inconsistency' was 'simply another example of Mill's attempts to stay within the general framework of classical economics' (Landreth and Colander, *History of Economic Thought*, p. 158).
68. Abrams, *The Origins of British Sociology*, p. 11.
69. Ibid.
70. Quoted by Abrams, ibid., p. 19.
71. Ibid.
72. Ibid., p. 21.
73. In this respect, Henry Mayhew's popular documentation of individual working-class lives, *London Labour and the London Poor* (London, 1861–2), was typical of its time.
74. See Abrams, p. 14.
75. Quoted in ibid., p. 11.
76. Abrams, ibid., p. 15.
77. Ibid., p. 17.
78. Ibid., p. 20.
79. Ibid., p. 27.
80. In response to this challenge, the Society retrenched, narrowing its interests by concentrating on mathematics rather than on social policy. In the 1890s new approaches to social reform developed outside the Society, and the influence of statistics diminished. It came to be seen as 'only one strand – more or less the official one, the mechanism of government action – in an increasingly diverse reaction to the problem of tying social knowledge to social change' (Abrams, p. 30). All this once again occurred several decades after the period in which the social-problem novels were written.
81. Quoted in Abrams, ibid., p. 39.
82. Ibid., p. 39.
83. Ibid., p. 38.
84. Quoted in ibid., p. 43.
85. Collini, *Liberalism and Sociology*, p. 32. Collini suggests three reasons why this situation changed 'very rapidly' in the 1880s: 'the first ... was the establishment of avowedly Socialist organizations ... The

second was the immense popularity of the ideas of Henry George,
widely perceived at the time as Socialist ... The third development
was the increasing radicalism of liberal legislation' (p. 33).

86. J. F. C. Harrison, *Robert Owen and the Owenites in Britain and America*
(London, 1969) p. 46. Harrison's is the standard study of Owen and
his followers, and I have drawn extensively upon it.

87. Ibid., p. 6.

88. *Cooperative Magazine*, I (1826) pp. 3–5; quoted in Harrison, *Robert
Owen and the Owenites*, p. 49. It is perhaps worth noting that Owen's
Utilitarianism was no less contradictory than that of Bentham. As
Harrison argues, Owen recognised that 'happiness is a condition of
man's self-realization as a complete human being', but he also
suggested that 'man should live for others as well as himself; the
individual has a duty to live for the happiness of the greatest
number, and in so doing will also promote his own highest
happiness'. Although this argument effectively 'abandoned'
Hedonism, it nevertheless left Owen with a 'theory of ethics which
was inconsistent', for it 'accounted for moral issues in non-moral
terms' (ibid., pp. 48–9).

89. Robert Owen, *Book of the New Moral World*, quoted in Harrison, p. 79.

90. Harrison, *Robert Owen and the Owenites*, p. 79.

91. William Thompson, *Inquiry into the Principles of the Distribution of
Wealth* (London, 1824) p. 300; quoted in Harrison, p. 80.

92. Harrison, *Robert Owen and the Owenites*, p. 62.

93. Ibid., p. 175.

94. Owen, *Report to the County of Lanark*, in *Life of Robert Owen*, Vol. 1A
(London, 1858) p. 282; quoted in Harrison, *Robert Owen and the
Owenites*, p. 56.

95. Owen, *New Moral World*, 28 May 1842; quoted in Harrison, pp. 56–7.

96. Harrison suggests that as early as 1819 Owenites had to defend themselves against the charges of 'Utopianism'. It is worth noting that
some elements of Owen's thinking resurface in minor literary works
(such as Walter Besant's and James Rice's *The Monks of Thelema*
(London, 1878)) which were published later in the century when
there was a renewed interest in socialism, and when socialist ideas
began to be taken more seriously.

97. As Harrison suggests, a fundamental weakness in Owen's thought
was a kind of intellectual belatedness – that is, Owen's adoption of a
'complex of ideas' which although considered 'commonplaces' of eighteenth-
century thought were considered 'démodé' by the 1820s, when 'the
Romantic reaction to the Enlightenment was in full swing' (Harrison,
Robert Owen and the Owenites, pp. 83–7). It is also worth noting
that nostalgia for an ideal community located in the past was a
commonplace in writing throughout the nineteenth century, occur-
ring in works across all shades of the political spectrum, from the
authoritarianism of Carlyle's model society in *Past and Present* to
William Morris's non-hierarchical socialist paradise in *News from
Nowhere*.

98. [Robert Torrens] 'Art. XI. Mr Owen's Plans for Relieving National Distress', *Edinburgh Review*, 32 (1819) pp. 453–77. The measured tone of Torrens's attack was set in the opening paragraphs: 'We can assure Mr Owen, that no particle of angry feeling mingles itself with our opposition, and that we cordially esteem the man whose projects we venture unequivocally to condemn' (p. 454). Harrison comments that labour historians, intent on tracing a link between Owenism and later socialist movements in Britain, have tended to exaggerate the significance of the 'Owenite critique of capitalism'. He argues that 'the number of Owenites who made original contributions to economic theory was very small, and the economic content of Owenism can be traced to a few key sources which were drawn upon many times' (Harrison, *Robert Owen and the Owenites*, pp. 63–4).

99. Ibid., p. 69.

100. Later in the century John Ruskin and William Morris used similar arguments in an attempt to redefine the value of labour and work, although it is perhaps worth pointing out that Ruskin and Morris nevertheless had very different political views. While Morris's theory of the value of labour was incorporated in a socialist perspective (and one much more radical than that envisaged by Owen), Ruskin used exactly the same argument to underwrite a hierarchical, authoritarian model of society.

101. Harrison, *Robert Owen and the Owenites*, p. 74.

102. Owen, *Book of the New Moral World*, Part 6 (London, 1844) p. 48; quoted in Harrison, ibid., p. 60.

103. Harrison, ibid., p. 217.

104. There were also more profound problems with Owen's view of character formation: they partly had to do with his terminology – what he meant by 'circumstances' and 'arrangements'; and partly to do with an apparent contradiction at the heart of his argument. As Harrison explains, 'even sympathizers with Owen professed difficulties in reconciling his statement that men were products of circumstances over which they had no control, with his apparent assumption that by acting rationally they could control those very same circumstances' (ibid., p. 82).

105. None of this is to deny the existence of a strong element of political or class prejudice in the rejection of Owen's ideas. The reader might, for example, suspect a connection between the general hostility to Owen (among a mainly middle-class intellectual establishment) and his involvement in the development of trades unions – circumstances which in turn may be linked to the largely negative portrayal of such collective bodies in the social-problem novels. At the same time, though, it is equally likely that one of the reasons why such political prejudices were so easy to exercise was precisely because intellectually and theoretically Owen's arguments were so unpersuasive. So, for example, it is no accident that the serious attention afforded to socialism in the last quarter of the century coincides not only with changes in the political climate but also with changes within

intellectual culture, particularly the development in Britain of a variety of new forms of social theory.

106. Charles Darwin, quoted in Ernst Mayr, *One Long Argument: Charles Darwin and the Genesis of Modern Evolutionary Thought* (Cambridge, Mass., 1991; Harmondsworth, 1993) p. 84. See also Sir Gavin de Beer (ed.), *Darwin's Notebooks on Transmutation of Species* (London, 1960).

107. Darwin, quoted in Mayr (ibid., p. 70); see Nora Barlow (ed.), *Autobiography of Charles Darwin 1809–1882* (London, 1958).

108. It is worth pointing out that neither explanation is incompatible with the other; indeed to interpret animal-breeding as a process of 'artificial selection' analogous to the process of selection which occurs in nature presupposes a certain conceptual set – a certain way of thinking – which in all likelihood is derived from the same nineteenth-century intellectual norms which defined contemporary explanations of industrialism.

109. Explanations of Darwin's thought are numerous and detailed. For the non-specialist, one of the most accessible and authoritative, which I have drawn upon here, is Ernst Mayr's popular and lucid account of the significance of Darwin to modern evolutionary biology, *One Long Argument* (see note 106). A more dramatic account is provided by Adrian Desmond and James Moore, *Darwin* (Harmondsworth, 1991). See particularly Chapter 18, 'Marriage and Malthusian Respectability' which tries to reconstruct what it might have meant for Darwin to read Malthus.

110. Mayr, in *One Long Argument*, documents this dispute on pp. 68–89; he advocates the first view.

111. Ibid., pp. 184 and 179.

112. Ibid., p. 184.

113. Desmond and Moore, *Darwin*, pp. 275–6.

114. Mayr, *One Long Argument*, p. 87.

115. [Unsigned review], 'A Triad of Novelists', *Fraser's Magazine*, XLII (1850) p. 574.

Notes to Chapter 4

With the exception of the Oxford editions of *Hard Times* and *Felix Holt* there are no standard modern editions of the social-problem novels referred to in this chapter. For convenience (and bearing in mind the needs of a student readership), I have therefore given all references to easily available paperback editions. *Hard Times* and *North and South* both appeared first in serial form in *Household Words*. In the case of *Hard Times* the book version differs only in very minor ways from the serialised version. By contrast, Gaskell made substantive revisions to the book version of *North and South*, the most important of which was the expansion of the concluding chapter into two new chapters (see note 52). She made further revisions to the second edition. *Felix Holt*, *Sybil*, *Mary Barton* and *Alton Locke* were all published originally as books; and in each case there are textual variants between the first edition and subsequent revised editions. It is clearly beyond the scope of this book to take account either of textual variants or of different forms of publication (but for a discussion of some of the theoretical issues involved here see, for example, Jerome J. McGann, *The Textual Condition* (Princeton, NJ, 1991) or D. F. McKenzie, *Bibliography and the Sociology of Texts* (London, 1986); and for some of the practical issues, see Allan C. Dooley, *Author and Printer in Victorian England* (London, 1992)). More importantly (and with the exception of *North and South* which I discuss later), the broad strategies of the novels are not affected by textual variants.

1. Critics such as Catherine Gallagher (*The Industrial Reformation of English Fiction* (London, 1985)) and Peter Keating (*The Working Class in Victorian Fiction* (London, 1971)) have included in the genre works such as Charlotte Elizabeth Tonna's *Helen Fleetwood* (London, 1841), Geraldine Jewsbury's *Marian Withers* (London, 1851), Harriet Martineau's *Illustrations of Political Economy* (London, 1832–4) and Frances Trollope's *Life and Adventures of Michael Armstrong, the Factory Boy* (London, 1840).

2. David Craig, 'Introduction', in Charles Dickens, *Hard Times* (Harmondsworth, 1986) p. 37.

3. Quoted in John Lucas, 'Mrs Gaskell and Brotherhood', in David Howard, John Lucas and John Goode (eds), *Tradition and Tolerance in Nineteenth-Century Fiction* (London, 1966) p. 178.

4. David Lodge, 'The French Revolution and the Condition of England: Crowds and Power in the Early Victorian Novel', in Ceri Crossley and Ian Small (eds), *The French Revolution and British Culture* (Oxford, 1989) pp. 123–40. Lodge attributes the use of revolutionary rhetoric to politics – to Dickens's middle-class fear of working-class agitation. However, it is worth noting that the fear of the mob was not simply class-based; in the eyes of many Victorians (particularly historians of the French Revolution) the collective consciousness of the mob undermined notions of individual responsibility and therefore of moral agency. In such a view, mob activity by definition would be immoral, anarchic and violent. See my account of revolutionary rhetoric in *The British Avant-Garde: The Theory and Politics of Tradition* (Hemel Hempstead, 1991) pp. 52–6; see also Hedva Ben-Israel, *Historians on the French Revolution* (Cambridge, 1968).

5. Raymond Williams, *Culture and Society, 1780–1950* (Harmondsworth, 1963) p. 106.

6. Lucas, 'Mrs Gaskell and Brotherhood', p. 185.

7. Ibid., p. 183.

8. Catherine Gallagher, *The Industrial Reformation of English Fiction*, p. 148.

9. Ibid., p. 153.

10. Dickens, *Household Words*, 4 Feb. 1854; quoted in John Halloway, '*Hard Times*: A History and a Criticism', in John Cross and Gabriel Pearson (eds), *Dickens and the Twentieth Century* (London, 1962, 1966) p. 166.

11. See Herbert L. Sussman, *Victorians and the Machine* (Cambridge, Mass., 1968).
12. Ibid., p. 55.
13. See, for example, David Craig's discussion of education in the Introduction to his edition of the novel, or Holloway's reference to Dickens's parody of volumes such as Charles Knight's *Store of Knowledge* (in Holloway, '*Hard Times*', pp. 161–3). It will be clear from the discussion which follows that I disagree with Holloway's censure of Dickens for failing to differentiate between different kinds of Utilitarian doctrines. I argue that the eclecticism of Dickens's sources – his failure to discriminate between, say, McCulloch or James Mill, together with his throw-away references to, say, the 'two younger' Gradgrinds, 'Adam Smith and Malthus' – is intrinsic to his polemic, to his claim that *all* the varieties of Utilitarianism and political economy are vitiated by the particular model of human nature which underwrites them.
14. See François Crouzet, *The Victorian Economy*, trans. A. S. Forster (London, 1982); and for a specific account of the relative technological developments in Britain and France, and the overall superiority of British manufacturing, see John Harris, 'The Transfer of Technology Between Britain and France and the French Revolution', in Crossley and Small (eds), *The French Revolution and British Culture*, pp. 156–86.
15. Dickens, *Hard Times*, ed. David Craig, p. 303. All subsequent references are to this edition.
16. Ibid., p. 304.
17. The possibility of divorce through reasons other than adultery was debated in the House of Lords in June 1854, although the Bill did not go to the Commons. The Divorce Act of 1857 simplified divorce procedures by establishing a new Court of Probate and Divorce, thus effectively making divorce a matter of civil rather than canon law. David Craig, following suggestions by John Butt and Kathleen Tillotson in *Dickens at Work* (Oxford, 1957), speculates that Dickens may have had a specific source in mind, a case presided over by a Judge Maule who, in 1848, showed his contempt for the law by sentencing a man to one day in prison for bigamy (see Craig, 'Introduction', p. 326).
18. Dickens, *Hard Times*, p. 77.
19. The troping of male kindness in terms of eccentricity may also be an attempt to find a 'safe' – that is, an unfeminised – way of talking about a caring masculinity.
20. See Kathleen Tillotson, *Novelists of the Eighteen-Forties* (Oxford, 1954) p. 202; Sheila Smith, *The Other Nation; The Poor in English Novels of the 1840s and 1850s* (Oxford, 1980) p. 84; and Lucas, 'Mrs Gaskell and Brotherhood', p. 162.
21. Jenny Uglow, *Elizabeth Gaskell: A Habit of Stories* (London, 1993, 1994) p. 3.
22. Ibid., p. 186. For the correspondence between Mrs Gaskell and Edward Chapman, see J. A. V. Chapple and Arthur Pollard (eds), *The Letters of Mrs Gaskell* (Manchester, 1966).

23. John Lucas, 'Mrs Gaskell and Brotherhood', p. 173.
24. Raymond Williams, *Culture and Society*, p. 102.
25. Catherine Gallagher offered an alternative view; she attempted to provide some kind of 'context' (a historical explanation) for *Mary Barton*'s formal and ideological contradictions. In particular she drew attention to the importance of Gaskell's Unitarian beliefs. The limitations of her argument can be glimpsed in her attempt to explain the relationship between Unitarian theology and the economic discourses in the novel. She seems to imply that a belief in determinism maps on to support for the tenets of political economy; so she argues that the providential plots of Harriet Martineau's stories correspond to the 'laws' of the free market: in both political economy and what Gallagher terms Unitarianism's 'first phase', 'religious and socio-economic determinism' coincide (*The Industrial Reformation of English Fiction*, p. 52). By contrast, a belief in free will enables the complacency of political economy to be questioned; so Gallagher links Gaskell's knowledge of James Martineau's work with *Mary Barton*'s moral critique of economics (p. 64). Gallagher finally implies that a confusion about economic issues (the failure of both these novelists to provide a coherent economic solution to social problems) maps on to a parallel confusion about the competing claims of free will and determinism. The limitation with this argument is that Gallagher takes for granted what she needs to prove: that there *is* a necessary relationship between debates about free will and determinism and debates about economics. Whether or not a certain religious debate corresponds to certain ways of understanding economic issues, such a conjunction of events does not *on its own* explain the limits to economic understanding. As I argued in Chapter 3, there were other, much more compelling reasons why it was difficult for any writer (Unitarian or otherwise) to articulate a coherent economic criticism of political economy.
26. For an account of the publication details of *Mary Barton*, see Uglow, *Elizabeth Gaskell*, pp. 181–8.
27. Ibid., p. 192.
28. Ibid., p. 44.
29. Ibid., pp. 86–8.
30. Ibid., p. 87.
31. Ibid.
32. My suggestion here is that Unitarian debates took place within certain limits, that arguments were formulated within certain intellectual paradigms. Catherine Gallagher is certainly correct to see a tension in Unitarian thought between determinism and free will, but her concentration on this opposition tends to obscure the fundamental point of continuity between the two doctrines: both take for granted the primacy of the individual, and both assume that the route to right understanding is through individual agency, guaranteed either by rational enquiry or by emotional intuition. Priestley's necessitarianism, for all its arid emphasis on a divine chain of predetermined causal laws, did not deny the potency of individual action. It is precisely this assumption about the primacy of the individual which I

argue placed limits on Unitarian responses to both social problems and political economy.

33. Uglow, *Elizabeth Gaskell*, p. 188.
34. See William Stevenson, 'The Political Economist: Essay First', *Blackwoods Magazine*, XV (1824) p. 524.
35. Ibid., p. 523.
36. See Stevenson, 'The Political Economist: Essay II – Part I', *Blackwoods Magazine*, XV (1824) pp. 643–55, and 'The Political Economist: Essay II – Part II', *Blackwoods Magazine*, XVI (1824) pp. 34–6.
37. Stevenson, 'The Political Economist: Essay III – Part I', *Blackwoods Magazine*, XVI (1825) p. 207 (emphasis added).
38. Stevenson, 'The Political Economist: Essay III – Part II', *Blackwoods Magazine*, XVII (1825) p. 208.
39. Ibid., p. 220.
40. Elizabeth Gaskell, *Mary Barton*, ed. Stephen Gill (Harmondsworth, 1970, 1985) pp. 455–6. All subsequent references are to this edition.
41. Ibid., p. 460.
42. Ibid., p. 457.
43. Ibid., p. 397.
44. Ibid., p. 152.
45. Martin Dodsworth, 'Introduction', in Elizabeth Gaskell, *North and South*, ed. Dorothy Collin (Harmondsworth, 1970, 1986) pp. 7–26. Dodsworth argues that the novel is better understood in relation to Charlotte Brontë's works, and that critics such as Raymond Williams and John Lucas were obliged to 'exaggerate the importance of the "industrial" and "social-problem" matter in *North and South* and *Mary Barton* in order fully to develop the more general themes of cultural history which are their true concern' (p. 9). However, it is also worth noting that with *North and South* (as with *Mary Barton*) the choice of title was again Gaskell's publisher's (in this instance Dickens). Gaskell initially offered *Margaret Hale*; Dickens's suggestion gives much greater emphasis to the 'social-problem' theme. See Edgar Wright, *Mrs Gaskell: The Basis for Reassessment* (Oxford, 1965) p. 131.
46. For example, David Lodge, in 'The French Revolution and the Condition of England', has argued that the mob violence in Chapter 22 functions as a symbol of the repressed sexual tensions between Margaret and Thornton.
47. Gallagher, *The Industrial Reformation of English Fiction*, p. 169.
48. Elizabeth Gaskell, *North and South*, ed. Dorothy Collin, p. 48. All subsequent references are to this edition.
49. Ibid., p. 113.
50. Ibid., p. 147.
51. Ibid., p. 208.
52. Gaskell, an unpublished letter to Maria James (Brotherton Collection); quoted in Uglow, *Elizabeth Gaskell*, p. 368.
53. As Uglow notes, Gaskell's disclaimer was a little disingenuous. Serialisation had been an unusually fraught process, but Gaskell had been as much to blame as her editor, Charles Dickens, for her

constant requests for more space and more time had disrupted Dickens's publishing schedule. For an account of their 'difficult' relationship, see Uglow, *Mrs Gaskell*, pp. 355–68; see also Edgar Wright, *Mrs Gaskell: The Basis For Reassessment* (Oxford, 1965) pp. 129–31.

54. Gaskell, *North and South*, pp. 183–4.
55. Ibid., p. 204.
56. Ibid., p. 293.
57. Ibid., p. 125.
58. Ibid., p. 526.
59. The antipathy of the English mind to a revolutionary understanding of social change is also voiced much earlier in the novel when Alton alludes to an English tradition of liberty articulated through 'Magna Charta and the Habeas Corpus Act, Hampden's resistance to ship-money, and the calm righteous might of 1688'. The mistake of the Chartists is to interpret this historical tradition as being analogous to the French conception of liberty. As British historians such as Burke and Macaulay had emphasised (and as Kingsley would later as an academic historian), the English 'revolution' of 1688 was about continuity and preservation, and not about wholesale change.
60. Charles Kingsley, *Alton Locke*, ed. Elizabeth A. Cripps (Oxford, 1983) p. 386. All subsequent references are to this edition.
61. Religious troping in *Alton Locke* refers to the orthodoxy of the Anglican church. Other forms of religious doctrine, particularly dissenting religions, are criticised in the novel for their divisiveness. So the chief reason for Alton's rejection of his mother's religion – her Calvinism – was the socially divisive nature of its model of humanity. Instead of providing a point of identification between individuals, the doctrine of the elect posits a rigid separation between the 'one human being out of a thousand' who is chosen, and the 'other nine hundred and ninety-nine [who] were lost and damned from their birth-hour'. Such a doctrine could hardy satisfy the working man's craving for 'some idea which gives equal hopes, claims, and deliverances, to all mankind alike' precisely because it posited a plural rather than a universal conception of human nature.
62. It is worth noting here that when in 1860 Kingsley became Regius Professor of Modern History at Cambridge, his inaugural lecture, *The Limits of Exact Science as Applied to History* (Cambridge, 1860), elaborated exactly this line of argument. So he attacked what he termed 'French philosophies of history' and the influence on history of 'positivist sciences', arguing that history properly belonged to the moral sciences and that historical laws, such as they were, only existed in 'persons; in the actions of human beings'. As one cultural historian has succinctly commented: in Kingsley's views, 'human history came about through the action of great individuals inspired by God'. See Ian Small, *Conditions for Criticism: Authority, Knowledge, and Literature in the Late Nineteenth Century* (Oxford, 1991) p. 50.
63. Kingsley, *Alton Locke*, pp. 364 and 378.
64. See Gallagher, *The Industrial Reformation of English Fiction*, pp. 88–110.
65. Kingsley, *Alton Locke*, p. 104.

66. It is worth noting in passing that the social 'experiments' carried out by Lord Lynedale are also dismissed as mere 'philanthropy' (although on a large scale). Moreover, Lynedale is explicitly identified with the forms of knowledge which the novel judges to be false; so he is described as thinking of himself as a 'Mirabeau', and he reads political economy: 'McCulloch on Taxation' lies on his desk, and when planning his model farm he brings in 'one of the first political economists of the day ... in order to work out for him a table of proportionate remuneration'. More significant, perhaps, is Eleanor's allusion to Lynedale's ambitions when she describes herself as wanting at one point to be 'a philanthropist, a philosopher, a feudal queen, amid the blessings and praise of dependent hundreds'. To realise that idea she turned the 'whole force' of her intellect to 'the study of history, of social and economic questions. From Bentham and Malthus to Fourier and Proudhon' (Kingsley, *Alton Locke*, p. 374).

67. Kingsley, *Alton Locke*, p. 376.

68. From the 'Prefatory Memoir' by Thomas Hughes included in the 1876 edition of *Alton Locke*; quoted in ibid., p. xix.

69. Benjamin Disraeli, *Sybil, or the Two Nations*, ed. Thom Braun (Harmondsworth, 1980, 1985) pp. 88–9. All subsequent references are to this edition.

70. Ibid., p. 440.

71. R. A. Butler, 'Introduction', in Disraeli, *Sybil*, p. 13.

72. In this respect it is significant that the most dangerous agitators in the strike as it affects Mowbray turn out to be not the miners, nor the disenfranchised power-loom weavers, nor indeed the exploited factory workers, but rather Bishop Hatton and the 'Hellcats'. Wodgate, with its division between 'aristocratic' employers and impoverished employees is an exaggerated version of the political system which in Disraeli's view had produced the 'two nations'. Hatton's involvement in the strike is to do with self-aggrandisement, rather than economic hardship. In this way, the strike and the mob violence which accompanies it serve to illustrate the general theme of political corruption, and consequently become dissociated from the more troubling idea that strikes might in part be justified by economic conditions.

73. Thom Braun, 'Appendix', in Disraeli, *Sybil*, p. 501. In his appendix to the Penguin edition Braun gives a useful summary of Disraeli's view of history. He also raises the interesting question that Disraeli's history might have been quite deliberately distorted; designed, as Robert Blake has argued, 'to puncture the balloon of early Victorian complacency, and by deliberate paradoxes to make people think'. Whether or not Disraeli was consciously rewriting history to serve his own particular political views, the practice was fairly common. For example, a liberal such as Edward Freedman (ironically originally a Tory), and a socialist such as William Morris, could both find in the medieval period precedents for their own political views. At the same time there is no reason to think that Disraeli (like Freedman and Morris) did not have absolute confidence in his version of the past.

For a more complex account of the problems in Disraeli's use of history, see Gallagher, *The Industrial Reformation of English Fiction*, pp. 200–18.

Notes to Chapter 5

1. [George Eliot], 'Art. II. – The Natural History of German Life', *Westminster Review*, n.s. 10 (1856) pp. 51–79.
2. Ibid., p. 52.
3. Ibid., p. 55.
4. Ibid., pp. 52 and 55.
5. Ibid., p. 54.
6. Ibid., p. 55.
7. Ibid., p. 71 (Eliot's emphasis).
8. Peter Coveney, 'Introduction', in George Eliot, *Felix Holt*, ed. Peter Coveney (Harmondsworth, 1972, 1987) p. 29. All subsequent references to *Felix Holt* are from this edition.
9. 'The Natural History of German Life', pp. 69–70. It is important not to confuse Eliot's famous comment in Chapter 3 of *Felix Holt* – that 'there is no private life which has not been determined by a wider public life' – with a form of social determinism. As the novel demonstrates, every form of public life is itself a product of the behaviours (usually selfish) of particular, but powerful individuals.
10. Ibid., p. 77.
11. Ibid. The *OED* locates the origin of the German term 'Philister' in the 1820s as a reference to a non-University educated member of the population. Acknowledging this derivation, Eliot is concerned with its wider, cultural use.
12. Ibid., pp. 64–5.
13. Eliot, *Felix Holt*, pp. 276–7.
14. Eliot, 'The Natural History of German Life', p. 69.
15. Gallagher's densely argued account of *Felix Holt* also connects Eliot's use of realism to the problematic relationship between her interest in 'facts' and her apparent separation of them from the realm of 'value'. However, Gallagher locates this feature of Eliot's work within a specific political debate about representation, rather than the broader context sketched in this book. See Catherine Gallagher, *The Industrial Reformation of English Fiction* (London, 1985) pp. 219–67.
16. For a detailed account of Eliot's research during the writing of *Felix Holt* see Fred C. Thompson, 'Introduction', in George Eliot, *Felix Holt, the Radical*, ed. Fred C. Thompson (Oxford, 1980) pp. xiii–xxx. See also Thompson's earlier article: 'The Genesis of *Felix Holt*', *PMLA*, 74 (1959) pp. 576–84. Eliot's notebook jottings reveal that she also consulted Parliamentary Reports on agriculture (1833) and on the Nuneaton rioters, as well as Samuel Bamford's *Passages from the Life of a Radical* (London, 1840). At this time she was also reading John Stuart Mill's *Principles of Political Economy* as well some of Comte's

'Social Science' in Harriet Martineau's edition (see Harriet Martineau, *The Positive Philosophy of Auguste Comte* (London, 1853)).
17. Eliot, *Felix Holt*, p. 399.
18. Ibid., pp. 623 and 625.
19. Ibid., p. 398.
20. Ibid., pp. 528–9.
21. Gallagher, *The Industrial Reformation of English Fiction*, p. 244.
22. Interestingly Eliot's argument here seems to point to a pattern in late nineteenth-century writing on ethical choices, where the good (or, more specifically, the reason to act morally) is simply invoked.
23. See Fred C. Thompson, 'Introduction', pp. xxii–xxv. Interestingly some modern editions of the novel have seen fit to provide the reader with a summary of the legal plot; see, for example, that provided by Coveney in the Penguin edition.
24. Thompson, 'Introduction', p. xiv.
25. Peter Coveney (ed.), *Felix Holt*, p. 38.

Select Bibliography

Abrams, Philip, *The Origins of British Sociology 1834–1914* (Chicago, Ill., 1972).

Althusser, Louis, *For Marx*, trans. Ben Brewster (London, 1969).

Althusser, Louis, *Politics and History*, trans. Ben Brewster (London, 1974).

Bamford, Samuel, *Passages from the Life of a Radical* (London, 1840).

Barlow, Nora (ed.), *Autobiography of Charles Darwin 1809–1882* (London, 1958).

Beer, Sir Gavin de (ed.), *Darwin's Notebooks on Transmutation of Species* (London, 1960).

Ben-Israel, Hedva, *Historians on the French Revolution* (Cambridge, 1968).

Bentham, Jeremy, *An Introduction to the Principles of Morals and Legislation*, eds J. H. Burns and H. L. A. Hart (London, 1982).

Besant, Walter and James Rice, *The Monks of Thelema* (London, 1878).

Blaug, Mark, *Ricardian Economics: A Historical Study* (New Haven, Conn., 1958).

Buckle, Henry, *History of Civilization in England* (London, 1857–61).

Butt, John and Kathleen Tillotson, *Dickens at Work* (Oxford, 1957).

Caporaso, James A. and David P. Levine, *Theories of Political Economy* (Cambridge, 1992).

Carlyle, Thomas, *Past and Present* (London, 1843).

Carlyle, Thomas, *Selected Writings*, ed. Alan Shelston (London, 1986).

Cazamian, Louis, *The Social Novel in England 1830–1850*, trans. Martin Fido (London, 1973).

Chapple, J. A. V. and Arthur Pollard (eds), *The Letters of Mrs Gaskell* (Manchester, 1966).

Collini, Stefan, *Liberalism and Sociology: L. T. Hobhouse and Political Argument in England 1880–1914* (Cambridge, 1979).

Crouzet, François, *The Victorian Economy*, trans. A. S. Forster (London, 1982).

Culler, Jonathan, *Structuralist Poetics* (London, 1975).

Danto, Arthur C., *Narration and Knowledge* (New York, 1985).

Darwin, Charles, *On The Origin of Species* (London, 1959).

Desmond, Adrian and James Moore, *Darwin* (Harmondsworth, 1991).

Dickens, Charles, *Hard Times*, ed. David Craig (Harmondsworth, 1986).

Disraeli, Benjamin, *Sybil, or the Two Nations*, ed. Thom Braun (Harmondsworth, 1985).

Doeser, M. C. and J. N. Kraay (eds), *Facts and Values* (Dordrecht, 1986).

Dooley, Allan C., *Author and Printer in Victorian England* (London, 1992).

Eliot, George, 'Art. II. – The Natural History of German Life', *Westminster Review*, n.s. 10 (1856) pp. 51–79.

Eliot, George, *Felix Holt, the Radical*, ed. Peter Coveney (Harmondsworth, 1987).

Eliot, George, *Felix Holt, the Radical*, ed. Fred C. Thompson (Oxford, 1980).

Foucault, Michel, *The Order of Things* (London, 1970).

Foucault, Michel, *The Archeology of Knowledge* (London, 1972).

Gagnier, Regenia, *Subjectivities* (Oxford, 1991).

Gagnier, Regenia, 'On the Insatiability of Human Wants: Economic and Aesthetic Man', *Victorian Studies*, 36, 2 (1993) pp. 125–53.

Gallagher, Catherine, *The Industrial Reformation of English Fiction* (London, 1985).

Gaskell, Elizabeth, *Mary Barton*, ed. Stephen Gill (Harmondsworth, 1985).

Gaskell, Elizabeth, *North and South*, ed. Dorothy Collin (Harmondsworth, 1986).

Greenblatt, Stephen, *Shakespearean Negotiations* (Oxford, 1988).

Greenblatt, Stephen, 'Resonance and Wonder', in Peter Collier and Helga Geyer-Ryan (eds), *Literary Theory Today* (Oxford, 1990) pp. 74–90.

Guess, Raymond, *The Idea of a Critical Theory* (Cambridge, 1981).

Guy, Josephine M., *The British Avant-Garde: The Theory and Politics of Tradition* (Hemel Hempstead, 1991).

Guy, Josephine M. and Ian Small, *Politics and Value in English Studies* (Cambridge, 1993).

Harris, John, 'The Transfer of Technology Between Britain and France and the French Revolution', in Ceri Crossley and Ian Small (eds), *The French Revolution and British Culture* (Oxford, 1989) pp. 156–86.

Harrison, J. F. C., *Robert Owen and the Owenites in Britain and America* (London, 1969).

Hollander, Samuel, *The Economics of John Stuart Mill*, 2 vols (Basil Blackwell, 1985).

Howard, David, John Lucas and John Goode (eds), *Tradition and Tolerance in Nineteenth-Century Fiction* (London, 1966).

Holloway, John, '*Hard Times*: A History and a Criticism', in John Gross and Gabriel Pearson (eds), *Dickens and the Twentieth Century* (London, 1962, 1966) pp. 159–74.

Hutchinson, T. W., *Review of Economic Doctrines 1870–1929* (Westport, Conn., 1975).

Hutchinson, T. W., *On Revolutions and Progress in Economic Knowledge* (Cambridge, 1978).

Hyndman, H. M., *England for All: The Text Book of Democracy* (London, 1881).

Landreth, Harry and David C. Colander, *History of Economic Thought*, 2nd edn (Boston, Mass., 1980).

James, Susan, 'Althusserian Materialism in England', in Ceri Crossley and Ian Small (eds), *Studies in Anglo-French Cultural Relations* (London, 1988) pp. 187–219.

Jewsbury, Geraldine, *Marian Withers* (London, 1851).

Keating, Peter, *The Working Class in Victorian Fiction* (London, 1971).

Kelly, P. J., *Utilitarianism and Distributive Justice* (Oxford, 1990).

Kettle, Arnold, 'The Early Victorian Social Problem Novel', in Boris Ford (ed.), *Dickens to Hardy: The Pelican Guide to English Literature*, Vol. 6 (Harmondsworth, 1958) pp. 169–87.

Kingsley, Charles, *The Limits of Exact Science as Applied to History* (Cambridge, 1860).

Kingsley, Charles, *Alton Locke*, ed. Elizabeth Cripps (Oxford, 1983).

Knight, Charles, *Knight's Store of Knowledge* (London, 1841).
Knights, L. C., *Drama and Society in the Age of Jonson* (London, 1937).
Leavis, F. R., *The Great Tradition* (London, 1948).
Lekachman, Robert, *A History of Economic Ideas* (New York, 1959).
Levinson, Marjorie, Marilyn Butler, Jerome McGann and Paul Hamilton, *Rethinking Historicism* (Oxford, 1989).
Lodge, David, *Language of Fiction* (London, 1966).
Lodge, David (ed.), *Modern Criticism and Theory: A Reader* (London, 1988).
Lodge, David, 'The French Revolution and the Condition of England: Crowds and Power in the Early Victorian Novel', in Ceri Crossley and Ian Small (eds), *The French Revolution and British Culture* (Oxford, 1989) pp. 123–40.
Lukes, Steven, *Individualism* (Oxford, 1973).
McCulloch, J. R., *The Principles of Political Economy* (Edinburgh, 1825).
McGann, Jerome J., *The Textual Condition* (Princeton, NJ, 1991).
McLellan, David, *Ideology* (Milton Keynes, 1986).
McKenzie, D. F., *Bibliography and the Sociology of Texts* (London, 1986).
Malthus, T. R., *An Essay on the Principle of Population*, ed. Patricia James (Cambridge, 1989).
Malthus, T. R., *An Essay on the Principle of Population*, ed. Donald Winch (Cambridge, 1992).
Martineau, Harriet, *Illustrations of Political Economy* (London, 1832–4).
Martineau, Harriet, *The Positive Philosophy of Auguste Comte* (London, 1853).
Mayhew, Henry, *London Labour and the London Poor* (London, 1861–2).
Mayr, Ernst, *One Long Argument: Charles Darwin and the Genesis of Modern Evolutionary Thought* (Harmondsworth, 1993).
Mill, John Stuart, *A System of Logic: Ratiocinative and Inductive. Collected Works of John Stuart Mill*, Vols VII and VIII (Toronto, 1967).
Mill, John Stuart, 'On the Definition of Political Economy; and on the Method of Investigation Proper to it', in *Essays on Economics and Society. Collected Works of John Stuart Mill*, Vol. IV (Toronto, 1967).
Mill, John Stuart, *Principles of Political Economy. Collected Works of John Stuart Mill*, Vols II and III (Toronto, 1967).
Morris, William, *News from Nowhere* (London, 1891).
Owen, Robert, *A New View of Society* (London, 1813).
Owen, Robert, *Book of the New Moral World* (London, 1836).
Owen, Robert, *Life of Robert Owen*, Vol. 1A (London, 1858).
Paley, William, *Principles of Moral and Political Philosophy* (London, 1785).
Plamenatz, John, *The English Utilitarians* (Oxford, 1966).
Plotkin, Henry, *The Nature of Knowledge* (London, 1994).
Ricardo, David, *On The Principles of Political Economy, and Taxation* (London, 1817).
Richter, Melvin, 'Intellectual and class alienation: Oxford Idealist diagnoses and prescription', *Archives européennes de sociologie*, VII (1966) pp. 1–26.
Roberts, David, *Victorian Origins of the British Welfare State* (New Haven, Conn., 1960).
Ruskin, John, *Unto this Last* (London, 1862).
Senior, Nassau William, *An Outline of the Science of Political Economy* (London, 1836).

Skinner, Quentin, 'Meaning and understanding in the history of ideas', *History and Theory*, 8 (1969) pp. 3–53.

Small, Ian, *Conditions for Criticism: Authority, Knowledge, and Literature in the Late Nineteenth Century* (Oxford, 1991).

Smith, Adam, *An Enquiry into the Nature and Causes of the Wealth of Nations* (Dublin, 1776).

Smith, Sheila, *The Other Nation: The Poor in English Novels of the 1840s and 1850s* (Oxford, 1980).

Sussman, Herbert L., *Victorians and the Machine* (Cambridge, Mass., 1968).

Taylor, M. W., *Men Versus the State: Herbert Spencer and Late Victorian Individualism* (Oxford, 1992).

Thompson, Dorothy, *The Chartists: Popular Politics in the Industrial Revolution* (Hounslow, 1984).

Thompson, Fred C., 'The Genesis of *Felix Holt'*, *PMLA*, 74 (1959) pp. 576–84.

Thompson, William, *Inquiry into the Principles of the Distribution of Wealth* (London, 1824).

Tillotson, Kathleen, *Novels of the Eighteen-Forties* (Oxford, 1954).

Tonna, Charlotte Elizabeth, *Helen Fleetwood* (London, 1841).

Torrens, Robert, 'Art. XI. Mr Owen's Plans for Relieving National Distress', *Edinburgh Review*, 32 (1819) pp. 453–77.

Trollope, Frances, *Life and Adventures of Michael Armstrong, the Factory Boy* (London, 1840).

Uglow, Jenny, *Elizabeth Gaskell: A Habit of Stories* (London, 1994).

Wheeler, Michael, *English Fiction of the Victorian Period 1830–1890* (London, 1985).

Williams, Raymond, *Culture and Society 1780–1950* (Harmondsworth, 1963).

Winch, Donald, *Malthus* (Oxford, 1987).

Wright, Edgar, *Mrs Gaskell: The Basis for Reassessment* (Oxford, 1965).

Index